Public
Speaking

An Introduction
to Message
Preparation

George Rodman
Brooklyn College, City University of New York

Holt, Rinehart and Winston
New York   Chicago   San Francisco   Dallas
Montreal   Toronto   London   Sydney

To Pat

Library of Congress Cataloging in Publication Data

Rodman, George R.
    Public speaking.

    Includes bibliographical references and index.
    1.   Public speaking.   I.   Title.
PN4121.R665   1981   808.5'1   80-22243

ISBN 0-03-051056-2

Preface

This book was written for performance-oriented public speaking courses. It is divided into four sections, each of which coincides with a major unit in most public speaking classes. The first section prepares the student for the first classroom speeches with overviews of message preparation and critical listening. The second section provides an analysis of the basics of message preparation, including focus, investigation, organization, language, and delivery. The third section examines the message strategies used by public speakers: audience interest, explanation, persuasion, and humor. The final section provides an overview of small group communication as it relates to group assignments in public speaking.

Each chapter begins with a brief outline of the material within it and a prediction that points out how that material relates to message effectiveness. Practical guidelines for speechmaking are then integrated with the rhetorical and behavioral theory that makes those guidelines intellectually valid. The writing style is informal, to reflect the conversational quality of public speaking. Examples are used extensively, including sample speeches that were originally given by myself, by my students, and by some well-known speakers. Each chapter ends with a short summary, questions for discussion, and probes that are designed to extend the reader's understanding of the concepts presented in the chapter.

An instructor's manual to accompany the text is available from your Holt representative or by writing the Communications Editor, Holt, Rinehart and Winston, 383 Madison Avenue, New York, N.Y. 10017. A taped self-study course to accompany the text is available from the author, Department of TV and Radio, Brooklyn College, Brooklyn, New York 11210. These tapes could be placed in your library or media resource center to be used by students who need extra help outside class.

It is almost obligatory to complain in a second edition preface that the second edition was nearly as difficult to produce as the first. However, this is not the case with this text. The first edition was torture, because I had to amend the way I approached the course to the way everyone approached the course, and everyone approached the course differently. Thrashing out the common ground was extremely difficult, and required several drafts, extensive criticism by twenty-six tireless reviewers, several screaming sessions with my editor, and hundreds of dollars worth of correcto-type.

This second edition, by comparison, was easy. I have simply added some material and made some changes that users of the text suggested. I included a new chapter on small group communication and new material on constructive criticism (Chapter 2), creativity (Chapter 3), special occasion speaking (Chapter 3), language improvement (Chapter 6), and logical reasoning (Chapter 10). The chapter on delivery was moved to Part Two, to emphasize the importance of preparation in good delivery. Minor rewriting and reorganization were done throughout the book, and a mini-anthology of speeches about public speaking was appended. In spite of these changes, though, I was careful to leave those sections intact that instructors found most helpful.

I originally wrote this book because I wanted to impart some of the enjoyment of public speaking without sacrificing the validity of the concepts involved. To do that I tried to present an explanation of human communication through an explanation of public speaking, rather than vice versa. In other words, rather than presenting an introductory chapter outlining the basic postulates of communication theory, I tried to present that theory when it was applicable to the task of speech preparation. I found this to be the best approach in my own classes, and I am heartened that enough of you agreed with me to justify this second edition. I hope you find it even more useful than the first.

Brooklyn, N.Y.   George Rodman
January 1981

Contents

Contents

Public Speaking

An Introduction to Message Preparation Second Edition

ONE
Introductory Overviews

Studying the variables of speechmaking can be like taking a canary apart to find the song. We can deprive ourselves of some of the fun and magic of the thing by looking at it too closely. So in a way, it's fortunate that students are called upon to start speaking before they have time to study all the variables involved. Still, it helps to have a general guide before you start work on your first assignment, so this section provides general overviews of message preparation and critical listening.

These overviews stress preparation. In speechmaking, as in life, there are three reasons for being prepared. The first is that *nothing is as easy as it looks.* Beginning public speakers are often misled because successful speeches look easy. But it takes a good deal of work to make a speech look easy. Which brings us to the second reason for being prepared: *Everything takes longer than you expect.* A successful speech is usually one that has had enough time budgeted to it. The final reason for being prepared is that *if anything can go wrong, it will at the worst possible moment.* It pays to be prepared for all foreseeable catastrophes when speaking. Lost notes, mental blocks, nervous twitches, and bored audiences can all be prevented if a speech is planned well enough. This section should give you a good idea of how to go about planning and presenting your first speeches, and how to listen to the speeches of your classmates.

Message Preparation

This chapter is based on the first prediction about message preparation:

A message that is planned in advance will be more effective than one that is not.[1]

AN OVERVIEW OF SPEECH PLANNING

Since you begin making speeches early in your public speaking course, you need to know about message planning right away. But since the principles of message planning require a certain depth of understanding, they must be developed in detail. A compromise will be attempted in this section. The entire process of creating a speech will be briefly overviewed, and each of the concepts will be developed in detail in later chapters.

Overviews like this are usually about as interesting to read as a set of assembly instructions for a do-it-yourself bookcase. In an attempt to liven this one up a bit, I will relate it to a speech I made not too long ago under circumstances that were at least as trying as those you face in your classroom speeches.

The circumstances were these: I was hired as a communication consultant to troubleshoot educational programs on overseas military bases. I was sent to Korea.

I landed at Kimpo Airport, 30 miles south of Seoul, on a warm Monday in June. On the ride to Seoul I was briefed by an enlisted man named Davidson, who told me that there were many classes open to American servicemen in Korea, but very few of the men took advantage of them. The men spent most of their off-duty time in bars and honky-tonks, and the officers were upset about it ("Probably because that's where they spend *their* time," Davidson commented).

According to Davidson, the director of the in-service education program did not understand why the program had been unsuccessful. To make matters worse, he was also defensive about it. He seemed to consider anyone with a solution a threat to his authority.

I thought about all that as Davidson drove past rice paddies carpeted with delicate green sprouts and through village streets crammed with tiny shops and signs with strange symbols. The city of Seoul was surprisingly modern, with only an occasional oxcart lumbering along next to the speeding buses and miniature taxis. Only a few people were dressed in the traditional clothes of the country folk. When we arrived at the U.S. Army Headquarters in the Yongsan section of Seoul, Davidson showed me to the director's office. "I'll wait outside," Davidson said. "Good luck."

The director was sitting behind his desk, staring out a window. He was a stout man with a bald head, red-faced, scowling. He addressed the window as I entered. "So you're the efficiency expert," he said.

"Well, not exactly. I'm a communication consultant."

"We don't need any communication consultants here. I don't know why you were sent." He began shuffling papers. After a minute or so I realized that I had been dismissed, so I left.

I dropped my luggage off at the BOQ—"Bachelor Officers' Quarters"—where my room turned out to be a duplicate of the dormitory room I had lived in as an undergraduate. Then I went out for my first Korean meal. I ate everything that was put in front of me, including one dish called "kimche," an unbelievably potent spiced cabbage. As I returned to my room I noticed an ungrateful rumbling in my stomach. There was a note from the director waiting: "Call me."

Over the phone the director seemed just as annoyed as he had in person. "I'd like you to prepare a fifteen-minute speech for oh-eight-hundred Wednesday," he said. "There will be an orientation briefing for a contingent of new recruits. Tell them about in-service education."

Click.

That was it. I had just a little more than a day to unpack and prepare a talk. I knew a lot about education, but next to nothing about the in-service programs offered in Korea. Luckily, I knew the steps involved in putting together a speech.

Choosing the Topic

Usually, the first step is picking a topic. But my topic had been chosen for me. It was a topic that interested me and one I considered important. After all, the service experience was a turning point for many recruits. Many of them would use the experience to turn unsuccessful pasts into successful futures. One important factor for them would be the education they exposed themselves to while in the service. I decided to learn more about the topic of in-service education.

Investigating

I went to G-1 (Administration), where I interviewed the colonel in charge of orientation briefings. He was extremely friendly, answering all the questions he could, giving me some pamphlets, and suggesting a visit to the Army Education Center on base. Unfortunately, I had been up for more than 24 hours and the jet lag and kimche were beginning to take their toll. I felt a supersonic heartburn on its way, so I went back to my quarters and slept for ten hours.

I was at the education center when it opened in the morning. I got some information there about the type of new recruit that I could expect in the audience. The counselor at the education center offered to lend me some slides she had used for a similar presentation. I chose three slides that listed available high school, college, and general-interest courses, and five others that showed men participating in various classes.

"If they want to find out more," the counselor told me, "you just send them over to me. In fact, just get me their names and I'll call them myself."

Next, I went to the base library and found some articles about trends and procedures in in-service education. I read material, took some notes, and then went over to the receiving center, where new recruits were processed into the base. I found a new group of men fresh in from the States. I asked them two questions:

1. Do you intend to take advantage of in-service education while in Korea?
2. Why or why not?

After that, I went out for lunch.

Thinking About It

Lunch is one of the most important steps in message preparation. For one thing, you need to eat so you will have the energy to create; but more important, if you go off alone somewhere for a long, leisurely lunch you have the time to *think*. And thinking is essential.

I bought a cheese sandwich and a container of milk from one of the base snack bars (I still hadn't recovered from the kimche) and sat in the bleachers that overlooked the empty parade ground. It was quiet. I flipped a few mental pinballs into my mind and waited for them to bump into the appropriate lights and buzzers.

Determining the General Purpose

Why was I making this speech, anyway? Because I was being paid? Certainly my check would not be withheld if I refused an assignment on my first day in the country. Well, then, was I trying to prove myself to the director? It was bad enough that I had traveled halfway around the world to be told I wasn't needed. Why should I play into the director's hands by setting myself up to be knocked down? All I had to do was make *one* mistake and the director would say, "Right. A communication consultant. What time is the next plane stateside, hotshot?"

But wait a minute. My purpose didn't have anything to do with pay, or with the director. My purpose was to get a group of new recruits to take advantage of in-service education. Even with only one day's research, I knew some things that the recruits probably didn't. I knew what courses they could take, how they could go about registering for those courses, and when the courses were offered. I also knew that most of them would not take any of the courses unless they were motivated to do so. In fact, I knew a lot more than I could possibly communicate in fifteen minutes. Before I decided what I would include in my talk, I would have to consider the audience and occasion.

Considering the Audience and Occasion

I knew from my various forms of investigation that there would be twenty-five people in the audience, and they would be all male. I knew that the average age of new recruits was 19, that on the average 15 percent had some college work, 40 percent were high school graduates with no college, and 45 percent were high school drop-outs; 15 percent of the drop-outs would need remedial-reading classes in order to succeed at high-school-level work. I knew that they had enlisted for "practical experience," "adventure," and "pay and benefits," in that order. I knew that 35 percent of them had failed at least one year in school. I knew that many of the men had enlisted because of an $18 million advertising drive, including one TV spot that had "a sexy stewardess welcoming young men aboard an airliner with breathy murmurs about the pleasures of sixteen months in Europe." [2]

I knew that most of the men who planned to take courses wanted to do so because they wanted to get ahead. The men who didn't want to take courses felt that the courses would be too difficult. These men preferred to relax in their free time.

I figured that the men would be nervous and confused about their new assignments in this strange land. They would probably also be tired. I knew that the briefing would take place in a quonset hut with no air conditioning, and that I would be the sixth person to talk to the men. The other five speakers would be:

1. A G-1 officer would talk about administrative procedures.
2. A G-2 officer would talk about security procedures.
3. A medical officer would talk about VD and other health problems.
4. A recreation officer would talk about the sports program.
5. A State Department representative would talk about the consequences of civil misconduct.

I thought about all these things. With them in mind, I considered the specific purpose of my talk.

Considering the Specific Purpose

I decided that I would have to limit my talk to three points:

1. Why the men should take courses during their stay in Korea.
2. What courses were available to take.
3. How they could find out more.

There would not be the time or attention available for more than that. In fact, I would have to plan my message strategy carefully if I wanted to hold their attention at all.

Considering the Message Strategy

I could see that I would have to *interest* my audience to hold their attention. I needed to *explain* clearly, too. My message was basic and could be easily understood, but it would be directed at men who were near the saturation point with other messages. I needed to *persuade* if I expected them to take the time to seek out educational opportunities when they could just as easily go to the bars and honky-tonks. Finally, I needed to *entertain* so I would leave the men with the feeling that education could be fun.

With these requirements in mind, I began to map out a plan, a *strategy*, to meet them:

To maintain the men's interest, I decided to analyze their needs and try to respond to those needs.

To explain clearly, I would use devices such as anecdotes, examples, descriptions, and visual aids (the slides) to illustrate what I told them.

To be persuasive, I would give the recruits reasons to seek out more information, and I would make it as easy as possible for them to do so.

To be entertaining, I would use humor when appropriate.

With this strategy in mind, I began to map out the message structure.

Considering the Message Structure

To give my speech a coherent structure I would have to organize my material and formulate an introduction, body, and conclusion.

THE BODY

I began by roughing out the body of the speech. I decided to organize my main points in a "why-what-how" order, since those questions would probably occur to my audience in that order. I outlined them as follows:

I. *Why* become involved in an education program during a tour of military duty?
   A. It saves you money.
   B. It is easier.
   C. It can increase your enjoyment of the country you are visiting.

(There were other points that I considered, like how education helps you "get ahead" in both civilian and military life. But after I thought about it, those points seemed too basic for an audience of adults. I decided to refer to them just briefly in my introduction.)

  II. What kind of courses are available?
      A. General-interest courses.
      B. High school courses.
      C. Remedial courses.
      D. College courses.

(These types were listed in order of decreasing demand. To the best of my knowledge, the largest number of men would be interested in the general-interest courses, and the least number of men would be interested in college courses. I hoped the high-interest courses would give the attention level of the audience enough momentum to carry them through the explanation of the other types of courses.)

 III. How to find out more.
      A. Talk to the education officer.
      B. Visit the education center.
      C. Sign up for an appointment.

THE CONCLUSION

In my conclusion, I intended to summarize my main points and re-affirm the main idea of my speech: In this case, I wanted to remind the men that their tour in Korea could be a turning point in their lives.

THE INTRODUCTION

I planned my introduction last; it's such an essential part of a speech, you really need to know what you're going to say before you know how to introduce it. I hoped to do three things with my introduction:

1. Get my audience's attention.
2. Establish the importance of my topic to them.
3. Preview the points I was going to speak about.

Preparing Speaking Notes

I put my speaking notes on one side of one 3 × 5 card. When I had refined them to the point where they were just enough to jog my memory but not complex enough to get lost in, they looked like this:[3]

```
Why—
    Cheap
    Easy
    Foreign country
Courses—
    G.I.
    H.S.
    Remedial
    College
Do It—
    Ed officer
    Ed center
    Sign it
```

I made changes in my notes as I practiced my speech.

Practicing the Speech

First, I practiced alone, trying to judge for myself whether my language would be clear, interesting, and appropriate to my audience. I also made sure that I could pronounce all the words I needed to, and that I could remember everything I wanted to say by glancing at my speaking notes.

By dinnertime, I thought the speech sounded pretty good. I found Private Davidson in the mess hall and asked him to act as a sample audience for one more rehearsal. Davidson listened, asked me to clarify a few items, and corrected me on a few points. Overall, though, he liked the talk, and I felt relatively confident about presenting it.

Presenting the Speech

Wednesday morning was cooler, the recruits were happier, and the other speeches were more stimulating than I had expected. The medical officer showed a series of full-color slides of untreated venereal sores, and the State Department representative showed slides of the Korean prisons that the men could be put into if they stepped out of line while away from the base. I began to think that those two would be tough acts to follow.

Finally the officer in charge introduced me.

Transcribed below, on the left, is a facsimile of my talk. Since the original talk was presented from brief notes, most of this one had to be reconstructed from memory. Some comments about the talk appear in the right-hand column.

Remember as you read this speech that it is a specific communication, rather than a general model. It is a man giving a simple, informal talk to a group of other men.

THE AUTHOR'S ADDRESS TO RECRUITS IN KOREA[4]

Some Comments

Nothing fancy in
the introduction.

I establish the importance of
my topic to them, and I try to
build some "common ground"
by stressing our similarities.
This seems to get their
attention, so I leave it at that. If
I had felt at this time that I did
not have their attention I might
have said something like
"What's the matter—you don't
like education? You want to
see some more slides of VD
sores?"

I preview my main points and
begin developing the first one:
Why the men should continue
their education.

First subpoint: It saves you
money.

Second subpoint: It's easier.

The Talk

I'm here to talk about education. I've been involved with
education all my life, as most of you have. I guess I don't
have to remind you how important education is, how it
can make the difference between being someone who
takes orders and being someone who gives orders, how
it can result in a richer, fuller life.

But did you know that you can continue your education
here in Korea? You can. There are many courses available, and they might be cheaper, easier, and more effective than the same courses if you took them stateside.
That's right—cheaper, easier, and more effective.

The courses are cheaper here because the government
pays some of your expenses for you.

The government is willing to do that to keep you out of
those pictures that the doctor and the State Department
rep showed you. For most of the courses, the government
will pay all of your tuition. For some courses, it will even
pay for your books and materials.
So you see, taking courses here in Korea saves you
money two ways. First, you get the courses free. Second,
you get something to do in your spare time, so you don't
have to go out and spend money. But that's not the most
important reason to study while you're here. Think about
this: The courses that you take here might be easier, too.

Some Comments	The Talk
	You might learn more because of that. After all, you are away from all the distractions and entertainments of home. You'll find it easier to spend an occasional evening in the library here. You'll find it easier to concentrate. You will, in short, find it easier to learn. There are courses available that will help you get more out of your Korean tour of duty, too.
Third subpoint: It can help you enjoy your tour in Korea.	You can study photography, drawing, or writing so that you can keep a record of your experiences. You can study the Korean language also. Have you ever heard it said that it is easier to learn a language if you actually live in the country where the language is spoken? Well, it's true. Not only will you be able to learn the Korean language rapidly here, but in just a few weeks you could understand some of the things that the people are saying about you on the city buses.
A few men chuckle and make comments here, so I respond directly to let them know that I appreciate the response.	
	Really—don't you ever wonder what they are saying? Are they saying "My, what a handsome foreigner" or "That dumb GI just sat on my groceries"?
A few men laugh cautiously.	Language, photography, art, and writing courses are available here for students at all levels.
I begin the second main point: What kind of courses are available?	But there are courses designed to help you complete your formal education, too. You can take high school completion courses that will lead to a diploma in much less time than it would take in civilian life. College courses are offered, also. And if you have a special problem, like low reading ability, there are even courses for that. All in all, there is something for everyone. Let me show you a partial list. (Private Davidson, will you hit the lights, please?)
(Davidson hits the lights.)	
Four subpoints: general-interest courses, high school courses, remedial courses, and college courses. They are introduced as the slides are shown.	

Some Comments	The Talk
	Here are some of the general-interest courses that you can take.
First slide: outline of general-interest courses. There are over 25 courses listed. It would have taken too long to mention them all, but the eye works faster than the ear.	
	You can see that in addition to the ones I have already mentioned, there are many others. Courses from karate to auto mechanics.
Second slide: men working with their instructor on a car engine.	
	You can learn to fix a car . . .
Third slide: karate instructor smashing three bricks with his bare hand.	
	. . . or demolish one with your bare hands.
Laughter here.	Some of these courses can even be taken for college credit.
Fourth slide: outline of high school courses.	
	Now, here are some of the high school courses that are available. You'll notice that with one program, if you qualify, you could earn a diploma by taking just three classes: math, government, and English.
Fifth slide: close-up of high school diploma. I hear some grumbles here, so I react to them.	
	That's a special program for you guys who joined the army to get *away* from school!
The grumblers laugh here, so my reaction was probably successful.	
	Not only that, but if you wanted to get away from school because of poor reading skills, remember: *We* have reading classes that are designed for *adults.*
Sixth slide: adult reading class in a clean, well-lighted classroom.	

Some Comments

The Talk

Seventh slide: list of college courses. Once again, it is quicker to show this list than to talk about it. The slide is projected long enough for the audience to scan the entire list.

Eighth slide: man being congratulated by commanding officer upon receiving diploma.

(Davidson has gone out for a smoke. He's heard the talk before.)

I don't get as much of a response as I want, so I push it a little.

I pick out one man to respond to. That keeps the rest of them on their toes thinking they might be next.

One or two men respond by pointing.

Finally, here is a list of just some of the courses that will be offered here by the University of Maryland.

These courses can count toward the completion of a bachelor's degree at any accredited college or university.

(Hit the lights, will you, Davidson? Uh, somebody hit the lights, will you? Thanks.)

That's just a brief summary of the kind of educational opportunities you can take advantage of during your tour of duty here. Now, I suppose the next thing you want to know is how you can find out more, right?

Is anyone interested in how you can find out more? Anyone? Is anyone still awake?

Ah ... you. You're interested in how you can find out more about these courses? What's the matter—you think people are talking about you on buses?

OK, listen: There are two things you can do if you want more information. The first is to talk to your education officer, Lieutenant Pike. You've all met Lieutenant Pike, haven't you? Also, you can go to your education center. It's in the center of camp, right between the bowling alley and the post office. Does everyone know where that is?

Right. It's in that direction, about five blocks. You can't miss it. At least, you won't want to miss it. There are some good people there. In fact, that's the only place I've met any single women in this country.

Some Comments	The Talk

This news seems to take them aback. One of them asks, "How long have you been here?" I glance at my watch and say, "Almost forty-eight hours." They laugh, apparently relieved.

I was over at the education center yesterday. The counselor there told me that if any of you were interested I could take your name and she would set up an appointment for you. I'm going to circulate a sign-up sheet. Just print your name on it and the counselor will get in touch with you.

Nothing fancy in my conclusion, either. I just summarize the main points and reaffirm my central idea.

Let me just review what I said. Your education is important. You can continue it during your tour of duty here. There are courses for everyone. And you can find out more from Lieutenant Pike, from your education center, or simply by putting your name on that sheet that's going around. Your tour of duty here could be the turning point in your life, especially if you take advantage of the educational opportunities you have here. So sign the paper.

I have time for a few questions. Do you have any?

Answering Questions

I answered three or four questions after my talk. I tried to answer each question as though it were intelligent, important, and evidence that the questioner had listened carefully to the talk. I responded as directly and briefly as I could. I didn't have the answer to every question, though. At one point I had to admit, "I don't know, but I think you'll be able to find out at the education center." Sometimes an honest "I don't know" is an extremely important (and infinitely welcome) response. Especially if you can suggest some other place to look for the answer.

THE PRINCIPLES INVOLVED

After the speech several men visited the education center, and the program director heard about it. He began to change his opinion about communication consultants, and he and I began to work together harmoniously. In time, attendance at in-service classes rose dramatically, and everyone lived happily ever after.

My Korea speech is offered as an example because it was do different from, and yet so similar to, a classroom speech. It was different because I was half a world away from home, in a military, all-male environment, a professional public speaker doing what I was paid to do. And yet that speech was surprisingly similar to a classroom speech in terms of audience size, resources for investigation, time available for preparation, presentation strategies that were necessary, and pressure I was under. Most important, the Korea speech was similar to a classroom speech in the way it was put together and presented. That process will be a little different for every speaker, every speech, and every speaking situation. The steps in the process occur in no set order, and often two or more are necessary at the same time. In fact, on some occasions, they all seem to happen at once. Still, to be successful you have to take each step into consideration. Briefly, the steps are based on the following principles:

Focus

You focus your *topic* by considering your own interests, the interests of your audience, the time available for your speech, and the occasion of the speech. Your topic should be interesting to you and important to your audience. It should be limited to something that can be dealt with thoroughly in the time available. It should be appropriate to the occasion. You focus your *material* by excluding all information that does not help develop that topic.

Investigation

You investigate general *ideas* and specific *facts* to support those ideas. You investigate the people who will be in your audience, also. You do all of this by speaking to people, by reading, and by observing.

Organization

You organize by choosing a limited number of main points and arranging them in a logical order. Your speech should have a recognizable introduction, body, and conclusion. Your introduction should preview your main points and establish their importance to your audience. Your conclusion should summarize your main points and reaffirm the central idea of your speech.

Use of Language

In wording your message, you should use language that is clear, interesting, and appropriate. You should experiment with different ways of expressing your ideas as you practice your speech. Your ideas should be expressed directly and simply.

Message Strategy

Most speeches will be a mixture of the basic strategies: audience interest, explanation, persuasion, and entertainment. You must decide how much of each to use, according to the audience response you want. When planning for audience interest you have to consider ways to hold your audience's attention. When planning for explanation, you have to consider how you will get them to listen, to understand, and to remember. When planning a persuasive strategy, you have to consider what you want them to do, and then you have to consider ways to make that behavior as desirable as possible. In planning for entertainment, you have to consider how to make the speech enjoyable to your audience.

Delivery

In presenting your speech, you should maintain the greatest possible contact with your audience. You should do this with a conversational speaking style that is natural in movement, posture, facial expression, eye contact, and tone of voice. The best way to achieve this naturalness is to become honestly involved in what you are saying. Although what you say is planned in advance, you must present it so that it is fresh to both you and the audience during the presentation. To accomplish this, your speech has to be practiced carefully, and presented with the idea that it is *important* to your audience.

These principles will each be developed in their own chapters.

SUMMARY

There is a process involved in preparing and presenting a speech. To be successful, you have to devote a certain amount of time to each of the steps involved in that process. The steps are interrelated; they happen in no set order, and often two or more steps will happen at the same time. These steps include preliminary tasks such as choosing the topic, investigating ideas, and thinking. They also include tasks such as determining your purpose, analyzing your audience, and analyzing the occasion of your speech. Putting the speech together requires time for considering message strategies and message structure. Finally, time is required for practicing the speech.

These steps are based on the principles of focus, investigation, organization, language, message strategy and delivery. These principles enable you to predict audience response; they are basic to all types of message preparation. Understanding their role in public speaking will enable you to use them in *all* forms of communication.

QUESTIONS FOR DISCUSSION

1. In preparing my speech on in-service education, I realized that my purpose "didn't have anything to do with pay, or with the director." My purpose was actually to influence the recruits. Think of two topics you might present in a speech assignment, in which your purpose would not only relate to a grade, or the instructor, but to a genuine desire to get a favorable response from the class. (In other words, what do you *really* want to discuss with your classmates?)

2. Do you agree that when answering questions about your speech, "an honest 'I don't know' is an extremely important (and infinitely welcome) response"? Why or why not?

3. Do you agree that the steps in the process of message preparation "occur in no set order, and often two or more are necessary at the same time"? Why or why not?

4. Before you go on and read any more of the text, check out your effectiveness *right now* at evaluating messages. Look again at the Korea speech. What statements, arguments, examples, and so on

do you think were probably most effective at entertaining, explaining, or persuading? What elements of the speech might have "turned off" the men? Explain your answers.

PROBES

1. Think about a time you had to plan a message—any message. It might have been a request you made to one of your parents, or a friend, or a teacher. (For example, you may have asked a teacher if you could turn in an assignment late.) How did the process of preparing that message compare with planning one for public speaking?

2. How do you think the principles of message preparation relate to the following kinds of communication?
   (a) Writing a term paper for one of your classes
   (b) Planning an advertising campaign for a new product
   (c) Cheering up a friend who has come to you with a problem

3. Pick up some of the recruiting "propaganda" from your school's admissions office. How do you think the principles of message preparation might have applied to the development of this literature?

4. (a) Watch three *different* television commercials for the *same* product. Do you notice any difference in strategies that might be designed to reach different audiences?
   (b) View the commercials for two different, but similar products. (For example, Coca-Cola and Royal Crown Cola.) Do the message strategies indicate they are both trying to reach the *same* audience, or do the ads seem to be aimed at *different* groups of viewers?

5. Interview someone who frequently prepares and delivers public speeches. Find out if the same message preparation principles discussed in this chapter apply. If *not,* how do the principles differ in this person's experience? If *so,* do the steps occur in the same order as in the author's experience, or can you cite differences?

6. As you prepare for your first speaking assignment in your class, keep a "diary" of the message preparation process. Compare the process you went through with the steps involved in the preparation of the author's speech in Korea. In what way or ways were the situations similar; in what ways did they differ?

NOTES

[1]Edward Rogge and James C. Ching, *Advanced Public Speaking* (New York: Holt, Rinehart and Winston, 1966), pp. 8–10.

[2]"Enlistment Blues," *Newsweek,* June 14, 1971, p. 29.

[3]These notes probably don't make much sense to you. But then, *your* notes probably wouldn't make much sense to me. They don't have to—your speaking notes are for you only.

[4]Reproduced from author's notes for a speech given in Korea in June 1973.

2

Critical Listening

This chapter deals with listening, and is based on a prediction that holds true for all oral messages:

The speaker and the audience will both get more out of a speech if the audience listens critically to it.[1]

LISTENING

Chapter 1 was written mostly from the *speaker's* point of view. In your speech class, however, as in life, you will spend more time listening than speaking. Learning to listen actively will not only make you more popular (good listeners are always more in demand at cocktail parties than those who consider themselves the "lives" of those parties), it will also enable you to learn more. It might even save you from moments of embarrassment. Dr. Ralph Nichols, who spent most of his life researching human listening, had an uncanny ability to catch audience members who weren't listening. His reaction was typical for a college professor:

> Frequently, as I look into their faces during a lecture, I will see a student, his chin resting on his hand, two unblinking, staring eyes fixed upon me. Occasionally, just for fun, I stop my lecture abruptly, call the student by name, and ask him: "What do you think of that?" The question has the same effect as throwing ice water in his face. He suddenly jerks to attention and tries to cover up his lack of listening with some hurried remarks: "Oh, yeah, sure, I guess that's a good, err . . ."[2]

As sadistic as this behavior seems, Dr. Nichols actually did these students a favor. He pointed out to them that "faked" listening wasn't *really* listening. Unfortunately, there is no human behavior that is so difficult to do well yet so easy to fake. We all have so much to think about. What are we going to do after class? How are we going to get out of our most recent predicament? Is the landlord going to evict us? Will we ever finish that project we started? It takes time to work through these things.[3] The easiest place to steal thinking time is in a nice, anonymous audience. We spend a lot of time as part of one audience or another. After a while, we learn how *not* to listen, how to turn off what's going on around us so we can concentrate on our thoughts. A problem arises when we do this too often. By blocking out messages, we barricade ourselves against any of the benefits those messages might have had for us.

Ideally, we should learn to listen when we want to and to *not* listen when we want to withdraw. Unfortunately, most of us find it easier to learn how to *not* listen. This is especially unfortunate in a public speaking class, where listening critically to others' speeches will enable you to improve your own. This chapter deals with three topics that are essential to learning how to listen: (1) the components of listening, (2) the objectives of listening, and (3) methods of enhancing listening.

THE COMPONENTS OF LISTENING

"Listen."

It's not as easy as it sounds. Listening is actually a complex neu-rological process that contains three major steps: *comprehension, interpretation,* and *evaluation.*[4] Understanding each of these steps will give you a basis for examining your own listening behavior.

Comprehension, the first step, is recognizing the words that are being presented. In order to comprehend a message you have to be able to hear it and concentrate on it.

The second step, interpretation, involves translating those words into ideas. In order to interpret a message, you mentally assign meaning to the words that are used.

The third step, evaluation, requires you to judge the worth of the speaker's ideas. In this step you judge whether the speaker's ideas are important to you.

These three steps might be represented by three questions that could act as listening guidelines:

1. The Comprehension Question: "What did the speaker say?"
2. The Interpretation Question: "What did the speaker mean?"
3. The Evaluation Question: "So what?"

We go through these three steps every time we truly listen, even in the most casual conversations. Imagine that one of your main in-terests in life is skiing. Imagine that you have a friend whose main interest is surfing. Imagine finally that you are listening to that friend tell you an anecdote about a spectacular "wipeout." To listen you must first *comprehend* what is said. Comprehension will break down if you can't hear, or if you are distracted by an interruption.

If you do comprehend what is said, you next *interpret* the story in light of your own experience: How "wiping out" in surfing might be similar to "wiping out" in skiing, for example. You can therefore attribute meaning to the various surfer terms that your friend uses, even though you are not a surfer.

Finally, you will *evaluate* the importance of your friend's story in light of your own interests; you might amend your ideas about "balance" and how it keeps you from falling over while skiing. Per-haps your friend's anecdote will provide some other appetizer on your menu of food for thought. In any case, when you evaluate it you place a judgment on it; "Good idea," you might think, or "Bad idea," or "Interesting story," or "Dull story." Whatever your judgment, if you have truly listened to what has been said, then you have gone through *all three steps:* Comprehension, interpretation, and evaluation. The listening process continues this way, hundreds of times during the average day. We go through these steps as we listen to radio, TV, friends, strangers, and speeches in class. And when we don't want to listen, we simply cut off the process before the steps are completed.

Recognizing these components of listening is a start, but you also have to think about what, specifically, you want to listen for. In a public speaking class, one of the things you want to take away from a classmate's speech is an idea of how to improve your own speeches.

THE OBJECTIVES OF LISTENING

As part of an audience in a public speaking class, you are entitled to be selfish. You are, of course, expected to accept the speaker as a human being, and treat him or her accordingly; but you also have the right to seek out and take away from a speech those things that are of personal importance to you. In fact, it is your responsibility to do so. If you accept the responsibility of what Nichols calls "enlightened self-interest,"[5] you will automatically become a better listener.

Five things that you should try to take away from a speech coincide with the principles of message preparation that will be presented in the final two sections of this book. Questions based on these principles become guidelines for listening to speeches. You could ask yourself about the following principles.

Focus

What is the *focus*—the one main idea—of this speech? Once you have answered that general question, you can ask some specific ones: Why is the idea important to *you?* What do you *need* or *want* to know about this topic? Remember that no topic is inherently uninteresting. The topic of the speech might be "Drunk Driving," and you might neither drink nor drive. Still, you *know* people who drink, and as a passenger you share the highway with some of them. Perhaps the speech will show you ways to protect yourself.

Investigation

How has the speaker investigated the topic? What has the speaker found that is of use to you? Has the speaker read things, conducted interviews, or made some personal observations that will help you better understand the things you are interested in? To return to the "Drunk Driving" example, perhaps the speech will supply you with some arguments you can use to help get a drunken friend out from behind the wheel of a car next New Year's Eve.

Organization

How has the speaker organized the speech material? How is the topic taken apart? Why are the main points important to you? Does the division or order of the ideas make them particularly interesting to you? The topic might be something as pedestrian-sounding as "Methods of Falling Asleep in Class," but the speaker's analysis of this topic might be unique. It might be something like this:

> There are three methods of falling asleep in class.
> I. The Tijuana Quick-Dip, in which the head dips forward and the sleeper is awakened just before hitting the desk top,
> II. The Rochester Roundabout, in which the head tips backward, rolls to the side, and wakes the sleeper up with a whiplash effect, and
> III. The Prop Failure, in which the head slides off the fist that is propping it up, and the sleeper is awakened as he or she receives that fist in the ear.

Even if you never indulge in such antisocial behavior as sleeping in class, the speaker's original analysis might supply you with a new perspective on the behavior, and you might therefore be able to relate it to your own interests.

Language

Does the speaker's use of language make his or her ideas clear and interesting? At the same time, is there new vocabulary being used that you can learn the meaning of from the context in which it is used? Is there vocabulary used that you can borrow to develop ideas of your own? Perhaps the speech is on "Sailing," and a few terms are used that are incomprehensible to a landlubber. But that's the way great vocabularies are built—by determining the meanings of words through the contexts in which they are used.

Delivery

Does the speaker seem honestly enthusiastic about the speech? If not, what is it about the delivery that causes you to doubt his or her enthusiasm for the topic or the audience? Eye contact, posture, and vocal clarity are just a few of the things that might distract from a speaker's contact with the audience.

An important caution is necessary here: Do not allow the

speaker's delivery to distract you from what is being said. The main reason you "listen" to delivery is to be able to help the speaker, and yourself, understand how delivery affects the audience's perception of the message.

Message Strategy

Is the speaker's message strategy based on a worthy purpose? Is it ethical? If so, does the message strategy cause you to respond the way the speaker wants you to? If the purpose of the speech is to arouse your interest, does it? If it seeks to explain something, are the ideas made clear with devices such as anecdotes, examples, and statistics? If the purpose of the speech is to change your attitude about something, are you given valid reasons for doing so? If the purpose is to entertain, is the speech relaxing and enjoyable?

Determining the focus, investigation, organization, language and message strategy are five "selfish" objectives of listening to others' speeches. In spite of the fact that these objectives are entirely in your self-interest, the behavior that derives from them (sitting up, smiling, looking at the speaker) will help the speaker present a better speech. As Dr. Nichols points out, "Nearly all of us have unconsciously developed a special set of senses that, in effect, measure the way people listen when we talk to them."[6] Nichols sums it up this way: "The more we take from the speaker through listening, the more he will give."[7]

METHODS OF ENHANCING LISTENING

Listening is an active process. It requires effort. You don't just sit there and wait for it to happen. There are four methods that are suggested for *making* listening happen. These methods are being prepared, controlling distractions, withholding evaluation, and taking notes.

Being Prepared to Listen

Just as you prepare messages, you can prepare to listen to a message. First, you can practice listening by exposing yourself to challenging messages. Discussing complex topics with friends, attending lectures, and tuning in to documentaries on radio and TV are just a few of the ways that you can exercise your ability to listen. If you exercise this ability regularly you will be better prepared to listen to a speech in class.

Another way to prepare to listen is to find out what the topic of a speech will be and then do some thinking about it. If one of your classmates is going to talk about nuclear energy, you could consider questions like this in advance: (1) Is nuclear energy safe? (2) Is it economical? (3) Is it practical?

Finally, you can prepare to listen by building up a positive attitude about the listening situation. Remember—you will be listening for your own benefit.

Controlling Distractions

A distraction is anything that directs your attention away from a message. There are two types of distractions: internal and external. Internal distractions are forms of daydreaming, like the personal plans and problems everyone dwells on from time to time. External distractions are changes in the environment: the sound of a book closing, the sight of a cloud passing over the sun, a whiff of cologne, or a speaker tripping over a podium.

You can minimize the effect of some distractions by planning for them in advance. One technique for doing that is to recognize those distractions, both internal and external, that you can predict in advance. Are you worried about your neighbor's complaints that your cat has been befouling their children's sandbox? That worry would be an internal distraction. Take note of it (mental or written). Do you have a social interest in one of your classmates? Take note of that, too. Do you have a cold? Take note: "Possible sniffles." Just *recognizing* these distractions helps you to fight them. Some of them you can take preventive action against—if you have the sniffles you can take an antihistamine before the speech starts. You can control other (unexpected) distractions *while* you are listening by recognizing them and making an effort to concentrate in spite of them.

Withholding Evaluation

You should not let your evaluation of a speech topic get in the way of your comprehension of the speech itself. Psychologist Carl Rogers has suggested that human beings have a natural tendency to evaluate a message before they hear all of it.[8] Thus, instead of going through all three steps of the listening process, we often skip the first one, comprehension, and then evaluate what we *think* is being said rather than what is really being said.[9] The character Emily Litella (Gilda Radner) on NBC's *Saturday Night Live* often satirized this tendency by demanding "equal time" for news reports about things like "making a steak out of Puerto Rico." As exaggerated as this example is, it is typical of the type of reaction caused by premature judgment. To truly listen you should withhold your evaluation of the message until

your comprehension of it is complete. In order to do this, you might keep two things in mind:

1. *Do not dismiss a topic as "uninteresting" until you have heard all that the speaker has to say.* Some topics just don't sound interesting at first, but if looked at closely enough they become fascinating. Ask "What is of interest in this topic?" rather than "Is this topic interesting?" The difference between those two questions is crucial, because the first one presupposes that there will be *something* of interest if we listen closely enough. Remember also that the things that will be of interest to you might not emerge until the speaker is well into the presentation.

2. Keep your criticism of the *speaker* separate from your criticism of the *speech*. Recognition of the speaker's delivery or physical appearance will be of use to you in improving your own speeches, but if you hold these things *against* a speaker you might "turn off" and miss the substance of what is being said. Don't let your feelings about the speaker interfere with your comprehension of the message.

The final method for enhancing listening, taking notes, will also help you to withhold evaluation and control distractions.

Taking Notes

A major problem in listening is allowing insignificant details to distract you from the main points of a speech. To keep everything straight during a presentation you should take notes on the main ideas, on the details that you consider important and interesting, and on questions that come up as you listen. It is impossible to keep all these things in your head and listen at the same time. If you record them in notes you can keep your mind on what is being said *when* it is being said.

One method of notetaking is as follows:

First divide a blank sheet of paper in half. Label one side "Main Ideas" and the other "Details and Questions."

Under "Main Ideas," list the topic or title of the speech, along with whatever seems to you to be a main idea. You do not have to put these notes in standard outline form. In fact, it would be distracting to try to do so. Simply list what seem to be main ideas, as they come up.

Since your first responsibility is listening to the speaker, it is important to keep your notes brief. If you take down too much you will be writing when you should be listening, which will be distracting for both you and the speaker. You have to learn to listen for general ideas, to jot them down briefly, and to return your attention as quickly as possible to the speaker. Sometimes you have to figure out the general idea from everything the speaker says. More often, though, the speaker will make a generalization about the idea before developing it. Other times, the generalization will appear after the development or right in the middle of it. It is important to listen for that general idea, no matter where it is. Suppose, for example, that you were in the audience when Governor Dan Walker of Illinois gave a speech on "Making Our Criminal Justice System Work." Governor Walker presented one idea this way:

> It's an understatement to say that the system is not working well. Take the problem of long delays before trial. In large metropolitan areas, criminals are out on bail for a year committing more crimes before they are tried for the first offense. In Chicago, the average—I emphasize average—period of time between arrest and trial of a felony is 360 days; New York, 292 days; Detroit, 208 days; Pittsburgh, 195 days; Los Angeles, 141 days; San Diego, 110 days. That means a large number of criminals are out on bail for considerable periods of time committing more crimes while awaiting trial on the original offense.
>
> There's another side to the coin: Innocent people languish in jail for months because they can't afford bail. And long delays cause prosecutors problems. Witnesses forget what happened. They become discouraged. They move. They die. And the criminal is free.[10]

If you were listening actively to that idea, you might reduce it to brief notes such as:

Trial delay: major problem

Jotting down general ideas in this manner allows you to review the previous points that the speaker made as a new point comes up. This will enable you to keep in touch with the focus of the speech.

On the opposite side of the same page under "Details and Questions," list those details that seem interesting to you, especially those that you might want to remember for your own use. Listening to that speech by Governor Walker you might jot down one or two details like this:

Guilty—go free w/ bail
Innocent—stay in jail w/out bail

or:

Chicago—360 days
New York—292 days

Also list in this column any questions that come to mind during the speech. If the speaker does not answer your questions in the course of the speech, ask for clarification during the question-and-answer period. Listening to Governor Walker's speech, you might realize that you had recently read conflicting figures. (You might have read an article stating, "The trial delay in New York City is around two years.") In that case, you might want to question the governor about the source of his statistics. To make a note of that, you simply jot down the statistic with a question mark after it. That way, if the question is answered during the speech all you have to do is cross out the question mark on your notes.

Using this method of split-page note taking, notes on a speech given about "Communication Between a Horse and Its Rider"[11] might look like this:

Details and Questions	Main Ideas
Great quote—where's it from?[12]	Horse-Rider Communication
	Humans use natural aids (voice hands legs seat) and artificial aids (whips spurs martingales)
Is the Lippizaner School in Austria?[13]	
	Horse Physiology— sensitive to touch; communicates with movements of ears, nostrils, back, and tail
Horses get insomnia?[14]	
	Horse Psychology— not smart good memory moody sociable

That is just one method of taking notes. There are many others. Nichols, for example, suggests a similar split-page format, with "facts" on one side and "principles" on the other.[15] Other methods commonly used in speech classes include taking notes on an outline provided by the speaker, and taking notes on a speech criticism form provided by the instructor. The method of note taking that you use is not terribly important. Use whatever method you like, but take notes. If you take notes, withhold evaluations, control distractions, and prepare for listening, both you and the speaker will get more out of the speech.

OFFERING CONSTRUCTIVE CRITICISM

One of your main responsibilities will be to offer constructive criticism after you have listened to a speech. We say that criticism is "constructive" when it helps the speaker improve. To offer this type of criticism you have to be *substantive*. Rather than saying, "I liked this" or "I didn't like that," provide the speaker with a detailed explanation of your reasons for liking or disliking parts of the speech. That will require some extra effort, which will be worthwhile because it will improve your own critical-analysis skills as well as the speaker's skills.

Also, be careful to point out what is *right* with the speech as well as what is *wrong* with it. If you don't, you run the risk of extinguishing the *positive* aspects of the speaker's behavior. In fact, negative criticism without positive criticism is often useless, because the speaker might become defensive and block out your criticism completely. It is a good idea, therefore, to offer your positive criticism first, and then tactfully offer your suggestions for improvement. For example, rather than saying, "Your ideas about horse psychology were completely unclear and unsupported," you might say, "I really enjoyed your explanation of horse physiology. It was clearly stated and well backed-up with examples and details. Your explanation of

horse psychology, however, left me a little confused. It might be my own fault, but it just didn't seem to be as well supported as the rest of your speech."

To encourage this type of criticism, I have my students use the speech evaluation form below (note especially the last two items).

Your instructor might prefer his or her own evaluation form, or you might want to amend this one to your own liking. That is all well and good. But whatever type of form you use, make sure it allows for positive, as well as negative, criticism.

SPEECH EVALUATION FORM

Name _____   Topic _____

Assignment # _____   Date _____

Please comment on each item:

	Good 5	4	3	2	Poor 1
Focus	—	—	—	—	—
Investigation	—	—	—	—	—
Organization	—	—	—	—	—
Language	—	—	—	—	—
Message Strategy	—	—	—	—	—

I especially liked _____

_____

However, improvement is needed in _____

_____

SUMMARY

This chapter dealt with listening, a human behavior that is as difficult to do correctly as it is essential to the learning that takes place in a public speaking class. The discussion included the components of listening, the objectives of listening, and methods of enhancing listening.

Listening is not as easy as it looks. It actually contains three components: *comprehension* (the process of hearing and concentrating on the words that are presented), *interpretation* (assigning meaning to those words), and *evaluation* (determining the value or importance of the ideas presented). Whenever we truly listen, we go through all three components of the act.

In a public speaking class, the objectives of listening are based on principles of message preparation. You listen for the *focus* of the speech, for the *investigation* that went into it, for the *organization* of the ideas, for the *language* that is used, and for the *message strategy.* You also observe the delivery traits, although it is important not to let them distract you from what is being said.

Methods of enhancing listening include preparing for listening (for example, by practicing), controlling distractions (by recognizing internal distractions such as daydreaming, as well as external ones such as noises in the room), withholding evaluation (until your comprehension of the speech is complete), and taking notes (to free yourself from remembering details, so you can concentrate on what is being said).

These methods, along with a recognition of the components and objectives of listening, can help you improve your listening skills.

After listening to a speech, it is important to offer constructive criticism. Constructive criticism includes positive as well as negative comments.

QUESTIONS FOR DISCUSSION

1. Do you agree that the objectives of listening coincide with the objectives of message preparation? Why or why not?
2. How do you interpret Dr. Nichols' statement "The more we take from a speaker through listening, the more he will give"? Do you agree or disagree? Why or why not?
3. Now that you understand the importance of developing listening skills, what do you think *speakers* can do in their presentations to *help* the audience listen more effectively?
4. Some people say, "If you don't have something nice to say, don't say anything at all." Do you think this "be nice or shut up" advice is sound, at least as it relates to the criticism of public speaking?

PROBES

1. Try this one only with a trusted friend or relative. To check on the possibility that people often don't listen, but only fake it, start telling someone a story about something you did yesterday or someplace

you went. At some point throw in a line such as "about then a pink rhinoceros walked in." If the person doesn't notice—and is obviously not listening—ask him or her to indicate what distractions led to the inattention.

2. Select a speech from the Appendix of this book or another source such as *Vital Speeches, Contemporary American Speeches,* or from the last set of speeches in your class. Were you able to learn any new words from the speech by determining their meanings from their context?

3. Check to see if there is an interesting documentary to be shown soon on television. (For example, it might be about the Middle East, the Bermuda Triangle, ESP, and so on.) What questions can you formulate in advance that might help you to be a more effective viewer or listener?

4. Recall the last speech you listened to in your speech class. Try to remember what *internal* distractions might have hampered your listening. What *external* distractions did you experience? What do you think you can do to avoid being distracted in the future?

5. People often tend to *evaluate* a message without first comprehending it. Recall an argument you recently had with a parent or a friend. Do you think the other person might have responded to what he or she *thought* you said rather than what you *really* said? If so, what might you have done to help that person hear you more accurately?

6. (a) Review your notes from the last class lecture you heard. Do they indicate that you may have missed some important points? If so, do you find that insignificant details might have distracted you? What are those details, and why do you think they are insignificant?

   (b) Try to take careful notes on the next speech you hear in your class. To what extent did insignificant details hamper your listening? Why are these details insignificant?

7. As you listen to the next two speeches in your class or the next two lectures in one of your courses, compare two methods of taking notes—your own, and the author's. Which method seems to work better for you, and why?

NOTES

¹Ralph A. Nichols and Leonard A. Stevens, *Are You Listening?* (New York: McGraw-Hill Book Co., 1957), p. 42.

²Ibid., pp. 104–105.

³A large body of classic experimental research suggests that numerous *other* factors, such as our prior experience and expectations, or our attitudes, affect how effectively we can listen or observe. Representative studies include R. Leeper, "The Role of Motivation in Learning: A Study of the Phenomenon of

Differential Motivation Control of the Utilization of Habits," *Journal of Genetic Psychology,* 45 (1935), pp. 3–40; R. Schafer and G. Murphy, "The Role of Autism in a Visual Figure-ground Relationship," *Journal of Experimental Psychology,* 32 (1943), pp. 335–343; A. H. Hastorf and H. Cantril, "They Saw a Game: A Case Study," *Journal of Abnormal and Social Psychology,* 49 (1954), pp. 129–134; E. E. Jones and R. Kohler, "The Effects of Plausibility on the Learning of Controversial Statements," *Journal of Abnormal and Social Psychology,* 57 (1958), 315–320; G. W. Allport and L. J. Postman, "The Basic Psychology of Rumor," in Eleanor Maccoby, Theodore Newcomb, and Eugene Hartley, eds., *Readings in Social Psychology,* 3rd ed. (New York: Holt, Rinehart, and Winston, 1958), pp. 54–65.

[4]Carl H. Weaver, *Human Listening: Processes and Behavior* (Indianapolis: Bobbs-Merrill, 1972) pp. 144–145.

[5]Nichols and Stevens, op. cit., p. 42.

[6]Ibid., p. 36.

[7]Ibid., p. 42.

[8]Carl R. Rogers, *On Becoming a Person* (Boston: Houghton Mifflin, 1971), pp. 331–337.

[9]Ample research evidence indicates that the strength of an audiences' attitude toward the topic, as well as their initial attitude toward the speaker, will markedly affect how a message is interpreted. For example, see S. Asch, "The Doctrine of Suggestion, Prestige, and Imitation in Social Psychology," *Psychological Review,* 55 (1948), pp. 250–276; M. Manis, "The Interpretation of Opinion Statements as a Function of Recipient Attitude and Source Prestige," *Journal of Abnormal and Social Psychology,* 63 (1961), pp. 82–86; and L. Berkowitz and R. Goranson, "Motivational and Judgmental Determinants of Social Perception," *Journal of Abnormal and Social Psychology,* 69 (1964), pp. 296–302. Similar studies are reported in C. Sherif, M. Sherif, and R. Nebergall, *Attitude and Attitude Change: The Social Judgment-Involvement Approach,* (Philadelphia: W. B. Saunders, 1965).

[10]Dan Walker, "Making Our Criminal Justice System Work," *Vital Speeches of the Day,* vol. 43 (September 15, 1976).

[11]My notes on a speech given by Elizabeth McEvoy in her public speaking class at the University of New Hampshire.

[12]The quote referred to here was: "The equestrian art, perhaps more than any other, is closely related to the wisdom of life. Many of the same principles may be applied as a line of conduct to follow. The horse teaches us self-control, constancy, and the ability to understand what goes on in the mind and feelings of another creature, qualities that are important throughout our lives." The quote comes from Alois Podhajsky, *The Complete Training of Horse and Rider* (Garden City, N.Y.: Doubleday, 1967).

[13]The answer was yes.

[14]The answer was also yes.

[15]Nichols and Stevens, op cit., p. 113.

TWO
The Basics of Message Preparation

This entire book is about message preparation, but this section concentrates on five concepts that underlie the basic process of putting a speech together: *focus, investigation, organization, language, and delivery.* You can look at *focus* as "deciding what to talk about," *investigation* as "finding information to back up what you say," *organization* as "arranging what you find," *language* as "making your ideas as clear as possible," and *delivery* as "presenting your ideas." At first glance, it looks as though these basics make up a set sequence: First you decide what to talk about, then you find information, and so on. Actually, these things happen in no set order, and sometimes they happen all at once; that's why it's important to study them as concepts *underlying* the process of speech preparation: If you decide, while practicing your delivery, to go back and change your organization or your language usage, you aren't doing anything wrong. In fact, if you do that you're probably using the process to its fullest advantage.

3

Focus

This chapter deals with focus, which is the process of concentrating on one idea that is appropriate to you, your audience, and the occasion of your speech. The importance of focus is based on a basic prediction about message preparation:

A message that is focused will be more effective than one that is not.[1]

SOME PRELIMINARY CONSIDERATIONS

Focus is the process of concentrating on one idea throughout your speech. This single idea should be appropriate to you, your audience, and the occasion of your speech. Focus requires thinking, creativity, and analysis, three processes that are closely related.

Thinking

The British novelist W. Somerset Maugham once observed that it is important to have lots of ideas so you can throw the unimportant ones away.[2] This process of throwing away unimportant ideas is especially helpful today. Modern people are inundated with more messages than ever before. The electronics revolution has made everyone a potential publisher or broadcaster, while our highly depersonalized and mobile society has increased our *need* to communicate. In our rush to express ideas, we sometimes don't wait for the good ones.

"Waiting for good ideas" is also known as thinking. Perhaps one reason why thinking tends to be difficult is that it is sometimes frowned upon in our society. I first noticed this tendency many years ago when, as a high school football player, I was chastised for thinking. I was, in the parlance of the day, a "pulling guard." That meant that I had to block out for the ball carrier by pulling back, running behind my own line, and knocking over the defensive end. This tricky maneuver was sometimes foiled because the lineman next to me was the only 97-pound tackle in the state, and he would be

pushed back and knocked down on every play. When it came time for me to "pull," both the offensive and defensive tackles would be piled up in my path. Rather than fight my way through both of them I would consider my options and then run downfield to see if there was anyone else who looked as though he wanted to be knocked down. Of course, pulling away from the pack like that made me rather visible, and my coach, who was well on his way to a coronary at twenty-five, would scream for me to report to the sidelines.

"You lunkhead," the coach would bark, with veins popping out all over his neck, "you were supposed to *pull* on that play. What in the name of the great Lombardi is wrong with you?"

"But Coach," I would say, "I thought—"

"How many times do I have to tell you, peabrain? *Don't think.* It hurts the team."

If I had a nickel in my pocket for every time my coach told me not to think, I wouldn't be able to hold my trousers up. But the coach wasn't the only one who believed thinking was dangerous. The notion was, and is, widespread. Try an experiment and see for yourself. Just sit down anywhere and think. Concentrate. Wrinkle up your forehead to increase the intensity of your concentration. See how long it is until someone walks up and asks, "What's wrong?"

This tendency is mentioned here so you can fight against it. Thinking is neither unpatriotic nor painful. It is not unmasculine, or unfeminine. It does, however, require time and concentration. To focus you have to give yourself the time and exert the energy necessary for thought.

Creativity

Creativity is a popular topic these days. We have best-selling books and franchised training programs on creative management, creative marriage, creative divorce, and even creative dying. In public speaking, creativity is important because it allows a speech to be perceived as "new" by both you and your audience; therefore, you will be more enthusiastic in giving it and the audience will be more enthusiastic in listening to it.

There are different types of creativity. One type is the discovery of some new relationship between two or more things you already know. If you were giving a speech on inflation, and you compared inflation to cancer or a multiple-car wreck, you would be using this type of creativity. You already know about inflation, cancer, and auto wrecks, but by discovering the relationship between two of them you have gained a vantage point that is potentially exciting to both you and your audience.

Another type of creativity is the discovery of order in something that appears to be chaotic. This is the type of creativity that Jacob Bronowski, the brilliant poet, scientist, and philosopher, best appreciated:

> Nature is chaos. It is full of infinite variety, and whether you are Leonardo da Vinci or whether you are Isaac Newton or whether you are modestly sitting down thinking about acts of revolt, there comes a moment when many different aspects suddenly crystallize in a single unity. You have found the key; you have found the clue; you have found the path which organizes the material. You have found what Coleridge[3] called "unity in variety." That is the moment of creation.[4]

This is the type of creativity that you'll experience when your speech finally "comes together." It is also the type of creativity that enables you to organize your speech.

Another type of creativity enables you to use available resources to do something that needs to be done. One of my friends is so well endowed with this type of creativity that he can practically rebuild a car with no more than a can opener and a rock. It is this type of creativity that enables speakers to choose a speech topic from their own realm of interests and experience. Students often experience a creative block about what to talk about; like kids wending their way through a room full of toys to complain that they don't have anything to do, they fail to see how many facets of their own lives are potentially interesting to their classmates. Every speech teacher has a favorite story about students who come in insisting that they can't think of a speech topic. When the teacher offers to discuss the problem with them, they explain that they don't have time because they have to get ready for a karate tournament, or they have to go work at a local clinic for autistic children, or they have to go feed a pet ostrich.

Obviously, then, creativity is important in public speaking—but can creativity be learned? Most theorists agree that it can at least be encouraged, since it is a natural ability that is systematically suppressed by football coaches, drill sergeants, and even some teachers. The best way to encourage creativity is to recognize it by its various phases, and then allow enough time and an environment that is conducive to letting those phases work. Most theorists agree that creativity has four phases: *preparation, incubation, illumination, and verification.*[5] An examination of these phases can give us an idea of how they relate to speech preparation.

1. Preparation.   In this stage thought and activity are expended on a problem that appears to require a creative solution. The problem is formulated, its components are defined, and various solutions are considered. The preparation stage is primarily a time of private thought and introspection. In speech preparation, this stage is seen in the time spent thinking about and investigating your topic. The preparation stage is often slighted by college students because of their predilection to put things off until the last minute. The result of that is almost always a noncreative speech.

2. Incubation.   This phase of the creative process is a period of escape from solitary thought about the problem. It is a time in which you step away from the task at hand and allow something other than your own thought processes to stimulate your unconscious.[6] The incubation stage, in effect, is a short vacation from the process of speech preparation. Obviously, this vacation won't be possible if you wait until the last minute to prepare your speech. The time set aside for incubation is important because it leads to illumination, the next phase of creativity.

3. Illumination.   This phase of the creative process is often referred to as the "Eureka!" phase. (*Eureka* is Greek for "I have found it.") It is a moment of sudden, concise, and certain insight into the problem. The literature is replete with stories of creative people who experience illumination at unpredictable—and sometimes embarrassing—times. Legend has it that Archimedes was in the bathtub when he came upon the method of determining the volume of solids by measuring the liquid they displace, and he got up and ran naked through the streets shouting, *"Eureka!"* It is hoped that you will experience the same type of excitement in the illumination you experience during speech preparation. It might happen when you hit upon the perfect topic, or an approach to that topic, or an organizational scheme, or anything else that will make your speech "work." It is also hoped that you will verify your insight before you announce it to the world. That is what the final stage of creativity is all about.

4. Verification. This is the phase in which the insight is validated and you find out whether your "Eureka!" is worth its capital "E" and exclamation point. People who have flashes of inspiration in the middle of the night often write down what they consider to be great ideas at 4:00 AM, only to find these same ideas worthless in the more critical light of day.

Verification is accomplished by taking a second look at your insight. Sometimes just re-examining an insight by yourself will turn the trick. Other times, you might need to tell someone else and see what they think about it.

These phases of creativity suggest that you can—in fact you *must—work* at creativity. One of the things we know about the working habits of most famous playwrights, painters, composers, and other creative people is that they set aside time and *work*, whether they feel creative or not. Creativity is a habitual way of thinking that must be learned, and the surprising thing is that once you learn it, you are often creative *without* knowing it. You can be creative, in other words, without the "flash."

Analysis

Thinking and creativity are the sparks that are needed to focus a speech. Analysis is the tool that controls that spark and makes it useful. *Analysis is the process of taking something apart and looking at each part in order to understand the whole.* That sounds simple, but actually analysis is more difficult today than ever before. For one thing, there is an unprecedented amount of information floating around for us to wade through. For another, we have a tendency to watch too much television.

"Now what," you might well ask, "does television have to do with our ability to analyze?" Marshall McLuhan would be glad you asked that question, because he was one of the first to equate the advent of television with a decline in analytical thinking.[7] McLuhan has suggested that the TV generation (a group consisting of nearly everyone under 35) has lost its ability to analyze. The print generation that came before them thought analytically, he says; when they had a problem before them they broke it up into simpler parts and examined each one of those parts. Today, McLuhan contends, because of our constant use of media that give us "everything at once," people attempt to look at things and understand them immediately, without taking the time to take them apart.

Robert Pirsig, in his book *Zen and the Art of Motorcycle Maintenance*,[8] seems to agree with McLuhan. He suggests that people are intimidated by technology because they no longer break up complex things into basic components. If they can't start a Honda by kicking it, yelling at it, or just staring sullenly at it, they give up. They don't sit down and *analyze* what might be wrong with it.

McLuhan and Pirsig might be right. You have to decide for yourself whether analysis is a problem for you. Do you sometimes find it difficult to examine things piece by piece? Do you sometimes feel like taking your *audience* apart limb by limb, but fail to see the necessity of taking it apart analytically, to understand it? Do you sometimes fail to take your *topics* apart before you talk about them, and therefore find yourself trying to talk about everything at once? Do you sometimes fail to analyze the circumstances surrounding your speeches, and wind up telling jokes when you should be serious? Or worse? If so, your problem might be a problem of focus.

Focus is essential in public speaking, and it relies on a thoughtful analysis of source, receiver,[9] and occasion. Figure 3–1 presents a model that clarifies the relationship between analysis and focus. The model is based on the idea that there is a similarity between optical focus and the focusing of ideas. Focusing an idea is like lining up three lenses in such a way that they produce a precise image. In order to be focused, a speech must have all three lenses simultaneously aligned. The lenses of the focus model include the source of the message (that's you), the receiver of the message (your audience), and the occasion for which the message is presented.

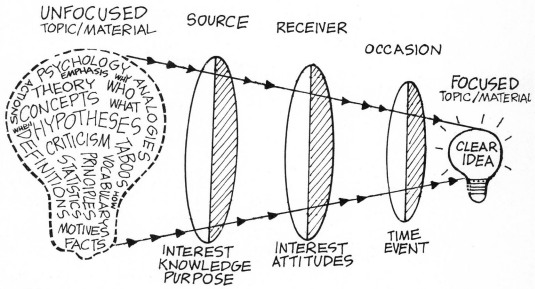

Figure 3–1

The model illustrates a procedure for focusing topics and material: Take them apart and view them through the lenses of yourself, your audience, and the occasion. Then use the topic or the material only if it "lines up" with all three lenses at once. A topic is focused only when it is focused from all three perspectives, or "points of view." Just being focused from *your* perspective is not enough. But you have to start somewhere.

FOCUS: THE SOURCE PERSPECTIVE

To focus topics or material from the source perspective you have to examine your own interests, knowledge, and purpose for communicating.

Interests

Until you become famous, a public speaking class will probably be the only place where you are asked to simply "give a speech." In the outside world, topics are usually chosen by whoever asks you to speak. If you're an expert on cooking you are asked to talk about cooking, and so on. But in a speech class you might be called upon to talk without being given a topic. When that happens, it helps to give some thought to your own interests and to try to analyze them.

Your topic must be one that you are interested in; otherwise it will be difficult for you to interest anyone else. Your interest in your topic will improve your ability to investigate it. It will also increase your confidence when it comes time to present it.

The same is true for all the material you use in a speech. If it isn't interesting to you, it will be difficult to make it interesting to your audience.

Knowledge

You will want to choose a topic you already know something about. However, the main problem for most people is not "knowing something" but knowing *what* they know. Recognizing what you know requires a certain amount of confidence. It is a mistake to think you don't know anything about your topic that your audience doesn't already know. That would not only be self-defeating, it would almost certainly be untrue. Your experiences, your thinking, and your investigation will be unique. Even if you talk about something your audience is familiar with, you will supply new information for them. You cannot help it. One of my students recently gave a speech on local blue laws that require stores to stay closed on Sunday. Every member of the class was familiar with these laws, but few realized how economically harmful they were, or what they could do about having the laws changed. These details were presented in the student's speech, and the class found it interesting.

But there is also the other side of the coin. Sometimes people think they know things that they do not. Worse yet, sometimes they stand in awe of that which they do *not* understand. This can cause problems when choosing material for a speech. The temptation to use material that is impressive because of its complexity is just about overpowering. By using it, the speaker feels he shares some of the intellectual prowess of the source of that information. Do not fall into this trap. Use only ideas, thoughts, and information you understand completely. Carefully collected scientific data you do not understand is much less valuable than ideas you can put into your own words and present from your own perspective. Ideas you have collected from other people must be totally within your control when you use them. You have to leave out those parts that sound good but that you don't understand. If you are interested in archaeology, a college audience will probably be more interested in your personal experiences at an excavation site than in a highly specialized, esoteric theory about an ancient Mayan culture—expecially if you do not completely understand the theory yourself!

Purpose

Determine your purpose for communicating and focus your topic accordingly. For example, "Maple Syrup" would be an unfocused topic until you attached a purpose to it. If your purpose is to entertain, you might speak on "Maple Syrup Fights and How to Clean up Afterward." If you intend to inform, "How to Make Maple Syrup" might be more appropriate. If you intend to persuade, your topic might be "Maple Syrup Should be Outlawed." In order to focus your topic, you have to determine which of the four basic message strategies (audience interest, explanation, persuasion, or humor) best suits the purpose of your speech. The strategies related to these basic purposes will be dealt with in detail in Part Three of this text. For now, they can be discussed in very general terms.

To focus your topic, you might want to formulate a "purpose statement." A purpose statement is an explicit declaration of *why* you are speaking. In fact, you might want to use one of these four fill-in-the-blank purpose statements:

1. My purpose is to interest by _____

    _____

    (Fill in specifically how you intend to interest your audience. Can you save them money or improve the quality of their life in some way?)
2. My purpose is to enterain by _____

    _____

(Fill in the precise method of entertainment. Do you want them to be intrigued by an adventure, relaxed with remembrances of things past, or amused by your story about an impossible mess-up at registration? State it simply and concisely!)

3. My purpose is to explain _____

_____

(Fill in specifically what you want to explain, whether it be the operation of a solar furnace or how you know for sure whether the light goes out when you close the refrigerator door.)

4. My purpose is to persuade my audience to _____

_____

(Fill in exactly what you want your audience to do. Make sure it is a reasonable action, though. Most audiences would not have it in their power to "repeal marijuana laws." They might, however, be persuaded to "write their congressmen to support the repeal of marijuana laws.")

Thus, the first lens of the focus model demonstrates how you focus an idea according to what you are interested in, what you know, and the purpose of your speech. You now have to give this idea a direction. If you don't, it could hit anywhere, like light streaming through a spinning prism. The first lens, therefore, has to be aligned with the second lens: your audience—the receiver.

FOCUS: THE RECEIVER PERSPECTIVE

In order to analyze topics or material in terms of the receiver of the message, you might want to examine the possible *interests* and *attitudes* of that receiver.

Audience Interests

Sometimes the easiest way to form an opinion on audience interests is through an analysis of audience demographics. Demographics are characteristics of your audience that can be labeled, such as age, sex, group membership, purpose for gathering, and so on. These characteristics provide clues to what the individual members of that audience will be interested in.

For example, it is generally accepted that young people and old people have different interests. Aristotle once observed that young people "have strong passions," that "their lives are spent not in memory but in expectation," and that they have high ideals "because they have not been humbled by life or learnt its necessary limitations."[10] This means that young people have a tendency to be less practical; they are interested in sports cars rather than four-door sedans, fashion rather than durability. Older people tend to be interested in the practical side of things. This might make a difference in how you approach a topic. For example, if you were speaking about "The World Food Shortage" with a young audience, the idealism of helping other people might be stressed. With older people, the practical advantages (such as the boost to our own economy that results from international charity) might be stressed. Either way, you have to make a conscious choice based on the best prediction you can make about audience interests.

The sexual composition of your audience provides another clue to their interests. Traditionally, men and women tend to be interested in different things. These different interests are becoming less prevalent as time goes on, because men and women are becoming conscious of sexual stereotypes and are rebelling against them. Still, the differences in interest that prevail are of concern to a speaker focusing a topic. There are still more men than women interested in automotive engineering, and more women than men interested in home economics. An important guideline for analyzing the sexual composition of your audience is this: *Do not exclude any portion of your audience on the basis of sex.* Recently, in a class composed primarily of men, one student gave a speech on "Picking Up Chicks." It was not a speech on methods of handling poultry. The women were offended by the speech, and the men, realizing the inappropriateness of the topic, sided with the women. Later, both men and women accused the speaker of being sexist and bigoted. The speech might more appropriately have been on "Meeting People." That way, it could have been treated in a manner that would be interesting to and appropriate for both men and women. This is true of topics like automotive engineering (which could be amended to "Car Designs of the Future") and home economics (which could become "Survival for Singles").

Organizations to which the audience members belong provide more clues to audience interests. By examining the groups to which they belong, you can surmise an audience's political leanings (Young Republicans or Young Democrats), religious beliefs (CYO or Hillel), or occupation (Bartenders Union or Speech Communication Association).[11] Group membership is often an important consideration in college classes. Consider the differences in "typical" college day classes and "typical" college night classes. This might not be true everywhere, but at my college the night students are generally older and they tend to belong to civic clubs, church groups, and the local chamber of commerce. Daytime students tend to belong to sororities and fraternities, sports clubs, and social-action groups.

Sometimes an audience is highly heterogeneous. In other words, the audience members have widely diversified interests. Also, sometimes audience interests are difficult to recognize. This is true in many public speaking classes, especially early in the semester before the interests of the various class members become known. When this is true, you can at least examine the audience's *purpose for gathering*. Audiences differ in reasons for gathering. Two audiences might be similar in age, sexual composition, and group membership, but their purposes for gathering could be completely different. In fact, this happens often on a college campus, where some classes are required and some are electives. The students in the required classes could be considered captive audiences, while the students in the elective classes are usually there because they are interested in the subject matter of the course. In fact, there are at least three different types of audiences that you are likely to run into on any college campus, and these audience types correspond closely to types of audiences found outside the ivory tower. The audience types might be called "passersby," "captives," and "involved citizens."[12]

"Passersby," as the name implies, are people who aren't much interested in what you have to say. To make matters worse, they are not even required to listen. A crowd milling around the student union, or one at a shopping mall, would fit into this category. "Captives" are audiences who have gathered for some reason besides the joy of gathering. That's why students in a required class make up a type of "captive" audience. Military formations, mandatory staff meetings, and other "required" gatherings fit this category, also. "Involved citizens" are audiences who have gathered together because of a common interest. Elective courses, especially those with long waiting lists, would fit into this category. So would most clubs, social organizations, or "action" groups.

Why your audience members gather is a big clue to the type of topic that would interest them. It is also a clue to the type of material you would need for presenting that topic. If you were attempting to explain a proposed gun-control law to a group of passersby, you would probably have to use some kind of "material" to make the audience aware that you wanted to speak to them. You might have to shout a snappy slogan or even fire a toy pistol.[13] For an audience of "captives," such as a required college class in U.S. government, such a drastic action is usually not necessary. The class members will probably be aware of you as a speaker. Your main responsibility before such an audience is to capture and maintain their interest. For an audience of "involved citizens," such as a group that has gathered specifically to support (or protest) gun control, you would have to be mainly concerned with an in-depth statement of your case.

You would have to maintain their interest, also. You never lose that responsibility. But when an audience is informed and involved, you have to treat your topic in greater depth.

This analysis of audience types is not included here to encourage you to stereotype audiences or try to make them all fit within one of the categories. It is presented to make you aware of possible differences in interest within audiences who have gathered for different purposes. Your audience's purpose for gathering can also be a clue to their attitudes, which are closely related to and just as important as audience interests.

Audience Attitudes

Characteristics such as age, sex, group membership, and reason for gathering help you determine audience attitude systems, also. The phrase "attitude systems" is useful because attitudes are often interrelated. You can often make a judgment about one attitude your audience members hold based on your knowledge of other attitudes they hold. If your audience is made up of undergraduates who have a positive attitude toward sexual-liberation movements, it is a good bet that they also have a positive attitude toward civil rights and ecology. If they have a negative attitude toward collegiate sports, they probably also have a negative attitude toward fraternities and sororities.[14] This should not only suggest appropriate topics, it should also suggest what kind of material can be used in discussing those topics.

I recently scheduled lectures on obscenity for both my daytime and my evening college classes. Though the topic was the same I had to prepare two separate lectures. The daytime college students were more familiar with the use of obscenity than the older, evening group. According to the value system of the older group, a person who used obscene language was untrustworthy. Because of this, I had to watch my language carefully. (Just try to lecture on obscenity sometime without using any). The attitudes that I had to consider when preparing the lecture were part of a system of attitudes that made the evening class more practical and conservative than the younger, day class.

The next point of focus is the audience's expectations, which are determined by the occasion of your speech.

FOCUS: THE OCCASION

The "occasion" of a speech is determined by the circumstances surrounding it. Two of the most important circumstances of an occasion are *time* and *event*.

Time

The time available for your speech is an essential consideration. You should choose a topic that is broad enough to say something worthwhile but brief enough to fit your time limits. "Sex," for example, might be an inherently interesting topic to a college audience, but it would be difficult to cover such a broad topic in a ten-minute speech and still say anything significant. But a topic like "How Sexual Stereotypes Are Established Through Television Advertising" could conceivably be covered in enough depth in ten minutes to make it worthwhile. All speeches have time limitations, whether they are explicitly stated or not. If you are invited somewhere to say a few words, and you present a few volumes, you will not be invited back.

Time must be considered when focusing your material, also. Any idea that takes too long to be made clear will have to be dropped, as well as any examples or statistics that take too long to explain fully. If you have too many ideas, you will have to drop all except the ones you have time to develop.

Event

Your speech is an event. It occupies a space in time that is surrounded by other events. For example, the "event" of a speech given in a public speaking class is usually a laboratory experience, before peers, followed by a critical evaluation in which the speakers are expected to learn from experience. This event might call for a learning orientation, a certain level of seriousness, and a certain level of thought. The learning orientation could mean that your topic and material will be most effective if it teaches something to the class. To do this, you might want to relate your topic directly to a theory[15] or a set of principles. For example, if you were soliciting contributions to have your cat neutered, you would not want to talk simply about how warm and cuddly your pet is, or how adorably it purrs right before it claws its way up your leg. It would be more appropriate to explain the beneficial relationship man and cat have enjoyed through the ages (rat control, etc.) or the dangers of uncontrolled overpopulation of domestic animals. The seriousness of the occasion might call for material that is well substantiated, and the appropriate level of thought would be one that is challenging enough for college students. If you were speaking at a sports banquet or before a social club, the event would be different and material that was less serious or challenging might be used.

In fact, "speeches of special occasion" are heavily influenced by event, so we should take a minute to consider them here.

Special Occasions

Special occasion speeches include (but are not limited to) after-dinner speeches, speeches of celebration, speeches of introduction, speeches of tribute, and speeches of appreciation.

After-dinner speeches are entertaining speeches. No one is eager for great profundity on a full stomach, so an after-dinner speech is expected to be light and humorous. A banquet following an annual club meeting is the kind of event at which this type of speech is likely to be heard.

Speeches of celebration are heard at events such as anniversaries, reunions, holidays, and commemorations. A speaker at events such as these is expected to be enthusiastic and well informed about the event.

Speeches of introduction acquaint the audience with a guest or a new member of their group. The speaker is expected to concentrate on the person being introduced, especially in terms of that person's importance to the audience.

Speeches of tribute are those that list the accomplishments and personal characteristics of an individual being honored. If the person is recently deceased, the speech of tribute is generally referred to as a *eulogy*.

Speeches of appreciation are those in which the speaker thanks the audience. The speech following the presentation of a prize or an award is typical of this type of speech. The speaker is expected to be courteous, and to honor both the audience and the thing that he or she is thanking them for. (For example, to say, "This is a dumb prize and you're all a bunch of clucks for giving it to me" would be inappropriate in this type of speech.)

PRACTICING FOCUS

Focusing according to you, your audience, and the speech occasion will continue for the entire time you are working on your speech. It is important to focus on a topic as soon as possible. As Wilson and Arnold point out,

> A consistent difference between good and poor college speakers is that the good speakers choose subjects carefully but swiftly and stick to them.[16]

It is important to focus when investigating your topic, too. Consider how you would feel if you decided to investigate inefficiency in the administration of your college. You might go to a well-known business-administration professor on your campus and ask her how your college measures up according to her standards of efficiency. She might tell you that it is not as good as Follage College, her alma mater. So you read up on Follage College and after taking seventeen pages of notes and missing two of the best parties of the year, you realize that Follage College is a private military academy. Since your college is a public liberal arts institution, most of the material you collected would be inappropriate for your topic. It would have to be thrown out.

Focus is meant to help you avoid this misery. If you keep a focused topic in mind as you collect your material, chances are you will have to throw less material away.

It is important to focus when organizing your speech. Everything you say must be perceived by your audience as relating to one thing: your topic. Whenever you present a speech you are presenting one basic idea, whether you know it or not, because your audience will have a tendency to reduce your message to a central theme anyway. Your audience should be able to leave the scene of your speech saying, "That speech was all about _____."

They should be able to fill in that blank with one idea. If they can't, they are likely to leave the speech saying, "I don't know what that speech was all about," or "That speech was about a little of this and a little of that, but I don't understand what those things had to do with each other."

Focus is even important when you are choosing the language you will use to express your ideas. Your language has to be appropriate to you, your audience, and the occasion of your speech.

So focus is a very general concept that relates to all the other areas of message preparation. One way to look at focus is as an adjustment on the screen through which you are viewing the other facets of message preparation. If the adjustment is correct, these other facets will be clearer and therefore easier to accomplish.

So keep focus in mind as you read the next three chapters and as you prepare your speeches for class. And don't be frustrated if, after finishing a speech, you recognize ways you could have focused even more. This is known as the What I Should Have Said Phenomenon, which is well known to anyone who has ever lost an argument. Don't let it worry you. That is, after all, what learning is all about.

SAMPLE SPEECH

The following is an example of a speech that used the procedure of focusing topic and material according to source, receiver, and occasion. This speech, like the sample in Chapter 1, was presented by me. The circumstances, however, were somewhat different. It was my first week as a college teacher. I wasn't much older than my students, and I was eager to please. I had just assigned the class their first speech: "Introduce yourself and tell the class why they should listen to you for the rest of the semester. Time limit: five minutes." I then asked for volunteers for the next class meeting, and received only an embarrassed silence in return.

"I don't really know what to say," one student said finally.

"And we really don't know anything about you," hinted another, with Mack-truck subtlety.

"How about a sample speech?" asked a third.

"Sure," said the ambitious young teacher.

Reconstructed below is a facsimile of the speech presented during the next class period. Some comments about the focusing process follow the speech.

CONFESSIONS OF A COMMUNICATION FANATIC[17]

At the last class meeting, I agreed to give you a sample speech of introduction. Almost immediately, I had misgivings. You see, the most successful speeches of self-introduction will deal with *your uniqueness* as a person. That's why we'll listen to you for the rest of the semester. You're unique. You've had unique experiences, you've thought unique thoughts, and you've become a unique person. And we *will* listen to you if you take advantage of that uniqueness, because you're going to tell us things that we couldn't learn any other way. The only way you can go wrong is if you hide your uniqueness. That's why I had misgivings about this sample speech. I don't want you to think that you have to be unique in the same way I'm unique.

You see, I'm unique because I am a communication fanatic. That means that I am, and have always been, fascinated by the way people speak, write, and relate with one another. Because of my fanaticism I've taken a few lumps, but I've learned a little bit, too. In fact, that's what I want to tell you about today—the lumps, and what I've learned from them.

The lumps came from all sorts of misadventures. For example, as a kid I got into dozens of fights that were none of my business, simply because I wanted to analyze what was going on. I remember one time when Bert Barrier and Joe Hanlon, two of the nastiest scrappers in school, were squaring off out by the bicycle racks late one afternoon. When I came on the scene both of them were saying "Yeah" to each other. Have you ever heard a dialogue like that? It goes like this:

"Yeah?"
"Yeah!"
"Yeah?"
"Yeah!"

So I asked them what they were fighting about, and if they realized that they sounded pretty funny saying "Yeah" to each other like that. Sure enough, before I knew it they were both beating on *me*!

I took quite a few lumps investigating human communication, so I naturally became obsessed with the phenomenon. I only took jobs, for example, that were communication-oriented. Eventually this fascination caused me to take a job with the U.S. Navy as a communication consultant. My job was to show shipboard instructors and administrators how to communicate better. I worked aboard ships at sea for months at a time. The problem there was that I was prone to seasickness. In fact, I was seasick every day I was at sea, and I got bounced around in a way that Bert Barrier and Joe Hanlon could never have managed. So the Navy job gave me some more lumps.

But I learned something important in that job. I learned that even seasoned professionals need to be constantly reminded about the things that are taught in public speaking classes. It was then that I realized that teaching public speaking is the best possible job for a dyed-in-the-wool card-carrying communication fanatic. You see, in a public speaking class you slow down the communication process so you can take a good look at it. You take each message apart and get in-depth suggestions for improving it. A public speaking class is one of the few places where you can be exposed to that much constructive criticism of your ability to communicate.

So that's why I'm here. I hope I can be of some service to you. I hope I can share some of the things that I've learned in fights and seasickness, without you having to take any of the lumps.

Comments

This assignment was designed to cause the students to focus a topic that they had practically limitless knowledge of: themselves. In order to do that, their topic had to be information about themselves that they felt good about expressing. It couldn't be boring or embarrassing to them. It had to relate directly to the audience. It had to be appropriate to the event of a public-speaking class. It also had to conform to the time limit of five minutes.

In order to focus the sample speech, I reviewed my own interests, which ranged from stickball to nuclear fission. When considering what I knew, my highly specialized mind immediately settled on communication. Thus, the topic area was determined while I was still working with the first lens of the focus model. My purpose, as reflected in the following purpose statement, helped limit my topic area:

> My purpose is to persuade my audience to listen to me for the rest of the semester.

I then considered my audience interests. Were they interested in graduate courses, doctoral dissertations, journal articles, and conference papers? Probably not. They probably had a negative attitude toward highly specialized research; they were young and the interests that they had in common would probably be far more general. So, I thought to myself, what would these people be most interested in, in terms of my qualifications to teach them something about communication? They were between 18 and 20 years of age, all of them freshmen or sophomores in college. Most of them lived on campus, where the big sport was hockey. An exciting sport, I thought—too bad I never played it myself. But wait—how about the limited excitement I *had* encountered as I "took my lumps" learning about communication?

The speech began to take shape. I was basically nonviolent, but had been involved in some experiences that could be used for audience interest as I stressed my main point, which was that my experiences had made me unique in a way that might be helpful to the class.

This is just one example of how the focus model can be used. It will be used a little differently, however, for any message to which it is applied.

SUMMARY

This chapter dealt with focus, which is the process of concentrating on one idea that is appropriate to you, your audience, and the occasion of your speech. Focus is essential when choosing a topic, limiting a topic, and choosing material for a speech. Focus requires thinking, creativity, and analysis, which means that it takes time, that it requires energy, and that there is a recognizable process involved. That process includes taking apart topics and material not only from your own perspective (your interest, your knowledge, and your purpose) but also according to your audience and according to the occasion. To focus according to your audience you have to consider their interests and attitudes. One way to visualize audience interests and attitudes is to look at audience demographics such as age, sex, group membership, and reason for gathering. To focus according to the occasion, you have to consider the time available and the "event" of the speech. As illustrated by the focus model presented on page 45, when all of the major considerations are aligned simultaneously, the topic and material will be focused. Focus is a process that is pervasive throughout the investigation, organization, and language choices of a speech. A more specific look at investigation is provided in the next chapter.

QUESTIONS FOR DISCUSSION

1. Do you agree that it is important to have lots of ideas so you can throw the unimportant ones away, or do you sometimes find that too many ideas make it difficult to decide what *is* important? Cite examples to support your answer.
2. Many people believe that television has hampered our ability to analyze, or to think in general. With this frequent criticism in mind, answer the following:

     (a) Do media really, as McLuhan contends, "give us everything at once"?

     (b) Are we primarily influenced by what the media give us, or are our own experiences and our interpersonal relationships more responsible for our modes of thinking?

     (c) Has television led us to slight *other* modes of investigating problems?

3. Do you agree with Robert Pirsig that we are intimidated by modern technology to the extent that we can no longer look at the basic components of complex ideas? What examples can you cite to support your position?

4. Several different "audience types" are mentioned in the text, along with advice as to how material might be varied for each audience. Can you think of any other audience types? If so, how would you vary the material in your speech for each of these types?

5. Reread "Confessions of a Communication Fanatic" and the comments about its development. After doing so, how well do you think the lenses of the focus model were lined up?

PROBES

1. "Do your thing" is a favorite slogan for some people. Roughly translated, it means do what you do best, or what you're most interested in, or what you most enjoy doing. Using that rough translation, what's *your* thing? How might you develop a speech on "your thing" for your speech class?

2. If your class is typical, you are probably preparing right now for one of your classroom speeches. How does your topic and situation compare with the topic and situation of the sample speech in this chapter?

3. What, in your opinion, are the three most important interests of the audience in your public speaking class? In what way(s) might one or more of your own interests be related to theirs?

4. Select a lengthy news story from the newspaper. Applying the focus model, rewrite the story so that its essence could be presented in a brief (5 min.) speech.

5. How well did one of your professors practice the focus model in his or her last lecture? What changes in the presentation do you suggest for an improvement in focus?

6. Today most television dramas or adventures are one hour in length, but in earlier days the detective and western shows usually were only a half-hour long. With this thought in mind, watch an hour-long episode of one of your favorite programs. How might you revise the script so that the same story could be told in only a half-hour? What aspects of the focus model will be most important as you work on this task?

7. Think about a topic that is familiar to you *and* your classmates. On the basis of your experiences and/or reading, what new information can you supply for the class?
8. After you have selected the topic for your next speech, write four explicit purpose statements, one for each purpose mentioned in the chapter: interest, entertain, explain, and persuade.
9. Suppose you were trying to persuade your class to accept a social or political change (for example, the passage of the Equal Rights Amendment). What advantages could you stress? What advantages would you cite if you were addressing an older audience, consisting of people in business and their spouses? Give reasons for any differences you note.
10. Select a topic that might still be interesting primarily to only one sex. Develop a title, and a list of main points and subpoints that would help you adapt your message to *both* sexes.
11. Select any very broad topic, such as drugs, South Africa, and so on. Write a title that focuses the topic for a 10-minute presentation. Do the same thing for a speech of only 5 minutes.

NOTES

[1]Edwin G. Boring, *The Physical Dimensions of Consciousness* (New York: Dover Publications, 1963), p. 200.

[2]W. Somerset Maugham, *The Summing Up* (Garden City, N.Y.: Doubleday, Doran and Co., 1938).

[3]Samuel Taylor Coleridge, English poet, 1772–1834.

[4]Jacob Bronowski, "On Art and Science," in Jack D. Summerfield and Lorlyn Thatcher, eds., *The Creative Mind and Method* (Austin, Tex.: University of Texas Press, 1960).

[5]The labeling of these phases is generally attributed to Graham Wallas, *The Art of Thought* (New York: Harcourt Brace Jovanovich, 1926), pp. 79–95.

[6]The role of the unconscious is generally accepted to be important in the creative process. See, for example, Erwin DiCyan, *Creativity: Road to Self-Discovery* (New York: Harcourt Brace Jovanovich, 1978), especially Ch. 15.

[7]See, for example, Marshall McLuhan, *Understanding Media: The Extensions of Man* (New York: Signet, 1964).

[8]Robert Pirsig, *Zen and the Art of Motorcycle Maintenance* (New York: Wm. Morrow & Co., 1974).

[9]"Source" and "receiver" are basic communication terms. The person who originates a particular message is in the role of a "source," whereas the person who perceives that message is in the role of a "receiver." "Source" and "receiver" are used for this model because the concept of focus pertains to *all* types of messages.

[10]Aristotle, *Rhetoric*, translated by W. Rhys Roberts (New York: Modern Library, 1954), pp. 122–123.

[11]The survey and experimental literature demonstrating the effects of group affiliation on an individual's attitudes—particularly when the group is highly attractive to the person, and expects opinion conformity for continued membership—is too extensive to discuss adequately in this text. An excellent basic review of the relevant research can be found in Daryl J. Bem, *Beliefs, Attitudes, and Human Affairs* (Belmont, Cal.: Brooks/Cole, 1970), Ch. 7, pp.

70–100. A more advanced discussion, including reprints of important research studies, is offered by D. Cartwright and A. Zander, *Group Dynamics,* 3rd ed. (New York: Harper & Row, 1968).

[12]A detailed analysis of audience types can be found in H. L. Hollingworth, *The Psychology of the Audience* (New York: American Book Company, 1935), pp. 19–32. Hollingworth's analysis is summarized in W. D. Brooks, *Speech Communication* (Dubuque: Wm. C. Brown, Co., 1974), pp. 259–260.

[13]Although this method has been applied in some college classes, it is absolutely not necessary. And it is not even suggested outside college classes, because of the high probability of arrest.

[14]Attitude systems, and how people maintain consistency among the various attitudes they hold, is covered in more depth in Daryl J. Bem, *Beliefs, Attitudes, and Human Affairs* (Belmont, Calif.: Brooks/Cole Publishing Co., 1970), pp. 24–39. An even more advanced analysis, from various points of view, is offered in R. P. Abelson, E. Aronson, W. J. McGuire, T. M. Newcomb, M. J. Rosenberg, and P. H. Tannenbaum, eds., *Theories of Cognitive Consistency: A Sourcebook* (Chicago: Rand McNally, 1968).

[15]A theory is a set of statements that seeks to describe, explain, or predict phenomena.

[16]John F. Wilson and Carroll C. Arnold, *Dimensions of Public Communication* (Boston: Allyn and Bacon, 1976), p. 66.

[17]Reproduced from author's notes.

4 Investigation

This chapter deals with investigation, which is the process of systematically collecting facts and ideas. The importance of investigation is based on another basic prediction:

A message that is based on investigation will be more effective than a message that is based merely on speculation or personal opinion.[1]

Why Investigate?

You investigate people, ideas, and facts early in speech preparation.

You investigate the *people* who will be in your audience. You try to learn as much as possible about their interests and attitudes, so you can make your message appropriate for them. You don't want to tell denture jokes at a senior citizens' club if the senior citizens are likely to be offended.

You investigate your *ideas* to improve their quality. This is especially important when you are choosing and focusing a topic. You begin with an idea that interests you and that you consider important. You limit that idea to what you can effectively deal with, given your audience and the time limitations of the speech. During the process of investigation you will mold that idea, take it apart, put it back together, expand it here, streamline it there. When you have finished, your investigation will be one of the differences between an idea that is clear and one that is gibberish.

You investigate *facts* to substantiate and help develop your ideas. Expert testimony, statistics, and examples support the substance and importance of your ideas.

Investigation is another one of those practices that is becoming more difficult because of our overabundance of information. People often do not bother to investigate because they think it requires too much energy. This problem was brought home to me recently when, after working late distilling volumes of classic wisdom into a public speaking text, I wandered out to my car and found a conspicuous hole in the dashboard where my radio had been a little while before. I beheld the theft with mixed emotions. I was upset, but I also felt a glimmer of excitement. I would now be involved in the investigation of a crime. I would get to see detective work in real life. Perhaps the police would let me help as they dusted the car for fingerprints and searched for possible eyewitnesses. After all, I was a specialist in getting people to talk.

I left the car where it was, careful not to touch anything, and called the police. They thanked me for calling and explained that there wasn't much they could do.

"We'll be sure to let you know if your radio turns up," they said. "In the meantime, would you mind coming in to fill out a report? We like to keep our paperwork up to date."

I was aghast. What would Kojak say? What ever happened to the American spirit of adventure, our belief in life, liberty, and the pursuit of stolen radios? I realized then that the police had the same problem that my students had. They didn't know where to go for the answers without investing more time and energy than those answers were worth. Like my students, the police were missing out on the most interesting part of their work. Someone, I said to myself, has to speak out for investigation. The answers are there, waiting to be uncovered with less time and energy than you would think. You can investigate without pain or injury through library research, interpersonal research, and personal observation, if you know how. Some practical guidelines for each one of those methods will be discussed in this chapter. First, though, consider the following note about taking notes.

Taking Notes

Chapter 2 presented a system for taking notes on someone else's speech (pp. 28–31). You will also have to take notes when you are researching your own speech. Everyone has a different system for taking notes. As you research you will be struck with ideas. If you are prepared for them, they won't hurt you. You should take notes on these ideas no matter how earthshaking and unforgettable they seem at the time. Half the time you will realize that your ideas are illogical or insufficient if you express them in writing. Other times, ideas that don't quite seem to make sense will jell on paper and become quite valuable. Write your notes as if you were writing them for someone else. Then leave them for a while. When you come back to them, if you still think they are worthwhile you can transcribe them onto index cards. You should also take notes on ideas, quotes, and facts that you get from other sources. Each note card should list a topic, the note, and a source, if necessary. For example, if you are researching the idea of cybernetics (communication between man and machine) you might be struck with an idea such as "Computers could eventually be taught how to think, like the one they called Hal in *2001: A Space Odyssey*." If, after you have researched the topic for a while, this thought still seems valid, you might transfer it to an index card.

Computers

      Could computers eventually be made to *think*, like Hal in *2001: A Space Odyssey*?

Later, you might find other items that relate to this idea:

Computers—Can they be made to think?

      "Rapidly, we approach the final phase of the extensions of man—the technological simulation of human consciousness . . ."

      —McLuhan, *Understanding Media*, p. 19.

      Placing your ideas and research on index cards in this manner will make the analysis and organization of that material easier later on. But if you don't feel like using index cards, don't let that deter you from taking notes. Take them on anything. The clean side of computer printouts, for example, is fine for investigative scribbling. Printouts can usually be obtained free at the computer center, and they will impress those who tend to be intimidated by the technology they represent.

Computers—Made to think?

"Everything a computer does is based on three functions:
(1) Math computation, (2) storage of information, and (3) re-
trieval of information. It will never be able to do more."
Smith, Interview
4/5/76

INVESTIGATING THROUGH LIBRARY RESEARCH

It is important, in this age of communication saturation, to understand that your intake of information is a form of nourishment. You
have to approach information in the same way you approach food.
You should try to take in a certain amount of high quality. If you
take in too much, you should diet for a while. If you have a deficiency, you should correct it, and if you are preparing for a special
exertion, you should alter your diet accordingly. Getting ready for a
speech is like getting ready for a sports event; you not only have to
make special preparations, you have to be in shape to begin with.

Staying in shape, in this sense, means regularly exposing yourself to stimulating ideas. One way to do this is to converse as much
as possible with people you consider knowledgeable. Another way is
through the selective use of the mass media. For example, when you
go to the movies you might consider a highly acclaimed film such as
All the President's Men rather than escapist fare like *The Hot
Nurses*. When watching television you might see what's available in
educational programs or documentaries before settling down to an
evening of repeated plots and gratuitous violence on weekly entertainment programs. When listening to the radio you might spin the
dial to an interview with one of our "great minds" rather than listen
to a DJ's mindless prattle in between hit songs and hyped advertisements. Most important, you should expose yourself to stimulating
ideas through daily reading. You should, for example, keep generally
informed by reading a good newspaper and a selection of magazines.
At least one of the magazines should be a national newsweekly such

as *Time* or *Newsweek*, which should be read from cover to cover and discussed with your friends and neighbors. Even if you keep yourself in top shape, though, you'll need a special workout or two to prepare yourself for a speech. That's where the library comes in. It's full of special pieces of equipment for communication athletes. The most important piece of equipment there is probably the card catalog.

The Card Catalog

The card catalog is an ancient and noble information-storing device. It is your key to all the books in the library; they are filed there according to subject, author, and title, so you can look for general topics as well as specific books or authors. Once you find a book, you needn't read the whole thing. You can check the table of contents and index for sections relating specifically to your topic.

Usually it pays to locate as many books as you can in this manner, and then select the one or two that have the best sections related to your topic. It is a good idea to give an in-depth reading to a limited number of pages. Do not concentrate on bulk. In order to read for understanding, read slowly and carefully. Pause from time to time to think about what you have read, and take notes as you read.

The card catalog can be used to find more than one book at a time. As a general rule, if you choose just one book from the catalog and then run to the shelves to locate it, it won't be there. There is no way to tell why that happens. It's just one of life's little mysteries, like the way toast always seems to fall jelly side down. You can guard against this heartbreak by locating, through the card catalog, the section of the stacks that seems to hold the books related to your topic. Once you find the general area, you can review the tables of contents and indexes of all the books there. If several of them seem to be important to your topic, choose the one or two that seem to be written the best and/or have the most recent copyright date. Remember to limit your reading and do it in depth. Read for understanding.

Reference Works

Reference works will also be listed in the card catalog, but it would be a better idea to spend some free time wandering through the reference room yourself. There are wonders there that could turn you into a trivia expert. There are encyclopedias galore, even specialized ones like *The Encyclopedia of Social Sciences* and *The Encyclopedia of American History*; there are statistical compilations, like *The World Almanac, Facts on File*, and *The Guinness Book of World Records*; you can even find out *Who's Who in America* or *Who Was Who*. You can collect a lot of facts in a short time in the reference room.

Periodicals

Periodicals (magazines, journals, and newspapers) are good resources for finding recently published material on interesting topics. Indexes like *The Readers Guide to Periodical Literature* will enable you to find popular magazine articles on just about any subject. *The Education Index* and *Psychological Abstracts* can be used to find more advanced, specialized articles, and *The New York Times Index* can be used to find microfilmed newspaper articles.

Both the microfilm machines and the indexes themselves are designed to be easy to use. Although you will need specific instructions for operating the microfilm machine in your library (your librarian will be glad to give you those instructions), there are general guidelines for using indexes. To investigate a general subject area using an index, use the following procedure:

1. List four or five possible titles or "headings" for your topic.
2. Arrange these headings from most to least specific.
3. Look up the most specific headings first.
4. If at first you don't succeed, look for your topic under one of the more general headings.

For example, if you had decided to investigate the mysterious "Legionnaire's Disease" that killed 27 people and hospitalized 155 following an American Legion convention in Philadelphia in 1976, you might formulate the following list:

Philadelphia Health Problems
American Legion
Disease Control
Respiratory Diseases
Legionnaire's Disease

The heading most specifically representing your topic would probably be "Legionnaire's Disease." The least specific heading would probably be "Disease Control." You could order the headings as follows:

1. Legionnaire's Disease
2. American Legion Convention
3. Philadelphia Health Problems
4. Respiratory Diseases
5. Disease Control

If you turned to *The Readers Guide to Periodical Literature* with this list you would find no articles listed under "Legionnaire's Disease." However, under "American Legion" you would find the subheading "Pennsylvania Convention, 1976." Under this heading you would find several articles on the subject. If you used *The New*

York Times Index, you would not find the articles until you looked under "Respiratory Diseases."

Once again, be selective. Pick the one or two articles that seem to be the most directly related to your topic, and digest them.

Nonprint Materials

The library is also a treasury of nonprint and audiovisual materials. Films, records, tapes, and videotapes can be used not only as research tools but as aids during your presentation. Your library probably has an orientation program that will acquaint you with what it has to offer. Take the tour! Do not be proud—even experts take an orientation tour before using a particular library. In fact, if you haven't taken the orientation tour at your library, do so immediately. It may be the most productive hour you ever spend!

Library Gnomes

Once you have done everything mentioned above, if you still can't find exactly what you need, seek out the gnome in your library. Every library has at least one. In folklore, garden-variety gnomes (the word comes from the Greek word meaning "to know") are ageless dwarfs that guard over precious ores and treasures. The library variety are real, though they may stand over six feet tall. These people seem to know where everything is. They can usually be found behind the reference desk, but they might be anywhere. Find the gnome in your library and you have half the battle won.

Talking with a library gnome is one way of using interpersonal communication as a method of investigation. That opens up a whole new realm of possibilities.

INVESTIGATING THROUGH INTERPERSONAL COMMUNICATION

Interpersonal communication can be used for investigation through *brainstorming* and *interviewing*.

Brainstorming

Brainstorming is a technique for generating ideas. It involves the spontaneous contribution of ideas from each member of a group. When the technique works, the contributed ideas lead to the creation of new ideas.

There are a number of ways to explain the creative effect of brainstorming. One is the idea of association; we associate one idea with another, and this allows us to retrieve ideas that would otherwise be too deeply stored away to use. Freud, however, would insist that creativity stems from the "freely rising" fantasy that noncreative people suppress and creative people accept. So if you happen to be a Freudian, brainstorming might work because you are encouraged toward "wild" ideas. Finally, there is the Gestalt view, which is that creativity is a reaction to "psychological incompleteness." You build *Gestalten*, or patterns, by a restructuring of the whole rather than a careful step-by-step analysis of components. Brainstorming, by stressing quantity, could help in building *Gestalten*. For our purposes here, however, it is only necessary to point out that brainstorming does work, and it can work either formally or informally.

INFORMAL BRAINSTORMING

"Brainstorming informally" means brainstorming in everyday conversations, using communication to generate ideas rather than just to kill time. When you go out for a beer after class, don't ask your friend whether the Dodgers will ever win the pennant or whether Mork will ever leave Mindy and return to his planet. Ask a question based on your topic instead. Informal brainstorming leads to the discovery of new and different materials, including films, television programs, popular books, magazines, or newspaper articles that might relate to your topic.

FORMAL BRAINSTORMING

In order to brainstorm formally you meet in a group of three to five people, pick a general topic, turn on a recorder (either the electronic kind or one of the group members appointed for that purpose), and start spilling out ideas. There are three rules for formal brainstorming, all of which are designed to facilitate the free flow of ideas:

1. No criticism of ideas—just get them out, record them, and go on to the next idea.
2. The wilder the idea the better.
3. Quantity, rather than quality, of ideas is stressed.

Later, after you've had the chance to cool down, review the ideas for quality. Throw the unimportant ones away.

Formal brainstorming is often an excellent procedure for generating speech topics and generating ideas about those topics. When you need more specific information, you might want to take advantage of an interview or two.

Interviewing

The interview is an especially valuable form of research on a college campus, where experts abound. The information-gathering interview allows you to view your topic from an expert's perspective, to take advantage of that expert's years of experience, research, and thought.

You can use an interview to collect facts and stimulate your own thinking. Often the interview will save you hours of library research and allow you to present ideas you could not have uncovered any other way.

WHY INTERVIEW?

An interview is more than a brainstorming session or a hunt for specific facts and quotes. It is a face-to-face interaction with an expert in which many ideas that otherwise would be unclear can become more understandable. Marshall McLuhan, for example, published a series of books and articles during the 1960s proposing complicated "probes" into the effects of mass media. To many, what he said made little or no sense until his 1969 interview in *Playboy* magazine. In that interview Eric Norden was able to pin McLuhan down on many of his ideas. Within that interview McLuhan told Norden:

> My purpose is to employ facts as tentative probes, as means of insight, of pattern recognition, rather than to use them in the traditional sense of classified data, categories, containers. I want to map new terrain rather than chart old landmarks.
> But I've never presented such exploration as revealed truth. As an investigator, I have no fixed point of view, no commitment to any theory—my own or anyone else's. As a matter of fact, I'm completely ready to junk any statement I've ever made about any subject if events don't bear me out, or if I discover it isn't contributing to an understanding of the problem.[2]

That turned out to be one of the clearest explanations of McLuhan's "probes" published anywhere.

One final advantage to the interview is that you can guide the expert on to new discoveries. This is the prospect that professional interviewers find most exciting. Digby Diehl (author of *Supertalk*, a book of celebrity interviews) has stated:

> I've become vaguely aware that what I'm searching for in some loony, unfathomable manner, are not the answers, but The Answers. Somewhere, sprinkled out amongst the best minds of the century, are clues. And someone's tongue is bound to slip.[3]

CONDUCTING AN INTERVIEW

To have a successful interview, you have to carefully plan out what to do before, during and after the interview.[4]

Before the Interview.   First, determine who the best available expert is. If you are truly ambitious, you might decide to visit or telephone a well-known celebrity. Unfortunately, you generally have to contact well-known people, at least at first, by mail. Even then the proportion of those who accept interviews to those who are contacted is very small, and much time can be wasted. Usually it is more practical to find successful authors, teachers, or administrators on your campus or in your community and contact them either personally or by phone. If your expert is willing to be interviewed, set up a specific time. Don't schedule the interview late in the afternoon or right before lunch, unless there is a chance that the expert might take you along.[5] Make sure you schedule a sufficient amount of time. Try to arrange for the least possibility of distraction.

After you have scheduled the interview, prepare the questions you would like to ask. Review these questions immediately before the interview, and keep them with you in case you need to refer to them during the interview.

It is a good idea to know as much as possible about both the person you are interviewing and the topic of the interview. If possible, collect background material that you could refer to during the interview.

Finally, consider the kind of person the expert is. Remember that everything you do has some effect. Try to plan for positive effects. The way you look (including the clothes you wear) and the way you act (including whether or not you seem to enjoy what you are doing) will influence the response you receive. Plan to dress and act in a way that your expert will consider appropriate.[6]

During the Interview.   During the interview, it is important to make the expert feel as comfortable as possible. When you begin, state the specific reason for the interview, explain what the answers will be used for, and ask if it is all right if you take notes or use a recorder (you should definitely do one or the other, unless you have a fantastic memory). Some interviewers suggest that you use the expert's name as often as possible. Others stress that the person being interviewed will be more comfortable if he or she can remember *your* name. They suggest that you give the expert a 3×5 card with your name on it.

Make sure you understand the expert's responses to your questions: Ask him or her (tactfully) to speak clearly, repeat, clarify, or use examples if necessary. Summarize or rephrase the answers yourself, if you have any doubt. Don't ask leading ("Don't you think . . . ?") questions or questions that can only be answered yes or no. Don't interject your own values into what the expert says. Don't get nervous about periods of silence; use them to collect your thoughts.

When you arrive at the scene of an interview, you should arrange yourself, in relation to the expert and whatever furniture is present, so that you will encourage communication. Try to make yourself and the interviewee as comfortable as possible.

Try to be sensitive to the nonverbal cues the interviewee gives you. Everyone has a need for a certain amount of personal space.[7]

SITTING ACROSS FROM SOMEONE WITH A DESK IN-BETWEEN, IS GOOD FOR VERY FORMAL INTERVIEWS

SITTING SIDE-BY-SIDE IS VERY INFORMAL AND WILL PROBABLY MAKE AN INTERVIEWEE UNCOMFORTABLE UNLESS HE OR SHE WANTS TO BE INFORMAL

Figure 4–1

Your expert will probably tell you with a raised eyebrow, a smile, or fidgeting behavior whether or not you have gotten too close. Figure 4–1 represents four ways you could sit during an interview. Different physical arrangements will work best with different people.

Don't refer to your notes during the interview unless you have to. Try to let the conversation run naturally. The questions you have prepared in advance are "lead" questions, to be used when the natural flow of conversation falters. "Follow-up" questions are those that relate directly to something the interviewee has said, to keep ideas flowing naturally. They can't be made up in advance.

If you feel you have to guide your expert back to an important idea that has been rambled away from, do so by supplying a transition. For example: "Yes, indeed, Professor Smith. Those are beautiful pictures of your grandchildren. Tell me—is it possible that computers might be able to think by the time those kids grow up?"

REMOVING THE DESK REMOVES SOME OF THE FORMALITY.

LEARN TO RECOGNIZE AND USE THE APPROPRIATE SEATING ARRANGEMENT.

Figure 4–1 *(continued)*

Make good use of the time you have scheduled. If one expert cannot answer your questions, see if he or she knows someone else who can. When experts give you printed material, ask them to point out the exact sections that would be most helpful. Don't waste time arguing over minor points. Make sure you have enough time so that you don't have to end abruptly; the best information is often saved for the end of the interview.

After the Interview.   Review your notes and/or recording as soon as possible after the interview. The more time you allow to elapse, the less sense your notes will make to you. Transcribe the main points and the important quotations onto index cards (or whatever system you prefer).

By now you should have a pretty good idea where your research is leading you. You might need some firsthand observation to bolster your evidence. The next section will deal with the collection of that type of data.

INVESTIGATING THROUGH PERSONAL OBSERVATION

Personal experience is one of the basic ingredients of any speech, but unsupported personal *opinions* can be detrimental. Personal observations, as a form of investigation,[8] gives some extra weight to your personal opinion. For example, if you were suggesting to an audience that the TV sets should be removed from the lounges of the dormitories at your college, you might say this:

> I think people in dormitories here would interact more if the televisions were removed from the dormitory lounges.

All you have there is personal opinion, which could be based on anything from scientific research to a purely emotional hatred of television—or of college students.

The use of personal observation, however, might allow you to say this:

> Last Wednesday, I spent 7:00 to 10:00 P.M. in the lounge of a dormitory here. Only three times during the evening did anyone attempt to start a conversation. Two of those attempts were met with a request for silence in deference to the television.

If you really wanted to prove your point, you could take personal observation one step further:

> This Wednesday, I received permission from the dormitory supervisor to remove the television from the lounge. During those same hours, 7:00 to 10:00 P.M., I observed the following behavior in that lounge, this time without television:
>
> 1. Thirty conversations were begun.
> 2. Twenty-four of these conversations continued, in depth, for more than ten minutes.
> 3. Seven groups of students decided on alternative entertainment for the evening, including table games, singing, dancing, and going to the library.
> 4. Four new acquaintanceships were made, one of which resulted in a TV date for the following Wednesday night.

This example illustrates a type of investigation known as *behavioral observation*. Behavioral observation is used to collect information about human beings. Since your job as a public speaker is communicating with human beings, and since human beings love information about themselves, observing behavior can be an extremely valuable form of investigation.

Observing Behavior

Depending on the behavior you intend to observe, your investigation can become quite involved. For example, some researchers in New York City wanted to see whether juvenile delinquents were responsible for stripping abandoned automobiles, so they left a car on a city street with the hood up and the license plates removed. Then they hid and waited to see what would happen. They observed (in an amazingly short time) that the auto strippers were predominantly middle-class adults.[9] More recently, students in Oregon collected data on wasted foods by measuring garbage from school cafeterias.[10] They were able to document an appalling amount of waste, and officials were forced to make changes in the school lunch programs. Admittedly, it takes a strong stomach for this type of research, but the results are sometimes worth it. There are also some ethical considerations to keep in mind.

The Ethics of Behavioral Observation

The "subjects" of behavioral observation are human beings and deserve to be treated as such. Always think ahead to the possible consequences of your research. Not too long ago some faculty members at a large midwestern university told their students in the basic communication course to "go out and create a communication event and observe the reactions to it." It wasn't long before the little campus town was in a state of near-panic because a group of students had faked a "shooting" on campus—carefully orchestrated with a blank-firing pistol and splattered ketchup wounds. State police were called in, the wire services were alerted, and the communication faculty was dragged onto several administrative carpets. The faculty members put all their communication skills to work and quieted things down in about a week. Some even say the whole thing would have been forgotten if only another student group had not decided to throw a dummy off a high-rise dormitory.

Both groups had failed to control the detrimental effects of their research, and therefore had ignored their ethical responsibilities. One form of investigation that is easier to control is survey research.

INVESTIGATING THROUGH SURVEY RESEARCH

One advantage of survey research is that it gives you up-to-date answers concerning "the way things are" in a fast-moving, constantly changing world. Survey questions can be asked of a specific group, also. This can be particularly important in public speaking. Consider the following ideas, which might be presented in an imaginary speech entitled "Corn Silk: The Killer Weed":

A survey run in 1970 suggests that 5 out of 10 college students will smoke corn silk during their stay in college. [Library-type data]

According to a survey I conducted last week, 9 out of 10

students in this class have tried corn silk, and fully half of you use it regularly. [Survey-type data]

The second statement would probably be of more immediate interest to an audience of students. That is another advantage of conducting your own survey. The major disadvantage is that your survey, being unpublished, may not have as much credibility as evidence found in the library.

Types of Surveys

The two most popular means of surveying people are (1) printed questionnaires and (2) telephone surveys.

PRINTED QUESTIONNAIRES

Printed (that is, mimeographed, photocopied, or whatever) questionnaires have the advantage of *standardization;* that is, you can be reasonably sure that each respondent has been asked the same question, without benefit of verbal or nonverbal urgings from the survey taker. Printed questionnaires can be mailed, but for the purposes of undergraduate research it is often quicker and easier to hand out the questionnaires and have them completed immediately. If you are looking for answers within a small group, like your public speaking class, it is possible to prepare a questionnaire for every member. For larger groups it may be necessary to take a *random sample.* A random sample is one in which every member of the group has, at least theoretically, an equal chance of being questioned. This means that if you wanted to randomly sample a population like the freshman class at your university, you could not do so at your favorite tavern or on one floor of a dormitory. You could, however, pass out questionnaires randomly during an orientation session that all freshmen attend.

TELEPHONE SURVEYS

Telephone surveys can make random sampling a bit more systematic, if you happen to have a telephone directory that lists everyone in the population you want to sample. You need only call every nth person on each page. The number n should theoretically be decided by a random drawing; that is, if there are 100 names on each page of your student directory, you should put the numbers 1 through 100 in a hat and pick out the number n at random. (For example, if you picked the number 10 you would call every 10th person). The main disadvantage of telephone surveys is that after all that work you might get no answer at all.

Types of Survey Questions

There are basically three types of survey questions: (1) those that can be answered yes or no, (2) multiple-choice questions, and (3) open questions that can be answered any way the respondent wants to answer them.

YES-OR-NO QUESTIONS

The yes-or-no question is best asked when you need a quick statistic: "Seventy-five percent of the students in this class have, at one time or another, smoked corn silk." A yes-or-no survey question produces responses that can be tabulated and expressed as percentages easily. However, it also requires you to "lead" the respondent and does not encourage detail which might be important. For example, if you asked the question "Have you ever smoked corn silk? Yes _____ No _____ ," the respondents would not have the opportunity to tell you if they just tried it once, experimentally, or if they have a habit that requires several pipes a day. Yes-or-no questions are especially valuable when you are trying to avoid a long-winded response. You might need to avoid this type of response in a controversial question of opinion, such as "Do you think corn silk should be legalized?" An answer to a question like that might be too lengthy.

MULTIPLE-CHOICE QUESTIONS

As a general rule, the more detail you ask for in your questionnaire, the more difficult the answers will be to tabulate and explain. One way to ask a question so the respondent can give some detail, without making tabulation difficult, is to establish the choices yourself. You might follow up a yes-or-no question such as "Have you ever smoked corn silk?" with a multiple-choice item such as

> If so, how often?
> ____ Once
> ____ A few times
> ____ Regularly
> ____ Other

and you might follow that one up with,

> If regularly, how often?
> ____ Once a month
> ____ Once a week
> ____ Daily
> ____ Other

You should arrange your choices so only a minimum number of responses will appear in the "other" slot, since those responses will be the most difficult to tabulate.

OPEN QUESTIONS

To encourage detailed, complete responses, you might want to use open questions: "What do you think of the practice of smoking corn silk?" It's a good idea to provide a limited amount of blank space after a question like this, once again to limit long-winded responses. Answers derived from this type of question will later need to be sorted into categories. The credibility of the sorting technique will be improved if you let an independent panel of expert judges, such as some of your classmates, decide what the categories should be and which responses belong in which categories. This could provide some surprises, though. You might find that rather than having "pro," "con," and "neutral" corn-silk categories, you'll wind up with "neutral," "pro," and "extremely pro," or "neutral," "con," and "extremely con."[11]

Survey research is important in public speaking because it is usually the best way to investigate your audience. Two hypothetical examples should help prove this point. Imagine first that you have just arrived at Honeysuckle State University, and before you really have a feel for the place, you are given a week to prepare a presentation for one of your classes. Just to make it interesting, make the class "Introduction to the Family" and your topic "Divorce." To get a better feel for your audience, you might run to the library and find the pamphlet "Student Life at Honeysuckle State," the magazine article "Honeysuckle State: Hotbed of Horticulture," or last year's most obscure master's thesis, "Student Attitudes at Honeysuckle State." If you examine that information carefully you will probably find that it refers to a more general audience than the one you will face. The information might also be out of date. So you might interview your instructor, or one of your classmates. Unfortunately, if you rely on only one or two people to speak for the entire class you may get a limited, and incorrect, view of that class. It would be more effective, therefore, to conduct a survey in the class and find out some pertinent information, such as the members' family backgrounds (were parents divorced?) marital status (maybe some of the class members are divorced themselves), religion, and attitude toward divorce.

Divorce, of course, isn't a particulary controversial topic these days. It's not like talking about dropping the bomb on Mexico or instituting capital punishment for landlords who refuse to return damage deposits. Still, audience investigation is immensely important. It will make the difference between talking about divorce in general and talking about how divorce affects *that particular audience.*

One more hypothetical example: Imagine that you have been invited to speak before the local chapter of the Gizmo Club. Your topic is to be "What College Means." If the Gizmos like you, you will be eligible for their annual scholarship, which covers room, board, books, tuition, and a lavish clothing allowance for an entire year. Unfortunately, you don't know anything about the organization. You might run to the library and look up "Gizmo" in the *Encyclopedia of Organizations,* or find the book *What It Means to Be a Gizmo* in the card catalog, or see how many articles thare are on "Gizmos" in the *Readers Guide to Periodical Literature.* This would give you a good idea of the traditional interests and attitudes held by Gizmos, but it would still refer to a very general audience. So you might interview the head Gizmo, or find a classmate whose parents belong. But then you have that limited perspective again. So you might conduct a survey at a Gizmo meeting. If you find out enough, you might be able to show that college means something to you that a typical Gizmo could appreciate—and that could mean success.

As you investigate, remember that it is the *quality* rather than the *quantity* of the research that is important. The key is to determine carefully what type of investigation will answer the questions you need to have answered. Sometimes only one type of research will be necessary. If you use some of the guidelines suggested here, your answers will probably be worth the energy you exert.

SUMMARY

This chapter dealt with the process of investigation, which includes the investigation of *ideas,* to improve their quality; the investigation of *facts,* to substantiate ideas; and the investigation of the *audience,* to make the message appropriate to its receivers. Investigation is aided by generally "staying in shape" by exposing yourself to stimulating ideas. It is also aided by understanding the functions of the library, brainstorming, interviewing, personal observation, and surveys.

The library is a labyrinth if you don't understand it, but it is a supermarket of speech material if you know how to shop. Getting to know your library involves making the acquaintance of the card catalog, the available reference works, the periodicals, the nonprint materials, and a library gnome or two.

Brainstorming is a technique for generating ideas in a group. It can be done informally, in everyday conversations, or formally, in a group assembled for that purpose.

Interviewing is especially useful on a college campus. This technique requires the selection of an expert, the preparation of questions, and a sensitivity to the nonverbal cues of the interviewee.

Personal observation, in order to be valid, should be done in a controlled manner. Personal observation as a form of investigation can make your personal opinions more valid in a speech.

Survey research is a useful way to gather up-to-date information about your audience. Survey methods include printed questionnaires and telephone sampling. Survey questions can be worded for yes-or-no answers, multiple-choice answers, or open answers.

Any or all of these methods can be used to investigate a speech topic. The important skill is using the appropriate type of research, rather than using as many types as possible. The appropriate investigation will make your information more valid, and therefore increase the effectiveness of your speech.

QUESTIONS FOR DISCUSSION

1. In your opinion, is it true that people often do not bother to investigate because it requires too much effort? Based on your experiences with people such as auto mechanics, teachers, registrars, store clerks, waitresses, and so on, how willing are people to look into a situation really thoroughly? How willing are *you,* for that matter?
2. In your opinion, how ethical or unethical is behavioral observation? Give examples of what you think to be acceptable or unacceptable instances of this method.
3. It was cautioned in this chapter that a major disadvantage of citing your own survey in a classroom speech is that such evidence, being unpublished, may not have as much credibility as evidence found in the library. Do you agree? Why or why not?

PROBES

1. You are advised to help yourself investigate a speech topic by regularly "staying in shape." What people and/or media events do you, or could you, use to stay in shape? What are the particular benefits you can gain from each source?

2. Take the orientation tour of your school's library. Compare the advice you receive from this tour with the author's advice. How do they differ? Which seems better, and why?

3. Select any topic of interest to you. It could be JFK's assassination, the Loch Ness Monster, U.S.–Cuba relations, King Tut, or anything else. If you were going to use an index to find sources of information, what headings might you list, and in what order of specificity? After pursuing these headings, which ones did you find to be most helpful in locating articles?

4. In your next conversation of an informal nature, how might you be able to steer the conversation away from the weather, or TV game shows, and to "brainstorming" about a possible speech topic? What ideas might you get from such a discussion?

5. Read or observe an interview with an expert in a particular area. Examples might be *Playboy* interviewing Marshall McLuhan or a TV interview by Barbara Walters or Dick Cavett. How well did the interviewer achieve the advantages of interviewing? What might he or she have done to make the interview more informative?

6. (a) Suppose you were interviewing an expert on your campus. What background information would you want *before* the interview? What questions would you prepare? What questions would you decide to definitely *not* ask?

   (b) Imagine that you will be interviewing a famous person. What background information would you find helpful before the interview with this particular individual? What questions would you prepare in advance? What questions would you definitely avoid? Explain your answers.

7. Who are the important gnomes in your library? What questions do you think you might need to ask such people? Why do you feel they are better sources, in some cases, than card catalogs, indexes, and so on?

8. What three questions could you ask your class, in survey form, to measure the students' attitudes toward your next speech topic? Which type of questions (yes-or-no, multiple-choice, or open) would you use? Why?

NOTES

[1]James C. McCroskey, *An Introduction to Rhetorical Communication*, 2nd ed. (Englewood Cliffs, N.J.: Prentice-Hall, 1972), pp. 158–161.

[2]Eric Norden, Interview with Marshall McLuhan, *Playboy*, October 1969, p. 54.

[3]Digby Diehl, *Supertalk* (New York: Doubleday, 1974), p. ix.

[4]The advice of noted television interviewers, such as Barbara Walters, David Frost, and Mike Wallace, is offered in "Some of TV's Best Interviewers Reveal the Tricks of Their Trade," *TV Guide*, 25, Aug. 13, 1977, pp. 6–10.

[5]Only go to lunch if the interviewee invites *you*. Don't do the inviting yourself. Besides the obvious financial advantage, if your interviewees invite you, the burden of entertainment will be theirs. They'll talk more. For other practical hints on interviewing, see John Brady, *The Craft of Interviewing* (Cincinnati: Writer's Digest, 1976).

[6]Those who are interested in an in-depth examination of the effects of clothes will want to read John T. Malloy, *How to Dress for Success* (New York: Warner Books, 1975).

[7]For a more thorough discussion of nonverbal cues and personal space, see Mark L. Knapp, *Nonverbal Communication in Human Interaction* (New York: Holt, Rinehart and Winston, 1972), pp. 41–46; and Edward T. Hall, *The Silent Language* (Greenwich, Conn.: Fawcett Publications, 1959).

[8]A more detailed analysis of personal observation as a form of investigation is provided in William L. Rivers, *Finding Facts* (Englewood Cliffs, N.J.: Prentice-Hall, 1975), pp. 56–75.

[9]This study is reported in Floyd L. Ruch and Philip G. Zimbardo, *Psychology and Life*, 8th ed. (Glenview, Ill.: Scott, Foresman and Co., 1971) p. 547.

[10]David J. Johnson, "Trash Tells a Tale," *The National Observer*, Dec. 20, 1975, p. 1.

[11]Survey research, as well as other forms of behavioral observation, can be far more complex and rigorous than what is suggested here for speech investigation. The complexity and potential of this type of research is covered more fully in books such as Fred N. Kerlinger, *Foundations of Behavioral Research*, 2nd ed. (New York: Holt, Rinehart and Winston, 1973).

5

Organization

This chapter deals with organization, which is the process of arranging something according to a plan. The importance of organization is based on the following prediction:

A message will be more effective if the information within it is organized. [1]

ORGANIZATION

The principle of organization is based on armchair theorizing that has been done since philosophers sat on rocks instead of armchairs. The fact of the matter is this: the human mind can deal with only a small number of ideas at any one time. Psychologist Jerome S. Bruner articulates the problem this way:

> One of the most notable things about the human mind is its limited capacity for dealing at any one minute with diverse arrays of information. It has been known for a long time that we can deal only with about seven independent items of information at once; beyond that point we exceed our "channel capacity," to use the current jargon. We simply cannot manipulate large masses of information.[2]

The scientific research upon which our knowledge of information processing is based began over 100 years ago with the experiments of a logician named Jevons. His experimental procedure was laughable by today's standards; he simply had an assistant throw various numbers of beans into a box. He would then, with a glance, estimate the number of beans for each throw. Jevons continued his experiment, faithfully recording his estimates, until he wore out three assistants and had produced the following percentages of correct guesses for various numbers of beans:[3]

No. of Beans	3	4	5	6	7	8	9	10	11	12	13	14	15
Percent of Correct Estimates	100	100	96	82	73	56	62	43	38	42	23	28	18

Jevons interpreted these results to mean that between four and five beans (or "pieces of information") could be dependably "processed" by the human mind at one time. In the last hundred years this experiment has been repeated hundreds of times with increasingly sophisticated electronic equipment and statistical techniques,[4] but the results have remained stubbornly the same. Psychologist George A. Miller summarizes his years of research in this phenomenon as follows:

> My problem is that I have been persecuted by an integer. For seven years this number has followed me around, has intruded in my most private data, and has assaulted me from the pages of our most public journals. This number assumes a variety of disguises, being sometimes a little larger and sometimes a little smaller than usual, but never changing so much as to be unrecognizable. The persistence with which the number plagues me is far more than a random accident. . . . Either there really is something unusual about the number or else I am suffering from delusions of persecution.[5]

The number that so tormented Miller as the irrefutable limits of human information processing was "the magical number seven, plus or minus two." Since ideas being expressed by a speaker are more difficult to keep straight than beans in a box, speakers have traditionally limited themselves to seven minus two (rather than plus two) ideas for a full-length speech. And since classroom speeches are generally shorter than full-length speeches, three or four ideas seems to be the rule for classroom speeches. In this case tradition and science heartily agree that if we are going to be able to communicate a reasonable amount of information at any one time, we have to break it up into a limited number of ideas. Speech organization is basically a process of breaking up information into a limited number of related chunks.

Organization will result in two major benefits for you as a public speaker. First, if your speech is organized it will be easier for you to remember everything that you want to say. One point will lead smoothly into the next, and you will be able to transmit more information than you would in a hit-or-miss, unorganized manner. Second, your audience will understand more of what you say, and remember more of what you say, if it is organized in a logical manner.[6] Three procedures are used to organize a speech: outlining; structuring the speech with an introduction, transitions, and a conclusion; and roughing the speech.

TYPES OF OUTLINES

An outline is a brief model of a speech. It contains the main ideas and it shows how these ideas are divided. Outlines come in all shapes and sizes, but they can generally be classified as either formal outlines or working outlines.

Formal Outlines

A formal outline generally uses the following symbols:

> I. Main point [Roman numeral]
>   A. Subpoint [Capital letter]
>   1. Sub-subpoint [Standard number]
>   a. Sub-sub-subpoint [Lowercase letter]

A formal outline can be used as a visual aid (on posterboard, for example, or distributed as a handout) or as a record of a speech that was delivered (many organizations send outlines to members who miss meetings at which presentations were given; in speech classes, outlines are often used by a teacher to analyze student speeches).

A formal outline contains only the structural units of a speech: main points (the main ideas) and subpoints (the division of those ideas, including sub-subpoints and sub-sub-subpoints). Thus, if you were speaking on the topic "The Causes of Modern Illness," you might divide your topic into the following main points:

    I. Poor Diet
   II. Pollution
  III. Stress

Each of these ideas might be further divided into subpoints:

    I. Poor Diet [Main point]
      A. Lack of Nutrition [Subpoint]
      B. Chemical Toxins [Subpoint]
      C. Irregular Intake [Subpoint]
   II. Pollution [Main point]
      A. Air Pollution [Subpoint]
      B. Water Pollution [Subpoint]
      C. Noise Pollution [Subpoint]
  III. Stress (Main point)
      A. Work-Related Stress [Subpoint]
      B. Day-to-Day Stress [Subpoint]

In formal outlines, *main points and subpoints always represent a division of a whole.* Since it is impossible to divide something into less than two parts, you always have at least two main points for every topic. If your main points are divided, you will always have at least two subpoints. The rule for formal outlines, therefore, is never to use a roman numeral I without a roman numeral II; never to use a capital A without a capital B; never to use a 1 without a 2; and never to use a small a without a small b.

Supporting points, or material that develops the ideas you present, are not usually listed on a formal outline. When they are, they are not given one of the standard symbols.[7] They are identified by type:

Definition:
Example:
Visual aid:
Quote:

And so on. Thus, if supporting points were included, the outline for the first main point of the "Modern Illness" speech might appear as follows:

    I. Poor Diet
      A. Lack of Nutrition
         Example: Breakfast cereals
      B. Chemical Toxins
         Visual aid: Chart showing use of chemical preservatives

C. Irregular Intake
    Definition: Meal schedule
    Quote: Adelle Davis

Since supporting points are not divisions of an idea, it *is* possible to have only one of them under a particular point on a formal outline.

Formal outlines can be full-sentence outlines or key-word outlines. The examples above are in the form of key-word outlines. This type of outline is often used for speaking notes, but is sometimes too brief when the outline is used to communicate the structure of the speech to someone else (as when an outline is used to substitute for a speech that someone missed). When a more complete model of the speech is necessary, a full-sentence outline is usually more appropriate.

A full-sentence outline for the "Modern Illness" speech might look like this:

I. Modern people often suffer from poor diets.
   A. Too many convenience foods can cause malnutrition.
   B. Too many chemical preservatives can cause toxic reactions.
   C. Irregularly scheduled meals can cause gastric disorders.
II. Modern people are subjected to more pollution than ever before.
   A. Air pollution contributes to respiratory diseases.
   B. Water pollution contributes to digestive diseases.
   C. Noise pollution contributes to nervous disorders.
III. Modern people are subjected to more stress than ever before.
   A. Work-related stress contributes to nervous disorders.
   B. The day-to-day stress of modern living contributes to circulatory diseases.

Working Outlines

Working, or "scratch," outlines are construction tools. Unlike a formal outline, a working outline is a constantly changing, personal device. You begin organizing your speech material from a rough working outline, and as your ideas solidify your outline will change accordingly.

A working outline is for your eyes only. No one else will have to understand it, so you can use whatever symbols you like. Just make sure that each type of symbol represents statements of similar importance, and that each symbol is indented the same distance as its counterparts. Your working outline can be written in any kind of personal shorthand that you find functional. In fact, it will probably become pretty messy by the time you have completed your speech.

PRINCIPLES OF OUTLINING

There are three principles that relate to all outlines, working or formal. These principles are (1) *division*, (2) *coordination*, and (3) *order*.

The Principle of Division

Plato recognized the importance of the principle of division. He said:

> First, you must know the truth about the subject you speak or write about; that is to say, you must be able to isolate it in definition, and having so defined it you must understand how to divide it into kinds, until you reach the limit of divisions.[8]

Plato had the right idea. The first principle of outlining is to divide your topic into main points that completely cover its essentials. In a classroom speech you should generally have no more than three or four main points, since that will allow for maximum audience comprehension. In the same manner, if you divide your main points you should try to have no more than three or four subpoints.

Chronological Division.   There are infinite ways to divide topics and points. Take a sample topic, "Public Speaking," and look at some of the ways you can take it apart. You might take it apart according to categories of time, or *chronologically*:

I. Public Speaking During the Classical Period
II. Public Speaking During the Early American Period
III. Public Speaking During Modern Times

All analyses that break up ideas into categories of time, whether stated in centuries or seconds, are chronological.

Spatial Division.   *Spatial analyses* divide things according to area, or space:

I. Public Speaking in Europe
II. Public Speaking in Asia
III. Public Speaking in Africa
IV. Public Speaking in North America

Analyses that divide ideas according to area, whether stated in continents or centimeters, are spatial.

Process Division.   If the idea involves a *process* (i.e., a series of actions), you could take it apart according to the *steps* in that process.

I. The first step: Focusing a topic.
II. The second step: Investigating facts, ideas, and your audience.
III. The third step: Organizing the speech material.

Division into Accepted Categories.   If the idea can be broken up into types, you could divide it according to *accepted categories:*

    I. The Speech to Entertain
   II. The Speech to Inform
 III. The Speech to Persuade

Accepted categories are those which are already well known. Familiarity has its advantages; audiences are generally more receptive to ideas that they can associate with their present knowledge. But familiarity also has its disadvantages. One disadvantage is the "oh-this-again" syndrome, which is what happens when members of an audience feel they have nothing new to learn from your topic, so rather than listening to you they just say, "Oh, this again."

Division into Original Categories.   To avoid the "oh-this-again" syndrome, you could invent *original categories.* To return to the "Public Speaking" example, you could talk about:

    I. The Good Head Speech (One That Entertains)
  II. The Egg Head Speech (One That Explains)
 III. The Get Ahead Speech (One That Persuades)

Original categories are often the best way to divide a topic, because they suggest an original analysis.

Chronological, spatial, process, accepted, and original categories are just some of the ways to divide topics and points. Other ways will become evident as you organize your material. Of course, more than one form of division can be used in the same speech. You might divide your main points chronologically, for example, and then divide one subpoint spatially and another by original categories.

No matter how you slice it, an idea should be divided so that its divisions are *exhaustive* and *essential*. "Essential" means that those three or four points are the most important parts of the idea. If you are speaking on jury selection, and are explaining that lawyers are able to recognize certain biases in prospective jurors, you might divide the idea of bias like this:

A. Racial Bias
B. Sexual Bias
C. Age Bias

If those three things are the most important parts of the idea of bias, then it can be said that the divisions of that idea are "essential."

"Exhaustive" means that all the necessary information concerning the idea can be included under the divisions of that idea. If you were speaking on "The Changing Climate in the Continental United States" you might want to arrange your discussion around four major geographical divisions:

1. Northeast
2. Southeast
3. Northwest
4. Southwest

If everything you want to say could be included under one of these subpoints, then the idea is properly divided. If not, the division of the idea would not be "exhaustive."

Finally, each division should contain one, and only one, idea. If you were discussing hangover cures your topic would be divided incorrectly if your main points looked like this:

I. "Preventive cures" help you avoid the problem.
II. "Participation cures" help you control the development of the problem, while "post-participation cures" help you get rid of the problem if you failed to avoid it or control it.

You actually have three ideas there, and thus three main points:

I. Preventive Cures
II. Participation Cures
III. Post-participation Cures

The Principle of Coordination

Coordination is the state of being equal in rank, quality, or significance. The principle of coordination requires that all your main points be of *similar importance* and that they be *related* to one another. The principle of coordination is reflected in the wording of your main points. Points that are equal in significance and related to one another can easily be worded in a similar manner. For example, if you are developing a speech against capital punishment your main points might be:

I. Capital punishment is not effective: It is not a deterrent to crime.
II. Capital punishment is not Constitutional: It does not comply with the Eighth Amendment.
III. Capital punishment is not civilized: It does not allow for a reverence for life.

This similarity of wording will help you create a clearer message than if you worded your main points so that their equality and relationship were not obvious:

I. Crime did not decrease during the 1950s, when capital punishment was enforced.
II. The Eighth Amendment of the U.S. Constitution protects against cruel and unusual punishment.
III. Most civilized countries have abandoned the notion of capital punishment.

The relationship of these points might seem "obvious" to the speaker, but chances are they would leave the audience confused. Similar wording of main points helps to guard against this confusion.

The Principle of Order

An outline should demonstrate a logical order for the points you want to make. There are as many different ways to order ideas as there are ways to divide them. In fact, the way you divide your ideas will help determine the order in which you will present them. For example, if you divide your topic *chronologically*, you might want to order your main points from the most recent to the least recent. That way, you will begin with the time period with which your audience is most familiar. If you are discussing the influence great scientists have had on the way people think, you might begin with today and work backward in time:

I. Everything is relative: The influence of Albert Einstein (1879–1955).
II. Everything has a cause: The influence of Isaac Newton (1642–1727).
III. Everything is systematic: The influence of Aristotle (384–322 B.C.).

If the opposite arrangement (least to most recent) seems to put the main points into a chronological order that makes the most sense, you will want to use that. This is especially true for topics that are easiest to comprehend if developed according to their historical backgrounds. If you are going to speak on the topic of employee-designed pay plans, you might arrange your ideas chronologically from the past to the future:

I. Early pay plans: Historically, employees have had little to say in the matter.
II. Current pay plans: Recent experiments show that some employee-designed pay plans increase morale, attendance, and productivity.
III. Future pay plans: Employee-designed reimbursement programs will be the wave of the future.

You always need to make a conscious choice about the order of your ideas. If you are speaking on the components of an automobile engine you might want to arrange your ideas according to *steps in a process.* Your first inclination might be to discuss the process of dismantling a complete engine, explaining what each piece does as you "remove" it in your discussion. However, if your audience is unfamiliar with engines to begin with, the idea of dismantling an entire engine might overwhelm them. It might be better to start with one major component—a piston, perhaps—and "build up" the engine around it. Your decision to use a building-up instead of a breaking-down process should be a conscious one based on your analysis of your audience.

Ordering According to Purpose.   One thing that will help you make the conscious choice of what goes where will be the purpose of your speech. If you seek primarily to interest your audience in what you have to say, you might want to build suspense with the order of your ideas. For example, you could construct a speech on the killer bees and order your points *spatially,* talking about the bees in faraway countries first and then in countries closer and closer to your audience. You could begin with a dispassionate report of killer bees in South America. You could then move northward to Central America, and report on North America last, after your audience has gotten the idea that killer bees can be serious business.

If your purpose is explanation, you might want to arrange your ideas according to *accepted categories.* One common set of accepted categories is based on six questions:

Who?
What?
When?
Where?
Why?
How?

One of these six questions will probably be most important to a given audience at a given point in a speech. If you were speaking before a college audience on "Euthanasia" (mercy killing), the first question on their minds might be "What?" In fact, if you said "euthanasia" to some college students that's probably the response you would get. But after you explain that "euthanasia" does not mean the young people of one of the continents, you could expect another question to arise in the collective mind of your audience: "Why?" After you answer that one the next question might be "Who?" Once again, the decision of what goes where is yours, and it should be based on audience analysis. The main points of my sample speech in Chapter 1 were arranged in a "Why—What—How" order. In that speech I believed that those questions would occur to my audience in that order.

If your purpose is to persuade, you might want to place your ideas in the order that has come to be known as Monroe's Motivated Sequence.[9] This order is based on five steps that are designed to motivate an audience to do what you want them to:

1. Attention Step: This step draws attention to your subject. (For example: "Have you ever sat in a nice restaurant and been choked by smoke from the table next to you?")
2. Need Step: This step establishes the need for a change. ("Wouldn't you like to do something about it?")
3. Satisfaction Step: This step proposes a solution. ("The State Clean Air Act will provide for separate smoking and non-smoking areas in restaurants.")
4. Visualization Step: This step describes the results of the so-

lution. ("Imagine—clean air in every public place, without denying smokers their rights in any way.")

5. Action Step: This step is a direct appeal for the audience to do something. ("Sign this petition and you will have done your part.")

If your purpose is to entertain, you might want to use original categories, and arrange them in order of least to most funny. For example, if you are talking on "Types of Students" you might want to make up the following categories:

Grinds—the students who go to every class and read every assignment before it is due, and are usually seen in dormitories telling people to turn their stereos down.

Renaissance students—the students who find a satisfying blend of scholarly and social pursuits. They go to most of their classes and do most of their assignments, but they don't let such things get in the way of serious partying.

Burnouts—the students who have a difficult time finding the classroom, let alone doing the work.

If you were arranging these categories for humorous effect you would probably want to end with your discussion of the grinds or the burnouts, since the potential for humor is greatest there.

Other topics and purposes will require other arrangements of ideas. The principle, however, remains the same: to arrange your ideas according to a plan that suits your purpose.

The principles of division, coordination, and order are generally used to outline the *body* of a speech first. The introduction and conclusion can be outlined separately when you are ready to structure the speech.

STRUCTURING THE SPEECH

A structured speech will have a recognizable introduction and conclusion, as well as transitions from point to point.

The Introduction

Traditionally, the most important function of an introduction is to capture audience interest. In fact, audience interest is such an integral part of a speech that Chapter 8 will be devoted to it. Here we are concerned with the introduction as a structural component. A well-planned introduction will usually preview the structure of a speech by telling the audience what your main points will be. It tells them what to listen for and it gives them an idea of what your method of organization will be. For example, Katherine Graham, the chairman of the board of the Washington Post Company, once addressed a group of businessmen and their wives. This was her introduction:

> I am delighted to be here. It is a privilege to address you. And I am especially glad the rules have been bent for tonight, allowing so many of you to bring along your husbands. I think it's nice for them to get out once in a while and see how the other half lives. Gentlemen, we welcome you.
>
> Actually, I have other reasons for appreciating this chance to talk with you tonight. It gives me an opportunity to address some current questions about the press and its responsibilities—whom we are responsible to, what we are responsible for, and generally how responsible our performance has been.[10]

Ms. Graham did not have to jump up and down to get her audience's attention. As head of one of the best-known media firms in the United States[11] her authority was well known. She did, however, feel it necessary to put the audience members at ease. That is why she joked with the men about a woman's traditional role in society. By beginning with this witticism she assured the men that she would not berate them or hold them personally responsible for the sexist traditions of their businesses. The most important part of this example, though, is the smooth way she previewed her main points:

> I.   To explain whom the press is responsible to.
> II. To explain what the press is responsible for.
> III. To explain how responsible the performance of the press has been.

Sometimes your preview of main points will be even more straightforward:

> "I have three points to discuss: They are _____ , _____ , and _____ ."

Sometimes you will not want to refer directly to your main points in your introduction. Your reasons might be based on a plan calling for suspense, or humorous effect, or stalling for time in order to win over a hostile audience. In that case you might preview just your main idea, in passing:

> "I am going to say a few words about _____ ."
> "Did you ever wonder about _____ ?"
> " _____ is one of the most important issues facing us today."

Remember: The audience will focus on one "central idea," anyway. Make sure they are able to recognize *your* central idea rather than one that they have to make up for themselves.

Transitions

Transitions join ideas together by showing how one idea is related to another. Transitions keep your message moving forward. They tell how the introduction of your message relates to the body of your message. They tell how one main point relates to the next main point. They tell how your subpoints relate to the points they are part of. They tell how supporting points relate to the points they support. Transitions usually sound like this:

> "Like _____ , another important consideration is _____ ."
>
> "But _____ isn't the only thing we have to worry about. _____ is even more potentially destructive."
>
> "Yes, the problem is obvious. But what are the solutions? Well, one possible solution is _____ ."

Transitions, like all components of messages, can be done artistically:

> "The relationship between my next point and _____ is like an Amazon: rough but conceivable. Bear with me, though, because the relationship is important. . . ."

Transitions make the difference between a grocery list of unrelated ideas and a recipe of structured thought.[12]

The Conclusion

The conclusion reviews the main points of your message and re-establishes the message's central idea. It lets an audience know that the message is over, and that the points can now be considered, used, or acted upon. The review of your main points can be done artistically if your audience is sophisticated enough to recognize that your main points are, indeed, being reviewed. For example, in the speech by Katherine Graham the conclusion sounded like this:

> . . . So instead of seeking flat and absolute answers to the kinds of problems I have discussed tonight, what we should be trying to foster is respect for one another's conception of where duty lies, and understanding of the real worlds in which we try to do our best. And we should be hoping for the energy and sense to keep on arguing and questioning, because there is no better sign that our society is still healthy and strong.[13]

Ms. Graham posed three questions in her introduction. She dealt with those questions in her speech and then reminded her audience, in her conclusion, that she had answered the questions:

I. Introduction: Who is the press responsible to? (Conclusion:

The press is responsible to its own conception of where its duty lies).

II. Introduction: What is the press responsible for? (Conclusion: The press is responsible for doing its best in the "real world.")

III. Introduction: How responsible has the press been? (Conclusion: It has done its best.)

The basics of message structure can be expressed in the aphorism, "Tell what you're going to say, say it, then tell what you said." This sounds redundant, but research in listening suggests that an audience will only remember 50 percent of what you've said immediately after you've said it, and a few days later that figure will be down to 25 percent.[14]

Structured messages seem to be especially important for college students. Minds wander. There's not much you can do about that. Several researchers have tried to discover why minds wander. One study, for example, suggests that college freshmen spend about 25 percent of their classtime daydreaming about sex.[15] Trying to compete with sexual fantasies is a difficult task. It forces you to decide what the main points of your speech actually are, because they should be the ideas that your audience retains. When you repeat your main points three times, you more than triple the chances that your audience will retain them. Audiences have a tendency to listen more carefully during the beginning and the end of a speech.[16]

Of course, introductions and conclusions usually do more than establish the basic structure mentioned here. Introductions usually relate the topic to the needs of the audience, but that idea will be covered in depth in Chapter 8. And conclusions are usually worded in such a way that they make the main ideas convincing and mem-

ALL I REMEMBER WAS: NICE TO BE HERE AND ANY QUESTIONS...

WHERE WERE YOU THE OTHER TWENTY MINUTES?

orable, but that idea will be covered in Chapter 7. This chapter is concerned with the organizational basics; more creative facets of the speech will probably arise naturally as you rough out your ideas.

ROUGHING THE SPEECH

"Roughing" means to shape in a preliminary manner. There are a number of ways to rough a speech. It can be done in the form of a complete written rough draft, in the form of brief notes, or in your head. This depends largely on the type of delivery you will use. Extemporaneous speeches are generally roughed first in outline form, and then out loud. The "roughing out loud" is generally done alone at first, and then later in front of a small sample audience such as one or two trusted friends.

All the time you were investigating, analyzing, and organizing your speech material you were "roughing" little sections of the speech in your head. That shaping process will continue right up until the time you actually present your speech. However, there will be one point in your speech development in which your main concern will be sitting down, in an environment that is suitable for quality thinking, and figuring out what goes where. That's roughing.

Roughing is a process of discovery. It is at this time that you test your ideas, your organization, and your potential audience appeal. Once you are before your audience, it is too late to test. A common plea of a beginning public speaker is: "Oops—forget I said that." Unfortunately, even if (indeed, *especially* if) the audience tried to forget that they heard something, they would remember it. A speech presentation is not well suited to trial and error. Roughing is. It is easy to deal with an idea that falls apart in mid-development when you are alone. It is impossible to do the same thing when you are speaking in front of an audience.

You should rough your speech and your working outline at the same time. Start with either the speech itself or the outline, but move back and forth, changing both the outline and speech as you go. As long as you maintain some form of organization, as evidenced by your outline, you can pour out your ideas as they come to you. The structure supplied by your outline gives you the freedom to experiment with new ways of expressing your ideas.

When you have finished roughing and outlining your speech you should have various trophies to show for your efforts. You should have a final outline. You should have (in your head, if nowhere else) a speech which you have been constantly trying out, changing, and generally fiddling around with during the entire time you worked with it. You should have a mass of scribbled notes, largely undecipherable, which will include several scratch outlines. The notes could, at your discretion, be written up as a manuscript, reworked into a term paper, or kept as a memento. Generally, however, they should just be shipped off to your nearest recycling center, to relieve tomorrow's public speaking student of the responsibility of killing a tree to complete an assignment.

SAMPLE SPEECH

Not too long ago Paul Urbanek, one of my students, expressed some suspicions about the simplicity of the basic principles of message preparation. "It can't be that simple," he said. "Do you mind if I try to prove in my next speech that some types of messages *don't* conform to these principles?"

I agreed, on two conditions. First, the speech would have to be based on investigation rather than personal opinion. Second, the messages that were used as examples would have to be *effective* messages.

Paul agreed and went to work. He began investigating with three main ideas in mind:

    I. Television Commercials
   II. College Lectures
  III. Political Speeches

It didn't take him long to realize that he was attempting too much. After consulting the focus model (Chapter 3) he narrowed his topic to college lectures. As he continued his investigation, though, his original idea changed in some fundamental ways.

Paul did an admirable job of researching his topic. In fact, because of the conditions I stipulated, he began organizing his speech around the various types of research he had done: the survey research he had found, his interviewing, and his library research.

As Paul roughed his speech he recognized that his most important ideas concerned the principles of message preparation that he was trying to debunk. The main points in his working outline, therefore, became the following:

    I. Are effective lectures focused?
   II. Are effective lectures based on investigation?
  III. Are effective lectures organized with an introduction, body and conclusion?

As he continued to rough his speech he arranged his main points for effect. He felt he should begin with the principle with which he had found the most agreement, and end with the principle with which he had found the most disagreement. He felt that this would increase audience interest as his speech progressed.[17] He also experimented with different ways of expressing each idea, and he roughed out an introduction, a conclusion, and some transitions from point to point.

By the time Paul gave his speech it was nothing like the speech he had intended. He titled his speech:

DO THE PROFS PRACTICE WHAT OUR PROF PREACHES?

Some
Comments

Paul first
establishes
audience
interest in his
introduction.

The Talk

How many times have you heard students say of one of their professors, "He's obviously brilliant, but I can't understand a word he says"? Richard Calish, writing in *The English Journal,* suggests that the communication gap between student and professor is a fairly common one. He blames it on (and I quote here) "the heartbreaking, head-aching, agonizing, scandalizing inability of the average pedagogically inclined, university-trained preacher, teacher, or educational creature to convey a message clearly, briefly, succinctly, openly, understandably, interestingly, in quasi-grammatical and pseudo-punctuational, intelligible, semi-formal, and close-to-normal English from the aura of his own consciousness to that of his thirty or so questioning, searching, listening young knowledge-intake organisms—the students." (Unquote).

He then
establishes the
focus of his
speech.

It was statements like these that led me to today's topic. I wanted to find out if good lectures use the principles we learn about in this class.

First I needed to find some of our best lecturers. I dug up the faculty evaluation surveys that are on file in the library. These forms are completed by students in each class each semester, and then filed in the library. Anytime you want to find out about your professors, you can look them up there.

One question on this survey seemed to be a good measure of a student's evaluation of his professor's ability to communicate. This item is "The instructor communicates well." The possible responses from students range from 5 (highly descriptive) to 1 (not at all descriptive). I chose three professors who were consistently rated as "5's" on this item: Professor Wheeler, the physics professor renowned for his in-class

Some Comments

The Talk

demonstrations of exploding gases; Professor Booker, the firebrand of the English Literature Department; and Professor Hartley, Professor of Psychology and Director of the University Counseling Center.

I then interviewed these professors. I asked them questions about three of the principles we learn about in this class: investigation, organization, and focus. Specifically, I asked them the following questions:

He previews his main points here.

1. Do you investigate new material for each lecture?
2. Do you organize each lecture with a clear-cut introduction, body, and conclusion?
3. Do you focus on one idea in your lectures?

End of introduction. First main point: investigation

Believe it or not, my model professors did not completely agree with these principles as we have learned them. They did agree, in reference to the first question, that a good lecture had to be based on investigation. But they generally found that their day-to-day research, reading, and interaction with colleagues kept them up-to-date enough in terms of the new material they presented.

Supporting point: Wheeler quote.

Professor Wheeler summed up the profs' opinion on investigation when he told me, "The new material is no problem. It is the standard material, like how many aspects of a particular phenomenon I have to cover, that I need to review before a lecture."

In other words, the professors reinvestigated what they already knew. They did that to make sure that the material was fresh in their minds, and also to make sure that it was presented in an organized manner. That brought me to my second question:

Transition to second main point: organization.

"Do you organize each lecture with a clear-cut introduction, body, and conclusion?" Here the professors divided according to their discipline. Professor Booker said, "Definitely," but Professor Wheeler explained that his introductions and conclusions were developed around "units," and a unit was impossible to cover in one class period. So, although he believed in organization, his introductions and

**Some
Comments**

The Talk

conclusions were often several days apart! Professor Hartley of the Psychology Department gave the most interesting answer to this question. He said that he didn't really believe in conclusions. He said that every one of his lectures began with a transition based on the previous lecture and ended with a transition to the next lecture. The course itself, he told me, ended with a transition to practical, everyday uses of what had been learned.

Transition to third
main point:
focus

By this time my faith in our revered principles was beginning to shake. It almost toppled when I asked the final question. That question dealt with focus, which has been introduced to us as a basic tenet of message preparation. All three profs gave me an identical answer when I asked them, "Do you focus on one idea only throughout a lecture?" They all told me, "No." They all told me that they concentrated on one idea at a time, but they seldom gave an entire lecture based on one idea only.

Conclusion.

I was confused, so I returned to the library. I started reviewing what some experts say about public speaking and how it relates to the college lecture hall. It didn't take me long to realize where I had gone wrong. Perhaps Shana Alexander, who presents "Point-Counterpoint" with James Kilpatrick each week on CBS Television's program *60 Minutes,* summed it up best. In an article entitled "Unaccustomed as I Am," she stated, simply enough, "A speech is not a lecture. The object of a 'Speech' is not to get points over; it is to try to make people feel something."

Paul begins his
conclusion by
telling where his
investigation led
him.

That hit me as such a revelation that I think I'll repeat it for you: "A speech is not a lecture. The object is not to get points over; it is to try to make people feel something." I considered that statement a revelation because it summed up an important point for this course and for this speech: *Good lecturers try to make their audiences feel something.*

He then reviews
his main points.

That is why professors Wheeler, Booker, and Hartley are such good lecturers. They don't just "get their points over." They make their audiences *feel* something. In order to do that, they make their lectures

Some Comments

The Talk

a series of related speeches. Each one of these speeches-within-a-lecture conforms to the principles of message preparation. They are all based on investigated material. They are all individually organized, and they all focus on one idea.

He reaffirms his central idea.

So the profs do practice what our prof preaches. I haven't been able to debunk the principles of message preparation yet. In fact, after this experience, I think I'll quit trying.[18]

Paul distributed a formal outline of his speech to the class. It looked like this:

Introduction
  I. The Problem
      quote: Richard Calish
  II. The Methodology
      A. Surveys
      B. Interview
          1. Investigation?
          2. Organization?
          3. Focus?

Body
  I. The Principle of Investigation: The profs all agree.
      quote: Professor Wheeler
  II. The Principle of Organization: The profs are divided by discipline.
      A. Prof. Booker: "Definitely"
      B. Prof. Wheeler: "Units"
      C. Prof. Hartley: "No Conclusions"
  III. The Principle of Focus: The profs seem to disagree.

Conclusion
  I. A Speech Is Not a Lecture
      quote: Shana Alexander
  II. The Basic Principles Revisited

SUMMARY

This chapter dealt with organization; with the organizational methods of outlining; with structuring the speech by means of an introduction, transitions, and a conclusion; and with roughing the speech.

Formal outlines are used as a model of the speech for other people. Working outlines are developmental tools for the speaker alone. Both types of outlines are governed by three principles. *The principle of division* requires that each idea (i.e., each topic, main point, or subpoint) should be divided into no more than five ideas. These divisions should cover all the essentials of the idea. Each division should contain one idea only. *The principle of coordination* requires that all the divisions be of equal importance and that they be worded similarly. *The principle of order* requires that the divisions be placed in a logical sequence.

The introduction of a speech gets your audience's attention and previews your main points. Transitions are used to show the relationship between each of your points. The conclusion reviews the main points and re-establishes the central idea of the speech. Roughing the speech is a process of trying out your ideas as you organize them. It can be done in writing, out loud, or in your head, but it should be done at the same time that you develop your outline.

Organizing your speech according to these guidelines will not only help you remember everything you want to say, it will help your audience understand and remember your ideas.

QUESTIONS FOR DISCUSSION

1. Do you agree that the working outline is an effective method for developing message organization? What other methods have you used that are also helpful?
2. It is stated that at times you might *not* want to refer directly to your main points in your introduction. Can you think of any topics and/or audiences for which an initial preview should be avoided? Explain your answer.
3. The text presents methods of "Division" and "Order": chronological, spatial, process, accepted categories, and original categories. From your experiences listening to or reading messages, can you think of any *additional* methods? If so, are they, in your opinion, more or less effective than those mentioned in the text?
4. Review the Paul Urbanek speech at the end of this chapter. After thinking about the evidence he presents, do you agree or disagree with his conclusion that "Profs" really *do* practice the principles of message preparation? Why or why not?

PROBES

1. To illustrate the point that receivers can process only a limited number of ideas, try a version of the "Telephone Game" on three of your friends. Tell a story (relatively complex) to one friend, with the others absent. Have that person repeat the story to the second

friend, and have that friend relate the account back to you. What deletions or distortions did you notice? Do these results verify or refute the studies of Jevons and Miller? Why do you suppose certain details were retained, while others were dropped or distorted?

2. Select a speech (or written message) from your class, *Vital Speeches, Representative American Speeches,* the local newspaper, or any other suitable source. Decide what you believe to be the message's *purpose,* and method of organization of main points (chronological, spatial, and so on). Do you feel the method employed was appropriate for the source's purpose? Why or why not?

3. Using the same (or a different) message from one of the sources listed above, reduce it to an outline following the outlining principles suggested in the chapter. After completing your task, do you feel that the "formal procedure" is effective? Why or why not?

4. Read (or listen to) a speech (from *Vital Speeches* or another source). Evaluate the introduction and conclusion. Did the speaker fulfill the objectives stated in this text? If not, how might these aspects of the message be changed in order to make the presentation more effective?

5. Observe three or four television commercials carefully. Do you feel that the principles of organization discussed in this chapter (introductions, conclusions, division, order, and so on) are followed in these presentations? *If not,* do any deviations from the suggestions in the text make these advertisements more or less effective?

6. Observe carefully several local or network newscasts. Are these programs organized according to any of the principles of division or order suggested in this chapter? Whatever their patterns of organization happen to be, why do you suppose they were selected?

NOTES

[1]James C. McCroskey, *An Introduction to Rhetorical Communication,* 2nd ed. (Englewood Cliffs, N.J.: Prentice-Hall, 1972), pp. 180–184.

[2]Jerome S. Bruner, "Learning and Thinking," in Richard C. Anderson and David P. Ausubel, eds., *Readings in the Psychology of Cognition* (New York: Holt, Rinehart and Winston, 1965), p. 77.

[3]Jevons' experiment, conducted in 1871, is reported in Edwin G. Boring, *The Physical Dimensions of Consciousness* (New York: Dover Publications, 1963), p. 195.

[4]George A. Miller, "The Magical Number Seven, Plus or Minus Two: Some Limits on Our Capacity for Processing Information," in Anderson and Ausubel, *op. cit.,* pp. 242–267.

[5]Ibid., p. 241.

[6]Studies have demonstrated that messages are, in general, not only better comprehended, but more persuasive, and the speaker more credible, when messages are well organized. See R. G. Smith, "Effects of Speech Organization upon Attitudes of College Students," *Speech Monographs,*

18 (1951), pp. 292–301; E. Thompson, "Some Effects of Message Structure on Listeners' Comprehension," *Speech Monographs,* 39 (1967), pp. 51–57; H. Sharp and T. McClung, "Effects of Organization on the Speaker's Ethos," *Speech Monographs,* 33 (1966), p. 182; and J. C. McCroskey and R. S. Mehrley, "The Effects of Disorganization and Nonfluency on Attitude Change and Source Credibility," *Speech Monographs,* 36 (1969), pp. 13–21.

[7]Different experts suggest different procedures for outlining, and often the rules are not this hard and fast. However, I have found the procedure presented here to be the most clear-cut and useful for formal outlining.

[8]Plato, *Phaedrus,* translated by B. Jowett, in *The Works of Plato* (New York: Tudor Publishing Co., n.d.), vol 3, p. 446.

[9]Alan H. Monroe and Douglas Ehninger, *Principles and Types of Speech Communication,* 7th ed. (Glenview, Ill.: Scott, Foresman and Co., 1974).

[10]Katherine Graham, "The Press and Its Responsibilities," *Vital Speeches of the Day,* vol. 42 (April 15, 1976).

[11]According to *Moody's Industrial Manual* (New York: Moody's Investors Service, 1979), the Washington Post Company publishes *The Washington Post, The Trenton Times* and *Sunday Times Advertiser,* and *Newsweek* magazine. It owns and operates four TV stations and two radio stations, and owns 30 percent of *The International Herald Tribune* and 50 percent of the Los Angeles Times–Washington Post News Service. *Moody's Industrial Manual,* by the way, is available in most library reference rooms, in case you ever wonder who owns what.

[12]Research suggesting that a message is better comprehended and accepted if transitions are employed is reported by D. L. Thistlethwaite, H. deHaan, and J. Kamenetsky, "The Effect of 'Directive' and 'Non-Directive' Communication Procedures on Attitudes," *Journal of Abnormal and Social Psychology,* 51 (1955), pp. 107–118; and E. Thompson, "Some Effects of Message Structure on Listeners' Comprehension," *Speech Monographs,* 34 (1967), pp. 51–57.

[13]Graham, op. cit.

[14]Ralph Nichols and Leonard Stevens, *Are You Listening?* (New York: McGraw-Hill, 1957).

[15]Study cited in Floyd L. Ruch and Philip G. Zimbardo, *Psychology and Life,* 8th ed. (Glenview, Ill.: Scott, Foresman and Co., 1971), p. 267.

[16]Studies indicate that ideas are better recalled by listeners if they are placed *either* at the beginning *or* at the end of presentation. This research is summarized in G. Cronkhite, *Persuasion: Speech and Behavioral Change* (Indianapolis: Bobbs-Merrill, 1969), pp. 195–196.

[17]The results of survey and experimental studies indicate that a source's credibility and the effectiveness of a message are *both* enhanced if arguments likely to gain audience acceptance are presented first. See J. C. McCroskey and S. V. O. Prichard, "Selective Exposure and Lyndon B. Johnson's January, 1966, State of the Union Address," *Journal of Broadcasting,* 11 (1967), pp. 331–337; and P. Tannenbaum, "Mediated Generalization of Attitude Change via the Principle of Congruity," *Journal of Personality and Social Psychology,* 3 (1966), pp. 493–500.

[18]References: Richard Calish, "Don't Talk, Communicate," *English Journal,* 62 (October 1973), pp. 1010–1011; Shana Alexander, "Unaccustomed as I am," in W. W. Wilmot and J. R. Wenburg, eds., *Communication Involvement: Personal Perspectives* (New York: John Wiley & Sons, 1974), p. 313, originally published in *Life,* May 19, 1967.

6 Language

Up to this point, most of the general aspects of message preparation have been covered. This chapter discusses what is perhaps the most important *specific* aspect of message preparation: our use, and occasional abuse, of language. The importance of language is another principle of message preparation, leading to the prediction:

A message expressed in clear language will be more effective than one that is not.[1]

LANGUAGE

The English language is amazingly complex. No matter what type of presentation you are using, you should take time to decide how to put your ideas into words. Even in an impromptu speech, you have time to consider more than one way of expressing your ideas. Language choices can be made even more carefully while preparing an extemporaneous speech. You make them while determining your main points, while roughing the speech, and while practicing the speech. You need not memorize exact wording: simply making your language choices in advance will lead to a clearer presentation. Language choices depend on two characteristics of language: vocabulary (the words we use) and syntax (the way we put those words together).

VOCABULARY

The words we use are said to have two distinct traits: connotation and denotation. Denotation is the literal meaning of the word (the meaning found in the dictionary), and connotation is what the word suggests to the listener. "Fat," "stout," and "portly" all denote superfluous body tissue, and yet the connotations of these words differ markedly. A "stout" person, for most audiences, would be strong and healthy. A "portly" person would probably be less strong but more dignified. The difference between connotation and denotation makes it necessary to carefully plan the words you use in a message. There are three basic guidelines for effective vocabulary: *appropriateness*, *vividness*, and *clarity*.

Appropriateness

The words you use must be appropriate to you, to your audience, and to your message. Three types of words are infamous for their inappropriateness: *obscenity*, *slang*, and *jargon*.

OBSCENITY
Obscene language is generally of a religious, sexual, or excretory nature. Society enforces strong sanctions against all three types of obscenity. Religious obscenity has been banned from Judeo-Christian cultures with the Third Commandment: "Thou shalt not take the name of the Lord thy God in vain." Other religious cultures have similar taboos. Sexual obscenity is considered taboo in our culture because of the beliefs of our Puritan forefathers and foremothers, who believed that such words were "designed to incite to lust and depravity."[2] According to Harold Vetter in his book *Language Behavior and Communication*, all societies need a short, concise term for copulation, and yet nowhere is a society as threatened by the term as in the

United States.[3] The intensity of our sexual taboos has lessened over the years, however. A list of words banned from U.S. movies in the 1930s included "eunuch," "courtesan," "harlot," "tart," "trollop," "wench," "whore," "sex," and "sexual."[4] Excretory obscenity is taboo in our culture because it evokes images of excretions, which most people do not like to smell, look at, listen to, taste, or touch.

Obscenity was commonly used in protest communication in the 1960s. Jerry Rubin, in his book *Do It*, explained why:

> Nobody really communicates with words any more. Words have lost their emotional impact, intimacy, ability to shock and make love.
>
> Language *prevents* communication
> CARS LOVE SHELL
> How can I say,
> "I love you"
> after hearing
> "Cars love Shell."
> Does anyone understand what I mean?[5]

Rubin believed that obscene language was needed to arouse emotion. He took this theory to the 1968 National Democratic Convention with him, and the Chicago police supplied proof of the emotional power of obscene words. The proof was supplied with such direct methods of feedback as billy clubs and Mace. There's a lesson to be learned in that: not to use obscenity unless you *want* the result that it is likely to provoke in your audience.[6]

SLANG

Slang words are those which are not yet an accepted part of the language. "Bus," "cab," "hoax," and "mob" were all slang terms at one time, but they later became standard. "Ripped off" (meaning "stolen" or "victimized"), "uptight" (meaning "anxious"), and "laid back" (meaning "calm") are currently slang terms. Slang is more appropriate in a spoken message than in a written message, but it is troublesome even when spoken. Slang should not be used unless all members of the audience find it acceptable. Otherwise, it should be replaced with a more standard usage. In the "Summer Vacation" example given later in this chapter, "ego trip" and "drag," are slang terms. "Conceited" might be better to use than "on an ego trip" (i.e., "they were very conceited" instead of "they were on real ego trips"), and "bore" might be better than "drag."

JARGON

Jargon includes words of a specialized nature that are used only by specific groups of people. Educators, for example, talk of "empirically validated learning" and "multi-mode curricula," and rather than saying that a child needs improvement, they say that "academic achievement is not commensurate with abilities." Doctors and military strategists are famous for their use of jargon, also. A heart attack is a "coronary thrombosis" or a "cardiovascular accident" for doctors, while air raids are "routine limited duration protective reactions" to the military. Business people, religious groups, sports enthusiasts, lawyers, and many other groups have semi-private vocabularies. *Words from these vocabularies are appropriate only when they are addressed to those who use them regularly.* Of course, the rule works in reverse, too. If you can use a limited amount of an audience's jargon to communicate ideas that they are not familiar with, you could be one step ahead in the make-yourself-clear game. You could explain gourmet cooking to a group of computer experts by referring to the input-output of recipe ingredients or by stressing the GIGO principle (garbage in, garbage out) in selecting ingredients.

It is important to recognize that making language appropriate does *not* mean making it dry and lifeless. That's where the idea of vividness comes in.

Vividness

A vivid vocabulary is one that gains your audience's attention because of the images the words evoke. Images are worth thousands of words; because of that, they help hold down the unnecessary verbiage. A vivid vocabulary is made up of words that are *original, action-oriented,* and *sensuous.*

ORIGINALITY

That first factor, originality, is the biggest problem encountered by college students in both written and spoken communication. An instructor at Mount Holyoke College claims that as a student she began seven years of English courses with some variation of the following theme:

How I Spent My Summer Vacation

When school let out I was happy as a lark. It was hot as hell and all I wanted to do was be as cool as a cucumber at the lake. I was brought back to reality with the profound realization that I was going to have to get a summer job. My parents said I was too old to be happy and carefree.

I got a job at an appliance store where I met some people as nutty as fruitcakes. . . . I got sick and tired of having dirty old men tell me I was as pretty as a picture. . . . They were on real ego trips.

The worst part of the whole summer was one day at work when I became as white as a sheet and my eyes overflowed with tears and then I slumped over with fatigue. I had to take a rest after that. Staying in bed was a real drag.

Soon though I was rosy with happiness and pretty as a peach. And I learned something over the summer that will start me on the yellow brick road to the end of my rainbow. Life is no bowl of cherries. The best things in life are those that come by starting out at the bottom of the ladder.[7]

Looking back on her years as a student, the author of this familiar-sounding passage remarks that the "How I Spent My Summer Vacation" assignment was usually "an exam on how many clichés we had remembered from the year before."[8] Granted, her example is overdone. But it is still a useful reminder of how boring some expressions are if we have heard them so many times that they no longer evoke an interesting image.

You don't have to know a lot of words to put them together in an interesting manner. You just have to be *honest.* You have to conjure up the image that *you* want to relate, and use *your own words* to describe that image.

The following "summer" passage is from the opening lines of Ernest Hemingway's *A Farewell to Arms.* It exemplifies the honest, original use of words we all understand.

In the late summer of that year we lived in a house in a village that looked across the river and the plain to the mountains. In the bed of the river there were pebbles and boulders, dry and white in the sun, and the water was clear and swiftly moving and blue in the channels. Troops went by the house and down the road and the dust they raised powdered the leaves of the trees. The trunks of the trees too were dusty and the leaves fell early that year and we saw the troops marching along the

road and the dust rising and leaves, stirred by the breeze, falling and the soldiers marching and afterward the road bare and white except for the leaves.[9]

Once again, the purpose is not to compare a mock college essay with the prose of a master. Especially this prose. Critic Robert Manning once said of these lines:

> One cannot estimate how many would-be writers, in a long generation since these lines were written by Ernest Hemingway, have looked at them, clean with discipline and pregnant with the sense of individual sensation, and then crumpled their own efforts with a sigh, and started over.[10]

There are no clichés in the Hemingway passage. Yet it is important to point out that Hemingway does not avoid common expressions completely. The very next paragraph of "A Farewell to Arms" begins, "The plain was rich with crops . . ." Using the word "rich" to describe horticulture is common; yet it works perfectly in that line. It is honest and precise, and Hemingway shows no fear of it.

The first example shows us how *not* to use figures of speech like similes and metaphors. "Happy as a lark" and "cool as a cucumber" are dead similes. They hold no more meaning for us than the simple words "happy" and "cool." Similarly, "life is no bowl of cherries" is a dead metaphor. We've heard the expression too many times for it to mean more than "life is hard."

Hemingway's passage does not use clichés or worn-out figures of speech. Hemingway didn't like them—he preferred to say what he wanted to say directly, and get on with whatever war or safari he was involved with at the time. What his passage lacks in clichés, however, it makes up in action orientation.

ACTION ORIENTATION

Notice that in Hemingway's prose nothing just sits around. The water moves swiftly, the dust powders and rises, the leaves fall, and the soldiers march. Even the village is not content to sit idly. It "looks across the river." That last phrase is also an example of personification. Personification, or giving human characteristics to inanimate objects, is one method of allowing objects to do more than just sit. Or set.

SENSUOUSNESS

Since we perceive reality through our senses, one method of evoking images is to use words that refer to sight, hearing, smell, touch, or taste. Objects have size, color, shape, and position that can be seen. The size has dimension, the color has brightness, the shape has contours, and the position has some relationship in space to other objects. Notice in the Hemingway passage that the water is blue, as well as moving, and the boulders are white, as well as dry. These are images based on the sense of sight. You can evoke images based on hearing by telling of the tone, rhythm, and melody of a sound. Sounds *do* things. They chime, chatter, clang, clatter, clink, crackle, crash, and creak. We can use words to duplicate sounds by using onomatopoeia. For example, you can describe the "blip" of a radar screen or the "hiss" of a distant waterfall. Words that evoke images of smell will tell us about the sharpness or intensity of an odor. Odors can be "moldy" or "musky." They can also be "balmy" or "woodsy." Words that evoke images of taste could describe the sweetness, sourness, bitterness, or saltiness of a flavor. Words that evoke images of touch could refer to pressure, texture, or warmth of contact. A touch could be "slimy" or "stinging." It could also be "satiny" or "smooth."

Appropriateness and vividness, then, are important considerations in language use. But our final consideration, clarity, is perhaps most important.

Clarity

Clarity is simply the process of saying what you mean. Many language experts suggest that it is becoming increasingly difficult for people to say what they mean. Peter Farb, in his book *Word Play: What Happens When People Talk*, describes America's present-day language trends this way:

> An entire generation has grown up that distrusts language's ability to express a true picture of reality and that relies upon the empty intercalations of like, you know, I mean. The world has grown inarticulate at the very time that an unprecedented number of words flood the media. The output has burgeoned, but speakers have retreated into worn paths and stock phrases.[11]

Saying what you mean requires careful word choice. When planning a message you have to become a wordsmith, a craftsman just like a silversmith or a watchsmith. Just as any other person involved in a craft, as a wordsmith you have to use the tools that are available to you. If you are the type of wordsmith who likes simple, all-purpose tools, you might like to use a good standard dictionary.[12] Dictionaries can be used for more than spelling and denotative meaning; they also supply word derivations, pronunciation guides, synonyms, antonyms, and word variations. All these things help you determine nuances of meaning.

If you are the type of wordsmith who likes specialized tools, you might like to use a thesaurus. A thesaurus is a dictionary of synonyms and antonyms. If you were planning a speech on "Poverty in America," you might find that the idea of "poverty" was repeated so many times, with different shades of meaning, that you need more than one word to describe it. If you looked up "poverty" in one thesaurus you would find this:

POVERTY

Nouns—**1,** poverty, inpecuniousness, indigence, penury, pauperism, destitution, want; need, neediness; lack, necessity, privation, distress, difficulties; bad, poor *or* needy circumstances; reduced *or* straitened circumstances; slender means, straits; hand-to-mouth existence; beggary; mendicancy, loss of fortune, bankruptcy, insolvency (see DEBT).

2, poor man, pauper, mendicant, beggar, starveling.

Verbs—**1,** be poor, want, lack, starve, live from hand to mouth, have seen better days, go down in the world, go to the dogs, go to wrack and ruin; not have a penny to one's name; beg one's bread; tighten one's belt. *Slang,* go broke.

2, render poor, impoverish, reduce to poverty; pauperize, fleece, ruin, strip.

Adjectives—poor, indigent; poverty-striken; poor as a church mouse; poor as Job's turkey; penniless, impecunious; hard up; out at elbows *or* heels; seedy, shabby; beggarly, beggared; destitute, bereft, in want, needy, necessitous, distressed, pinched, straitened; unable to keep the wolf from the door, unable to make both ends meet; embarrassed, involved; insolvent, bankrupt, on one's uppers, on the rocks. *Colloq.,* in the hole, broke, stony, looking for a handout.

Antonym, see MONEY[13]

Each of these terms for "poverty" will have a fine shade of connotation. Some of them might also be hopelessly out of date. Most college audiences, for example, would not understand expressions like "poor as Job's turkey" or "stony." But the thesaurus is a handy tool for finding an appropriate synonym to use for a specific reason. The thesaurus is particularly handy when you have the word "on the tip of your tongue" but you can't quite think of it. If you were looking for a more formal term for "poor man," and you knew there was such a term but for some reason you had a mental block and couldn't think of it, the thesaurus would give you "pauper." If you were looking for a descriptive expression for "a life of poverty," the thesaurus would give you "hand-to-mouth existence."

Whether you are using a thesaurus or a standard dictionary, there are two characteristics of clarity that, if you recognize them, will help you make the best word choice. These characteristics are *specificity* and *concreteness.*

SPECIFICITY

A specific word is one that restricts the meaning that can be assigned to it. "Specific" is therefore the opposite of "general." General words name groups of things; specific words name the individual things that make up that group. The term transportation is general. "Automobile," "sports car," and "Porsche 911-S Targa" are increasingly specific terms. Someone who says, "I had an automobile accident the other day" is likely to evoke less sympathy from a sports car enthusiast than one who says, "I demolished my 911-S Targa the other day."

One of the reasons some people distrust politicians is that politicians often do not speak in specifics because of the broad audience they attempt to please. Candidate X favors "law and order." What does that mean? Does the candidate favor registration of firearms, enforcement of busing for integration, or the suspension of the Fourteenth Amendment? (That's the one that guarantees "due process of law.") Advertisers also shy away from specific language. They use words like "virtually." It sounds so virtuous: "Zitsaway will give you *virtually* clear skin in 90 days." In that sense, "virtually" means "almost." You can bet they wouldn't sell as much Zitsaway if they advertised that it would give you "almost clear skin."

Specificity (or "accuracy" or "precision") in word choice is one characteristic of clarity. Another is concreteness.

CONCRETENESS

Concrete words are words that refer to things in actual physical reality, things that we can perceive with our senses. "Concrete" is therefore the opposite of "abstract." Abstract words refer to concepts that we can't see, hear, taste, touch, or feel. "Freedom," "democracy," "capitalism," and "communism" are typically abstract concepts, while "hot fudge sundaes," "skinny bodies," and "the smell of rotten garbage" are more concrete.

An understanding of symbolization—the relationship between words, perceptions, and reality—helps one understand concreteness.

SYMBOLIZATION

Words are symbols. A symbol is something that stands for something else. Words merely represent reality. Words are labels. Some of those labels refer to things we can perceive. We can't, however, perceive everything. No one has eyes in the back of the head. What we do perceive is distorted; we all perceive according to our prior experience. To make matters worse, we each assign different labels to what we perceive.[14] The buzzing confusion of "reality" is like a garbage dump, at which we are all pickers. Some of us pick out some things, some of us pick out others. Even if by some stroke of luck two of us pick out the same thing, one of us might call it "a piece of trash" and the other might call it "a charming antique."

Words are labels, and labels are generalizations for the way one person perceives reality. Since no two people perceive reality in exactly the same way, you should be very careful about labeling *your* reality. One heartbreaking story of the effects of improper labeling goes like this:

> There once was a brilliant but poverty-stricken entomologist who spent years breeding an uncommonly intelligent breed of housefly. One day, through a loophole in the laws of genetics, there appeared in his collection a young fly who could actually talk. Elated, the entomologist set about teaching the fly to sing, tell jokes, and play a few simple tunes on a small rubber band. When the fly had been sufficiently primed for a career in show business, the entomologist set off to find an agent. Since he would soon be wealthy, he decided to celebrate at a tavern along the way. He sat down at the bar and proudly displayed the fly to the bartender.
>
> "See that fly?" he asked.
>
> "Yup," said the bartender, slapping his hand on the bar and squashing the fly. "What'll ya have?"

It is an old story. But don't let that obscure the point. The label "fly" meant something entirely different to the entomologist than it did to the bartender. They were, as we say in the language business, operating on two different levels of abstraction. Levels of abstraction for the word "cow" are illustrated in Figure 6–1.[15]

This figure shows how confusing levels of abstraction can be. If you wanted to tell someone that you milked a cow, it would be just as confusing to say "I milked the atoms yesterday" as it would be to say "I milked the wealth." The key here is recognizing the level of abstraction that you are dealing with and choosing words that are appropriate to that level.

An example might clarify this piece of advice. Recently, one of my students attended an intensive communication session that lasted an entire weekend. When she returned, she wanted to tell the class what she had learned.

"I learned how to be really real," she bubbled. "I learned that each of us is the only one who can give each of us what we really need. I learned that the only way to self-actualization, self-realization, and true human dignity is through being really real. I learned that what is, is."

The class favored her with the polite, easygoing attention that one would give to a song sung in an unknown language. The class members believed that what she said was true, but they didn't feel that they understood what she was talking about. They still didn't know what she had done over the weekend or what she had learned by doing it. Her audience had no way of knowing what she meant by expressions like "really real," "what we really need," or "what is, is." For her second try, she decided to talk about an actual exercise that she had been involved in, and what that exercise had accomplished. Her second try went something like this:

"ASSETS"

8. Or, at the most abstract level, an anonymous item of value.

"WEALTH"

"FARM ASSETS"

7. or a salable item in general.

6. or merely a salable item from a particular farm.

"LIVESTOCK"

"COW"

5. or just another farm animal.

4. To someone else, Bessie might be just another female domesticated bovine.

"BESSIE"

3. If you've been introduced, you'll know Bessie according to characteristics like her loving expression and her amiable, if somewhat unimaginative, personality.

INFINITE CHARACTERISTICS

MOOO?

1. At the most concrete level, Bessie has infinite characteristics. These characteristics include everything from electrons to buttermilk, and it is impossible to perceive them all at once.

2. Strangers who perceive Bessie might ignore those characteristics in which they are not interested.

Figure 6–1

"Last weekend I attended a communication training session. In one exercise we all dressed in swim suits and painted each other's bodies. It was a great feeling. We felt really close. We learned how to be really real. We learned that what is, is. We learned—"

"Wait a second," one of her classmates pleaded. "You're making it sound like an orgy that turned into a religious experience. What exactly went *on* up there?"

The speaker's problem was her use of abstract terms. *She* knew what she was talking about, but she used terms that were much too abstract to describe her experiences for her audience. In order to recognize the problem, she made up the following abstraction ladder by substituting the various levels of "Bessie" with the various levels of "a group of people body painting."

8. A group of people being really real.
7. A group of people controlling barriers to everyday communication.
6. A group of people recognizing and controlling communication barriers in a group exercise.
5. A group of people involved in a group exercise.
4. A group of people interacting with a purpose.
3. A group of people body painting.
2. A group of people with characteristics we perceive.
1. A group of people with infinite characteristics.

Then, using the levels of abstraction that were appropriate for her audience, she formulated a clear message. Her next explanation went something like this: "Last weekend, as part of a 48-hour communication training session, I was involved in a group exercise that was designed to break down our barriers to effective communication. We often worry too much about what we look like to interact honestly and openly in a group of people. We worry more about our clothes and grooming than about our personalities. In this exercise we wore only bathing suits and we were painted—from head to toe—by the other people in our group. Who could worry about *looks* in a situation like that? The exercises helped us recognize the kind of barriers we put up in everyday communication. We hope recognition of these barriers will help us control them."[16]

Vocabulary, then, must be clear, vivid, and appropriate. The next language consideration is syntax.

SYNTAX

Syntax refers to the way we put our sentences together. Two of the most important considerations for effective syntax are *directness* and *variety*.

Directness

There are two ways to express ideas: in a direct style or in a complex, intricate style. The most effective style for a public speaker is usually the direct style. There are three things to keep in mind if directness is your goal: (1) use a simple construction, (2) use an active voice, and (3) use a simple tense.

Usually if a sentence is not constructed simply, it is because it contains too much. Generally, you can either throw away superfluous words or break a long, complex sentence into shorter, simpler ones. Some complex sentences contain two or more thoughts sitting too closely together:

> The registration of firearms is being considered by some members of Congress because they are owned by criminals.[17]

This statement is confusing because it sounds as though the members of Congress are owned by criminals, which is another issue entirely. The issue of gun control is better expressed by breaking this sentence up into two simpler ones:

> Unregistered firearms are often owned by criminals. Because of this, some members of Congress are considering legislation that would require firearms to be registered.

Sometimes, all you need to do to simplify a sentence is to throw away words that you don't need. One way to check for excess wording is to see how long it takes you to get to the point you want to make:

I'm not completely sure about all sides of the issue, but I think in the final analysis the registration of firearms is a procedure that we might want to support.

That is superfluous wording. Your audience will not be interested in the mental processes that brought you up to the point you are making. They just want to hear the point:

The registration of firearms should be supported by us.

This statement can be made even more direct by using the active rather than the passive voice. The active voice has the subject of the sentence perform action rather than be acted upon:

We should support the registration of firearms.

Also, you should use the simplest possible verb tense: Stick to the present, past, and future tenses if at all possible, and stay away from the present perfect, past perfect, and future perfect. Compare the following verb tenses in active and passive voices. The simple tenses in the active voice are generally the most direct:

	Tense	*Active Voice*	*Passive Voice*
simple tenses	present	I ask	I am asked
	past	I asked	I was asked
	future	I will ask	I will be asked
not-so-simple tenses	present perfect	I have asked	I have been asked
	past perfect	I had asked	I had been asked
	future perfect	I will have asked	I will have been asked

Keeping your sentences simple will help you to keep them direct, and keeping them direct will help you to keep them clear. Of course, you should also want to make your syntax interesting. That is where variety comes in.

Variety

Variety is interesting. It keeps people waiting to see what will happen next. It also helps to emphasize ideas. Variety in syntax is accomplished by using sentences of different *length, type,* and *structure.*

SENTENCE LENGTH

If your sentences are all the same length they will have a tendency to lull your audience to sleep. Your audience will be less interested in what comes next because they will already have a subconscious feel for how long each sentence will be. Even, steady rhythms are too smooth, too reassuring. Keep them guessing. Throw in some shorter sentences now and then. Do it for emphasis. It helps.

SENTENCE TYPE

Have you ever noticed that an occasional question seems to spice up a speech? A *rhetorical question* is one that does not require a direct response from your audience—it simply gives them something to think about. Questions should not be just "thrown into" the speech, though. They should be planted carefully, with enough room between each one to allow it to germinate. You should not give your audience too much to think about at any one time. You should, of course, answer a rhetorical question once you ask it, or at least give your audience enough information so they can answer it for themselves.

You can also use an occasional imperative sentence to keep your syntax interesting: "Take the initiative!" for example, rather than "We should take the initiative."

SENTENCE STRUCTURE

Finally, you can vary the structure of your sentences occasionally to give them a snappy, memorable sound. It was mentioned in Chapter 5 that one of the things a conclusion can do is to state the main idea of the speech in a convincing and memorable way. There will be other places besides the conclusion for memorable wording, though, so it would be a good idea to look at some of the methods for achieving it. One method, for example, is parallel sentence structure. Parallel sentence structure allows one idea to balance with another, such as John F. Kennedy's "Ask not what your country can do for you, ask what you can do for your country."[18] With a little less care J.F.K. might have said, "You should ask what services you can perform for the United States, rather than looking to the government to help you." That would have been far less snappy and memorable.

You could also vary your sentence structure so you put two or three words together with the same first letter or sound. This is alliteration, a device that former Vice President Spiro Agnew was famous for. He used to talk about "middle-aged malcontents," "effete intellectuals," and "nattering nabobs of negativism." Not that Agnew is such a great model, but at least his phrases were memorable. Assonance, the repetition of similar vowel sounds, is more difficult to do well. In fact, assonance is often accomplished accidentally, and it winds up sounding silly. William W. Watt, in *An American Rhetoric*, complains about "tone-deaf experts in several fields" who insist on using phrases like "the evaluation of the examination with relation to integration in education."[19] The repetition of all those "ations" gives the phrase the pleasant, empty cadence of a nursery rhyme. No word or phrase is stressed for importance because they all fall in with the pattern of the tune.

Of course, some memorable expressions are not memorable because of a recognizable device like parallelism, assonance, or alliteration. They are simply memorable because the speaker has experimented with different ways of saying something and then said it the way it sounded best. Consider the following expressions and see if they ring a bell:

> "Eighty-seven years ago . . ."
> "You wouldn't be Dr. Livingston by any chance, would you?"
> "Don't fire until they get right up next to you."
> "Old soldiers don't die, they just leave."
> "Why, I'd sooner die than not have liberty."

Varying the length, type, and structure of your sentence syntax will make your message sound more interesting, and will help you emphasize points you want to emphasize. That, along with direct syntax and clear, vivid, appropriate vocabulary, should allow you to *design* an effective message. This is generally true for all types of messages that use language, written or spoken. However, there are some important differences between written and spoken language.

WRITTEN AND SPOKEN STYLE

Effective spoken language is generally less formal. It contains more sentence fragments, more colloquial language, more contractions, and more interjections such as "well," "oh," and "now" than written language.[20] Spoken language is generally more personal, too. More references are made to yourself ("I," "me," "mine") and to your specific audience. There are subtle stylistic differences, too. As Shana Alexander points out, "The very weakness of writing, which is adjectives, is the strength of speaking."[21]

Spoken language is also more redundant. You are required to repeat yourself, because your audience can't go back and look over your words. The structured introduction, body, and conclusion of a speech might seem unnecessarily repetitive if the same message were written out.

So not all the rules of language apply to all messages, but the rules pertaining to clarity, vividness and appropriateness of vocabulary, and directness and variety of syntax are essential in spoken messages.

GUIDELINES FOR LANGUAGE IMPROVEMENT

"You are what you speak" might be the war cry of the time-honored school of self-improvement that teaches that if you improve your ability with language, you improve your chances for success, however you define it. Here are the traditional guidelines for language improvement:

1. Read and Listen.   We improve our language skills most efficiently by taking an interest in thoughtful writing and speech. As we read and listen we learn new words through their context, and we learn new and graceful constructions through our observations of how professionals use them. Read and listen to the best and the most challenging material you can. This guideline is most helpful when combined with guideline #2, below.

2. Get into the Dictionary Habit.   When you see or hear a word you are unsure about, look it up. Check the meaning, the derivation, the pronunciation, and the root of the word. The root is especially important. It will help you remember the word, and it will also give you a better understanding of words you already know that contain that root. In fact, the root might acquaint you with a whole new family of words you don't know yet.

For example, you might look up *vertigo*, and find that it means "dizziness, a feeling that everything is turning." The Latin root for the word is *vert-*, Latin for "turn." You therefore have a clue to the meaning of all the words in the "vert-" family, including (but not limited to) the following:

DOLT... adoll, dol., doll., dull., a dull stupid fellow, a blockhead; numbskull.,

extrovert: a person who turns his attention away from self.
introvert: a person who turns his attention away from others.
revert: to turn back to a former habit, belief, etc.
divert: to turn aside.
vertex: turning point.
convert: to turn something into another form or use.
invert: to turn upside down.

Some experts suggest that you should go as far as reading the entire dictionary page-by-page. Although I've never had the patience for that myself, I have to admit that it's good advice. It's one of those things that I mean to get around to someday.

3. Experiment with Language.   Use new vocabulary and new constructions in conversation and in writing, especially when you are in an environment in which someone will correct you if you are wrong. William Safire tells the following anecdote about how Governor Jerry Brown of California follows this advice:

> The Governor, who likes to use unfamiliar words to clothe fresh ideas, was talking about space-age projects in California "as a synecdoche for the world's future space interest." He used the word "synecdoche" correctly, as a part to be taken for a whole—as one speaks of "head" for cattle. But he pronounced it wrong. He said "SY-neck-doash," when the Greek-rooted word should be pronounced "sin-EK-doe-key," roughly rhyming with "Schenectady" . . . Later in the interview, I asked a question using the word as if repeating his own use, but pronouncing it correctly. . . . "If the pen is mightier than the sword—to use a couple of synecdoches, Governor, as you did before . . ." I dribbled off onto another subject, but the Governor stopped me: "Is that how you pronounce it? I'd seen the word in print, but I never heard anyone pronounce it before."[22]

Safire goes on to admit that "not all speakers are so willing to learn." But the implication of his anecdote is clear: It pays to be willing to use language incorrectly once, so you can use it correctly the next time. I remember my own college years as a long series of trials and errors in language use. I remember the day I learned that you don't pronounce the "c" in "indictment," after I had pronounced it incorrectly at a political rally. I remember a kindly professor explaining to me that I had used the word "placenta" when I meant "placebo." And I remember another professor pointing out that "forte," when it means a person's strong point, has only one syllable, and that the first consonant in "chasm" is pronounced as a "k" rather than a "ch." In fact, this trial-and-error learning of my native tongue goes on to this day.

So, all in all, your observation of clarity, vividness, and appropriateness in language is essential to your own language improvement. Observe the way these traits are put to work in the sample speech that follows.

SAMPLE SPEECH

Susan B. Anthony of New York was arrested in 1872 for voting in a presidential election. She was, to say the least, annoyed. It seemed to her that there was a very basic issue that people did not understand. This issue was based on two ideas:

1. The Constitution guarantees citizens the right to vote.
2. Women are citizens.

Eventually, enough people got the message and women got the vote. It probably would have taken consideraly longer had it not been for people with language skills like Ms. Anthony's. As you read it, you will notice that there is nothing flowery or ornate about her language. The speech is simple, clear, direct, and effective. Some comments accompany it, and additional comments follow it.

ON WOMAN'S RIGHT TO SUFFRAGE[23]

Some Comments

The Talk

FRIENDS AND FELLOW CITIZENS:—I stand before you tonight under indictment for the alleged crime of having voted at the last presidential election, without having a lawful right to vote. It shall be my work this evening to prove to you that in thus voting, I not only committed no crime, but, instead, simply exercised my *citizen's rights*, guaranteed to me and all United States citizens by the National Constitution, beyond the power of any State to deny.

Concrete statement.

The preamble of the Federal Constitution says:

"We, the people of the United States, in order to form a more perfect union, establish justice, insure *domestic* tranquillity, provide for the common defense, promote the general welfare, and secure the blessings of liberty to ourselves and our posterity, do ordain and establish this Constitution for the United States of America."

Specificity.

It was we, the people; not we, the white male citizens; nor yet we, the male citizens; but we, the whole people, who formed the Union. And we formed it, not to give the blessings of liberty, but to secure them; not to the half of ourselves and the half of our posterity, but to the whole people—women as well as men. And it is a downright mockery to talk to women of their enjoyment of the blessings of liberty while they are denied the use of the only means of securing them provided by this democratic-republican government—the ballot.

Some Comments

The Talk

For any State to make sex a qualification . . . is to pass a bill of attainder, or an *ex post facto law*, and is therefore a violation of the supreme law of the land. By it the blessings of liberty are for ever withheld from women and their female posterity. To them this government has no just powers derived from the consent of the governed. To them this government is not a democracy. It is not a republic. It is an odious aristocracy; a hateful oligarchy of sex; the most hateful aristocracy ever established on the face of the globe; an oligarchy of wealth, where the rich govern the poor. An oligarchy of learning, where the educated govern the ignorant . . . might be endured; but this oligarchy of sex, which makes father, brothers, husband, sons, the oligarchs over the mother and sisters, the wife and daughters of every household—which ordains all men sovereigns, all women subjects, carries dissension, discord and rebellion into every home of the nation.

Parallel construction. Variation in sentence length. Assonance.

Vivid language.

Webster, Worcester and Bouvier[24] all define a citizen to be a person in the United States, entitled to vote and hold office.

Variation in sentence structure. Alliteration.

The only question left to be settled now is: Are women persons? And I *hardly* believe any of our opponents will *have* the *hardihood* to say they are not. Being persons, then, women are citizens; and no State has a right to make any law, or to enforce any old law, that shall abridge their privileges or immunities. Hence, every discrimination against women in the constitutions and laws of the several States is today null and void, precisely as is every one against Negroes.

Effective language, like all aspects of effective message preparation, does not need to call attention to itself. In this speech, Ms. Anthony is *specific:* she talks about "a bill of attainder, or an *ex post facto* law." This is clearer than a vague reference to "unjust laws" or "legislated oppression." Not only does the audience know what she is talking about (i.e., a law that takes away established rights) but they know that *she* knows what she's talking about. The language is *concrete* when it needs to be. We know, for example, that she *voted* and was *arrested.* Consider how much clearer this is than an abstract wording such as "I performed a democratic duty in the interest of liberty and was persecuted for it." The language is vivid, also. We can almost see the oligarchy of sex "carrying" dissension into our homes. The length of the sentences varies for effect. Because most of the sentences are long, short ones like "It is not a republic" and "Are women persons?" stand out emphatically. The language of the speech contains no clichés, slang, jargon, or (and this is commendable, considering her emotional involvement in the issue) obscenity. Ms. Anthony's word choice showed careful thought that was reflected in the use of assonance ("odious aristocracy") and alliteration ("hardly . . . have the hardihood").

Effective language is timeless. This speech, given over a century ago, is as meaningful today as it was then.

SUMMARY

Language use is a specific problem in message preparation. This discussion centered around *vocabulary* (the words we use) and *syntax* (the way we put those words together). Three aspects of vocabulary were discussed. *Clarity*, the process of saying what you mean, includes the ideas of *specificity* (using words that restrict meaning) and *concreteness* (using words that refer to things that can be perceived through the senses). *Vividness* includes the ideas of *originality* (avoiding clichés), *action orientation*, and *sensuousness* (using words that evoke images). The discussion of appropriateness warns against the use of obscenity and slang, and warns that jargon should be used only with groups that are familiar with it.

Two aspects of syntax were discussed. *Directness* is accomplished through the use of simple, active sentence constructions, and *variety* results from the manipulation of sentence length, type, and structure. A consideration of these characteristics of language should help you make effective language choices. Three guidelines for language improvement were suggested: (1) reading and listening, (2) dictionary use, and (3) language experimentation.

QUESTIONS FOR DISCUSSION

1. Do you agree that phrases such as "like," "you know," and "I mean" make clear expression difficult? Why?
2. Specificity and concreteness are two important aspects of effective language. Which of these characteristics do you think is most often ignored in writing, public speaking, or informal conversations?
3. Do you agree that a lack of originality is the biggest problem college students encounter in their communication? If you agree, what are some of the overworked phrases or words that annoy you? If you disagree, what arguments can you raise against this statement?
4. Slang and jargon may be appropriate in some cases, but often they are not. When slang and jargon are used *in*appropriately by organizations and individuals, what do you think the reason might be? Is the purpose to conceal meaning or confuse or awe the listener, or is it simply careless word choice?
5. Can you think of any situations in which obscenity might be effective? If so, why do you think such language might work in these instances?

6. When you read or hear a message are you influenced by the quality of the syntax? For example, do complex sentences, or sentences that use the passive voice give you trouble? Why or why not? Do you think other people generally share your reaction?

7. Evaluate the Susan B. Anthony speech according to the criteria for effective vocabulary and syntax. After doing so, do you agree or disagree with the criteria? Explain your answer, using examples from the speech.

PROBES

1. For practice at selecting your vocabulary carefully, write two versions of the *same* event, object, or person. Keep the *facts* exactly the same in each version, but change (where necessary) the *wording* so that a positive attitude is conveyed in one case, and a negative viewpoint in the second version. For example, the first time you might refer to "a plump, relaxed, easy-going maintenance man," and in the second version you could write about "a fat, lazy janitor."

2. Select one main point from one of your previous speeches, or from a speech you have found in a source such as *Vital Speeches.* Reword the point in three different ways. Which one is the clearest wording? Why?

3. Select the same main point (or a different one). Using the characteristics of *vividness,* add more of this quality to the point.

4. If possible, obtain a copy of a jargon-filled business or government memo. After you ascertain its meaning, try rewording it according to the characteristics of effective language stressed in this chapter.

5. This one is similar to #4. Select any article from any issue of a professional journal in your major. (For example, if you are a psychology major, you could select something from the *Journal of Personality and Social Psychology.*) With the suggestions from this chapter in mind, rewrite a paragraph from the article so that it is clear and interesting to the layman.

NOTES

[1] Peter Farb, *Word Play, What Happens When People Talk* (New York: Knopf, 1974).

[2] *Webster's New Collegiate Dictionary,* 1973.

[3] Harold Vetter, *Language Behavior and Communication* (Itasca, Ill. Peacock Publishers, 1969), p. 170.

[4] Ibid.

[5] Jerry Rubin, *Do It* (New York: Simon and Schuster, 1970), p. 99.

[6] The more general concept, known as "language intensity," includes "sex metaphors," such as "getting screwed." The experimental evidence suggests that such language usage hampers a message's effectiveness, and the speaker's credibility, if the audience initially holds attitudes strongly opposed

to those of the source. See J. W. Bowers, "Language Intensity, Social Introversion, and Attitude Change." *Speech Monographs,* 30 (1963), pp. 345–352; M. Burgoon and L. King, "The Mediation of Resistance to Persuasion Strategies by Language Variables and Active-Passive Participation," *Human Communication Research,* 1 (1974), pp. 30–41; and M. Burgoon, S. B. Jones, and D. Stewart, "Toward a Message-Centered Theory of Persuasion: Three Empirical Investigations of Language Intensity," *Human Communication Research,* 1 (1973), pp. 240–256.

[7]Cindy Limauro, "The Student's Epidemic." *College English,* vol. 37 (April 1976), p. 813. © 1976 by the National Council of Teachers of English. Reprinted by permission of the publisher.

[8]Ibid.

[9]Ernest Hemingway, *A Farewell to Arms* (New York: Charles Scribner's Sons, 1929), p. 3.

[10]Robert Manning, "Ernest Hemingway," in Louis Kronenberger, ed., *Brief Lives: A Biographical Companion to the Arts* (Boston: Little, Brown and Co., 1965).

[11]Peter Farb, op. cit., p. 193.

[12]Preferably a full-sized, current, *college* edition.

[13]*Roget's College Thesaurus in Dictionary Form* (New York: Signet, 1962), p. 271. From *The New American Roget's College Thesaurus in Dictionary Form* by Albert Morehead. Reprinted by arrangement with The New American Library, Inc., New York, N.Y.

[14]Research studies demonstrating that persons from differing backgrounds or differing age groups assign different labels to concepts are reported by C. F. Vick and R. V. Wood, "Similarity of Past Experience and the Communication of Meaning," *Speech Monographs,* 36 (1969), pp. 159–162; and R. V. Wood, J. Yamauchi, and J. Bradac, "The Communication of Meaning Across Generations," *Journal of Communication,* 21 (1971), pp. 160–169.

[15]Adapted from a diagram in S. I. Hayakawa, *Language in Thought and Action,* 2nd ed. (New York: Harcourt Brace Jovanovich, Inc., 1964), which was adapted from a diagram in Alfred Korzybski, *Science and Sanity* (Lancaster, Pa: Science Press Printing Co., 1933).

[16]A true classroom experience in which not even the footnoted name of the student, Margo Bradden, has been changed to protect her innocence.

[17]This is an example of a dangling construction. For a more in-depth description of these and other common grammatical mistakes, see William W. Watt, *An American Rhetoric* (New York: Holt, Rinehart and Winston, 1964), or any other writing text in that section of the library shelves.

[18]From John F. Kennedy's Inaugural Address, delivered January 20, 1961.

[19]William W. Watt, *An American Rhetoric* (New York: Holt, Rinehart and Winston, 1964), p. 224.

[20]Studies pertaining to the differences between written and spoken language are reviewed in John F. Wilson and Carroll C. Arnold, *Dimensions of Public Communication* (Boston: Allyn and Bacon, 1976) pp. 195–198.

[21]Shana Alexander, "Unaccustomed As I Am," *Life,* May 19, 1967.

[22]William Safire, "The Wiseguy Problem," *New York Times Magazine,* March 25, 1979, p. 12.

[23]From Lewis Copeland and Lawrence Lamm, eds., *The World's Great Speeches* (New York: Dover Publications, 1958), pp. 321–322.

[24]Compilers of the standard dictionaries of the day.

7 Delivery

This chapter deals specifically with preparing for the presentation, or *delivery,* of a speech. It is based on another prediction about message preparation:

A delivery style that is perceived as natural will be more effective than one that is not. [1]

DELIVERY

It is difficult to talk about the problems of presenting a speech, because everyone's speeches (and everyone's delivery) are unique. In fact, if you have ever sought out advice on how to give a speech, you probably ran up against the same confusing bits of advice that journalist Shana Alexander heard when she was preparing to make a speech at a banquet:

> Friends rallied round with all sorts of advice, mostly contradictory. Don't be afraid to write it out. Read it. Memorize it. Put it on cards. Speak it off the cuff. Start funny. Start dull—an early joke lets them off the hook of curiosity. Turn from side to side so they can all see you. Find one nice face in the audience and tell it all to him. Get a new dress. Get a little drunk. By the afternoon of the speech, trying to follow all the advice at once, I sat stupefied with terror in my room in the hotel where the banquet was to be held. . . .[2]

As Ms. Alexander points out, too much advice can be stifling. A speaker concentrating on all the classic bits of advice becomes like the centipede who, when asked how it operated all its legs, thought about it and found that it couldn't. Besides, as Wilson and Arnold point out, "No one has ever found prescriptions for delivery in speech which work for everyone and which are appropriate for all speaking situations—even public ones."[3]

The purpose of this chapter is to supply some background that will help you prepare an effective delivery. Specifically, this chapter will discuss (1) nervousness and how to control it during a speech, (2) some nonverbal aspects of delivery, and (3) the advantages and disadvantages of different types of delivery.

CONTROLLING NERVOUSNESS

Everyone is nervous in a public-speaking situation. I've been a professional public speaker for years, but I still get nervous when I get up to speak in front of a group of people. Right before speaking my mouth gets dry and, as though to make up for it, my palms get wet; my knees feel weak and my heart gets into the balancing act by pumping stronger than ever.

It's only natural.[4] When you are preparing to speak you are preparing to be observed, to have your ideas and intelligence evaluated. It's a threat, and your body braces you for it as it would brace you for any other threat. It shoots some extra adrenaline into your system, which temporarily gives you some extra energy. The trick, then, is to control this extra energy and get it to work for you rather than

against you. There are three generally accepted ways to control nervousness about speaking:

1. Be Receiver-Oriented.   Concentrate on your audience rather than on yourself. The time to worry about yourself, including how you are dressed and groomed, is before your presentation. Once you get up in front of an audience, worry about *them.* Worry about whether they are *interested*, worry about whether they *understand,* and worry about whether or not you are maintaining human *contact* with them.

2. Be Positive.   It is important to build and maintain a positive attitude toward your audience, your speech, and yourself as a speaker. One communication consultant[5] suggests that public speakers should concentrate on three statements immediately before speaking. The three statements are:

> "I'm glad I'm here, I'm glad you're here." ("You" being the audience.)
> "I know I know." (About the topic of the speech.)
> "I care about you." ("You," once again, being the audience.)

Keeping these ideas in mind will help you maintain a positive attitude.

3. Be Prepared.   If you are fully prepared, your speech will represent less of a threat. Devote enough time to each of the steps of message preparation so you can feel secure. Especially, make sure you leave enough time to *practice* your presentation. And when it comes time to give your presentation, keep in mind that nervousness is normal. Expect it and remember that its symptoms, even shaky knees, are more obvious to you than they are to the audience. Beginning public speakers, when congratulated for their poise during a speech, are apt to make such responses as "Are you kidding? I was *dying* up there."

Being prepared, positive, and receiver-oriented will help you control your nervousness. Still, there may be facets of your delivery that detract from the ideas you are trying to get across.[6] It will be very difficult for you to recognize these distractions, but your instructor and your classmates will probably be able to point them out with ease. The next section is designed to help you make sense out of your instructor's and your classmates' comments about some problem areas that both reflect and cause nervousness while speaking.

NONVERBAL ASPECTS OF DELIVERY

Your nonverbal (i.e., non-word) characteristics are perceived by the audience at the same time as your words. Often, nonverbal aspects of a message change the meaning that is assigned to the spoken word, and in some cases negate that meaning entirely. In fact, if an audience wants to interpret how you *feel* about something, they are likely to trust your nonverbal communication more than the words you

say.[7] If you tell an audience, "It's good to be here today," but you stand before them slouched over with your hands in your pockets and with an expression on your face that would be appropriate if you were about to be shot, they are likely to discount what you say. This might cause your audience to react negatively to your speech, and their negative reaction might make you even more nervous. It's a vicious cycle, but you can pedal it in the opposite direction if you want to. Become familiar with the following visual and auditory aspects of delivery so you will understand your instructor's and classmates' comments concerning them.

Visual Aspects of Delivery

Visual aspects of delivery include such things as appearance, movement, posture, facial expressions, and eye contact.

APPEARANCE

Appearance is not a presentation variable as much as a preparation variable. Some communication consultants suggest new clothes, new glasses, and new hairstyles for their clients. In case you consider any of these, be forewarned that you should be attractive to your audience, but not flashy. Research suggests that audiences like speakers who are similar to them,[8] but they prefer the similarity to be shown conservatively. For example, studies run in 1972, when long hair on males was a relatively new phenomenon, showed that even long-haired listeners considered long-haired speakers less credible than shorter-haired speakers.[9]

MOVEMENT

Movement is an important visual aspect of delivery. Nervous energy can cause your body to shake and twitch, and that can be distressing both to you and to your audience. One way to control involuntary movement is to move voluntarily when you feel the need to move. Don't feel that you have to stand in one spot or that all your gestures need to be carefully planned. Simply get involved in your message, and let your involvement create the motivation for your movement. That way when you move you will emphasize what you are saying, in the same way you would emphasize it if you were talking to a group of friends. If you move voluntarily you will use up the same energy that would otherwise cause you to move involuntarily.

People have a tendency to be bored by things that do not move. If you don't believe that, just visit your local games room. People who are reasonably intelligent and sane can sit and watch one of those TV tennis games for hours. As long as it moves it keeps their attention. So don't worry about moving. But one word of caution:

Don't move without a reason. Move because you feel the need to do so, or because you want to emphasize something you are saying. *Always* let your involvement in your message create the motivation for your movement.

Movement can help you maintain contact with *all* members of your audience. The audience members closest to you will probably feel the greatest contact with you. Not only that, but the people who are less interested will have a tendency to sit farther away to begin with. This creates what is known as the "action zone" of audience interaction.[10]

Without overdoing it, you should feel free to move toward, away, or from side to side in front of your audience. That way, you can maintain contact with those outside the action zone.

Move with the understanding that it will change or add to the meaning of the words you use. It is difficult to bang your fist on a podium or take a step without conveying emphasis. Make the emphasis natural by allowing your message to create your motivation to move.

POSTURE

Generally speaking, good posture means standing with your spine relatively straight, your shoulders relatively squared off, and your feet angled out to keep your body from falling over sideways. There are speakers who are effective in spite of the fact that they sprawl on table tops and slouch against blackboards, but their effectiveness is usually in spite of their posture rather than because of it. Sometimes speakers are so awesome in stature or reputation that they need an informal posture to get their audience to relax. In that case, sloppy posture is more or less justified. But since awesomeness is not usually a problem for beginning speakers, good posture should be the rule.

Good posture can help you control nervousness by allowing your breathing apparatus to work properly. It will also help you get a positive audience reaction, because it makes you more visible. Your audience contact will be increased because the audience members will feel that you are interested enough in them to stand formally, and yet relaxed enough to be at ease with them.

FACIAL EXPRESSIONS

The expression on your face can be more meaningful to an audience than the words you say. Try it yourself with a mirror. Say "College is neat," with a smirk, with a warm smile, deadpan, and then with a scowl. It just doesn't mean the same thing. When speaking, keep in mind that your face might be saying something in front of your back. Remember also that it is just about impossible to control facial expressions from the outside. Like your movement, your facial expressions will reflect your involvement with your message. Don't try to fake it. Just get involved in your message and your face will take care of itself.

EYE CONTACT

This is perhaps the most important nonverbal facet of delivery. Eye contact not only increases your direct contact with your audience, it also should increase their interest in you by making you more attractive.[11] Eyes are beautiful things; much more beautiful than eyelids, foreheads, or scalps. Futhermore, and contrary to popular opinion, eye contact can be used to help you control your nervousness. Direct eye contact is a form of reality testing. The most frightening aspect of speaking is the unknown. How will the audience react? What will they think? Direct eye contact allows you to test your perception of your audience as you speak. Usually, especially in a college class, you will find that they are more "with" you than you think.[12] I found that out through personal experience. When I first began teaching, I was terrified of students who would slither down in their chairs, doodle, and generally seem bored. These students upset me so thoroughly that I usually would try *not* to look at them. And that made matters worse. Eventually, by deliberately establishing eye contact with the apparently bored students, I found that actually they were interested; they just weren't *showing* their interest because they didn't think anyone was looking. Once bored-looking students realized that I was actually looking at them, noticing their existence, they made their attention more obvious by sitting up and looking *back* at me. The more eye contact they had, the more interested they became.

To maintain eye contact you might try to meet the eyes of each member of your audience, squarely, at least once during any given presentation. Once you have made definite contact, move on to another audience member. You can learn to do this quickly, so you can visually latch on to every member of a good-sized class in a relatively short time.

The characteristics of appearance, movement, posture, facial expression, and eye contact are visual nonverbal facets of presentation. Now consider the auditory nonverbal messages that you might send during a presentation.[13]

Auditory Aspects of Delivery

How you use your voice, or *paralanguage*, is extremely important in controlling nervousness. It's another cycle: controlling your vocal characteristics will decrease your nervousness, which will enable you to control your voice even more. But this cycle can also work in the

RATE! "CHECK!"
PITCH! "CHECK!"
VOLUME! "CHECK!"
ARTICULATION!
"CHECK!"

vicious direction. If your voice is out of control, your nerves will probably be, also. Controlling your voice is mostly a matter of recognizing and using appropriate volume, rate, pitch, and articulation.

VOLUME

Volume—the loudness of your voice—is determined by the amount of air you push past the vocal folds in your throat. The key to controlling volume, then, is controlling the amount of air you use. The key to determining the *right* volume is audience contact. Your delivery should be loud enough so that your audience can hear everything you say, but not so loud that they feel you are talking to someone in the next room. Too much volume is seldom the problem for beginning speakers. Usually, they either are not loud enough or have a tendency to fade off at the end of a thought. Sometimes they lose faith in an idea in midsentence, so they compromise by mumbling the end of the sentence so it isn't quite coherent. That's an unfortunate compromise, like changing your mind in the middle of a broad jump.

RATE

Rate is your speed in speaking. Normal speaking speed is around 150 words per minute. Faster, and you will tend to be unintelligible. Slower, and you will tend to lull your audience to sleep. Once again, your involvement in your message is the key to achieving an effective rate.

PITCH

Pitch—the quality of highness or lowness of your voice—is controlled by the frequency with which your vocal folds vibrate as you push air through them. Because taut vocal folds vibrate with a greater frequency, pitch is influenced by muscular tension. This explains why nervous speakers have a tendency to occasionally "squeek," whereas relaxed speakers seem to be more in control. Pitch will tend to follow rate and volume. As you speed up or become louder, your pitch will have a tendency to rise. If your range in pitch is too narrow, your voice will have a singsong quality. If it is too wide, you may sound overly dramatic. You should control your pitch so your listeners believe you are talking *with* them, rather than performing in front of them. Once again, your involvement in your message should take care of this naturally for you.

When considering volume, rate, and pitch, keep *emphasis* in mind. You have to use a variety of vocal characteristics to maintain audience interest, but remember that a change in volume, pitch, or rate will result in emphasis. If you pause or speed up, your rate will suggest emphasis. Words you whisper or scream will be emphasized by their volume. One of my students recently provided an example of how volume can be used to emphasize an idea. He was speaking on how possessions like cars communicate things about their owners. "For example," he said, with normal volume. "A Lincoln Continental says, 'I've got money!' But a Mercedes-Benz says, *'I'VE GOT MONEY!'* " He blared out those last three words with such force that the podium shook. His audience got the point.

ARTICULATION

This final auditory nonverbal behavior is perhaps the most important. For our purposes here, articulation means saying all the parts of all the necessary words, and nothing else.

Regional or ethnic dialects are not included within this discussion. Native New Yorkers can continue to have their "hot dawgs" with their "cawfee," and Southerners can drawl as much as they please. You *should* know, however, that a considerable amount of research suggests that regional dialects can cause negative impressions.[14] But it is also true that an honest regional accent can work in your favor. For example, one linguist recently pointed out that Jimmy Carter's pure Gulf Coastal Plain Georgian accent showed that he "does not seem to have messed around with his language very much. That's the sign of a person who's got his head on straight."[15] The president of the Federal Reserve Bank of New York used his accent to his benefit when he began a recent speech this way:

> Fellow New Yorkers: I am emboldened to use that simple salutation tonight for more than one reason. At the most personal level, I was reminded the other day where my own roots

lay. I heard a tape recording of some remarks I had made. After spending three quarters of the past 16 years in Washington, I confess to being startled by what I heard—the full, rounded tones of a homegrown New York accent.[16]

The purpose of this discussion is to suggest *careful,* not standardized, articulation. Incorrect articulation is nothing more than careless articulation. It usually results in (1) leaving off parts of words *(deletion),* (2) adding parts to words *(addition),* or (3) *slurring* words together.

Deletion.   The most common mistake in articulation is deletion, or leaving off a part of a word. Since you are thinking the complete word, it is often difficult to recognize that you are only saying part of it. The most common deletions occur at the end of words, especially "-ing" words. "Going," "doing," and "stopping" become "goin'," "doin'," and "stoppin'." The ending "-th" is another problem. This sound is sometimes replaced at the end of a word with a single "t," as when "with" becomes "wit'."

The "th-" sound is also a problem at the beginning of words, as "this," "that," and "those" have a tendency to become "dis," "dat," and "dose." Parts of words can be left off in the middle, too, as in "natully" for "naturally," and "reg'lar" for "regular."

Addition.   This articulation problem is caused by adding extra parts to words that are already perfectly adequate, such as "regardless." "Irregardless" is not a word, and should only be used to parody substandard speech. Other interesting additions that are often heard include "incen*ta*tive" instead of "incentive," "ath*a*lete" instead of "athlete," and "orien*ta*ted" instead of "oriented." The worst, however, is "anda." "Anda" is often stuck between two words when "and" isn't even needed. If you find yourself doing that, you might want to just pause or swallow instead. Other words that are often needlessly added onto the beginning or end of other words include "you know," "like," and "right?" To have every sentence punctuated with a barely audible superfluous word (there are others, too, like "you see?" or "huh?") can be maddening.[17]

Slurring.   Slurring is caused by trying to say two or more words at once. Word pairs ending with "of" are the worst offenders in this category. "Sort of" becomes "sorta," "kind of" becomes "kinda," and "because of" becomes "becausa."

Word combinations ending with "to" are often slurred, as when "want to" becomes "wanna." Sometimes even more than two words are blended together, as when "that is the way" becomes "thatsaway." Careful articulation means biting your words off one at a time to prevent slurring.

There is no hard-and-fast rule for good articulation. Simply accept your instructor's evaluation of whether or not you add, drop, or slur words together. Then "mend your speech a little."[18]

This discussion of behaviors that affect the quality of delivery should, when considered along with the requirements of your speech, enable you to choose the type of delivery that is best for a particular speaking situation.

TYPES OF DELIVERY

There are four basic types of delivery: *extemporaneous, impromptu, manuscript,* and *memorized.* Any speech may incorporate more than one of these types of delivery. For purposes of discussion, however, it is best to consider them separately.

Extemporaneous Speeches

An extemporaneous speech is planned in advance but presented in a direct, spontaneous manner. This text and most public speaking courses stress extemporaneous speaking. This style of speaking is generally accepted to be the most effective, especially for a college class. In a classroom you generally speak before a small audience (five to fifty people) made up of people with diverse backgrounds. Spontaneity is essential with this type of audience, but so is careful message planning. Extemporaneous speaking allows you to benefit from both careful planning and spontaneous delivery. A speech presented extemporaneously will be focused, organized, and planned out in advance, but the exact wording will not be memorized or otherwise predetermined. Because you speak from only brief, unobtrusive notes, you are able to move and maintain eye contact with your audience. Extemporaneous speaking is not only the most effective type of delivery for a classroom speech, it is the most common type of delivery in the "outside" world. The Korea speech in Chapter 1, for example, was an extemporaneous speech. Most of those involved in communication-oriented careers find that the majority of their public speaking is done in situations that resemble a college classroom in size of audience and diversity of interests represented within that audience. Professional public speakers recognize the advisability of both careful planning and spontaneity with such an audience.

The extemporaneous speech does have some disadvantages. It is difficult to keep exact time limits, to be exact in wording, or to be grammatically perfect with an extemporaneous speech. Therefore, if you are speaking as part of a radio or television broadcast, or if your speech will be reproduced "for the record," you might want to use a manuscript or memorize your speech. Also, an extemporaneous speech requires time to prepare. If you don't have that time, an impromptu speech might be more appropriate.

Impromptu Speeches

An impromptu speech is given off the top of one's head, without preparation. An impromptu speech is often given in an emergency, such as when a scheduled speaker becomes ill and you are suddenly called upon:

> Grunt Johnson couldn't make it this evening, folks, but I notice in our audience another Sioux U student leader who I am sure would be glad to say a few words.

Impromptu speeches are sometimes given when speakers forget they are scheduled for extemporaneous speeches. This happens so often, in fact, that a certain amount of confusion exists between the terms "extemporaneous" and "impromptu."

The problem with an impromptu speech is that it is given on the spur of the moment and, as Monroe and Ehninger have pointed out, "Too often the 'moment' arrives without the necessary informed and inspired 'spur.' "[19] There are, however, advantages to impromptu speaking. For one thing, an impromptu speech is, by definition, spontaneous. It is the best delivery style for informal talks, group discussions, and comments on others' speeches. It also can be an effective training aid; it can teach you to think on your feet and organize your thoughts quickly. To take full advantage of an impromptu speaking opportunity, remember the following things:

1. Take advantage of the time between being called on to speak and actually speaking. Review your personal experiences and

use them. Don't be afraid to be original; you don't have to remember what every other expert says about your topic—what do *you* say about it? If nothing else, consider the questions "Who? What? When? Where? How?" and formulate a plan to answer one or more of them. Even if you have only a minute, you can still scribble a few brief notes to protect against mental blocks.

2. Observe what is going on around you and respond to it. If there were other speakers, you might agree or disagree with what they said. You can comment on the audience and the occasion, too, as well as on your topic.

3. Keep a positive attitude. Remember that audience expectations are low. They know you haven't prepared in advance, and they don't expect you to be Patrick Henry.

4. Finally, and perhaps most important, keep your comments brief. Especially, do not prolong your conclusion. If you have said everything you want to say or everything you can remember, wrap it up as neatly as possible and sit down. If you forgot something, it probably wasn't important anyway. If it was, the audience will ask you about it afterward.

Manuscript Speeches

Manuscript speeches are necessary when you are speaking "for the record," such as at legal proceedings or when presenting scientific findings. The greatest disadvantage of a manuscript speech is the lack of spontaneity that may result. Manuscript readers have even been known to read their directions by mistake. This leads to extreme embarrassment, and sometimes ulcers.

Manuscript speeches are difficult and cumbersome, but they are sometimes necessary. If you do find occasion to use one, here are some guidelines:

1. When writing the speech, remember the differences between written essays and speeches. Speeches are usually less formal, more repetitive, and more personal than written messages.

2. Use short paragraphs. They are easier to return to after establishing eye contact with your audience.

3. Type the manuscript triple-spaced, in all caps, with a dark ribbon. Underline the words you want to emphasize.

4. Use stiff paper, so it won't fold up or fly away during the speech. Type on only one side, and number the pages as visibly as possible.

5. Rehearse until you can "read" whole lines without looking at the manuscript.

6. Take your time, vary your speed, and try to concentrate on ideas rather than words.

Memorized Speeches

Memorized speeches are the most difficult and often the least effective. They usually seem excessively formal. They tend to make you think of words rather than ideas. However, like manuscript speeches they are sometimes necessary. They are used in oratory contests and on very formal occasions such as eulogies or church rituals. They are used as training devices for memory. They are also used in some political situations. For example, in the 1980 presidental debates the candidates were allowed to make prepared speeches, but they were not allowed to use notes. Thus they had to memorize precise, "for-the-record" wording.

There is only one guideline for a memorized speech: Practice. The speech won't be effective until you have practiced it so you can present it with what actors and term-paper recyclers call "the illusion of the first time."

You will want to choose the appropriate delivery style for the type of speech you are giving. The best way to assure that you are on your way to an effective delivery is to practice in front of a small sample audience—perhaps one or two friends—and have them comment on it.

SUMMARY

This chapter provided an overview of speech delivery. It dealt specifically with controlling nervousness, recognizing visual and auditory nonverbal variables, and choosing the best delivery style for a particular speaking situation.

There are three generally accepted methods for controlling nervousness. The first is to be receiver-oriented by concentrating on your audience rather than on yourself. The second is to maintain a positive attitude. The third is to be prepared.

Visual nonverbal aspects include your appearance (things like your clothes and your grooming), your movement (steps and gestures), your posture, your facial expressions, and your eye contact. All these things have an effect on how your message is received, and they can all be controlled to a certain extent. Mostly, though, they are taken care of naturally when you become involved in your message. Auditory nonverbal aspects refer to the way you use your voice. Volume, rate, and pitch can all be used to emphasize important points in your speech. Careful articulation makes your message clearer. A consideration of visual and auditory nonverbal variables helps you determine the method of delivery to use.

There are four basic types of delivery. Extemporaneous speeches are planned in advance and then presented in a spontaneous manner. Impromptu speeches are given without preparation. Manuscript speeches are read word for word, usually "for the record." Memorized speeches are learned word for word and then recited as naturally as possible.

QUESTIONS FOR DISCUSSION

1. It is often said that good, smooth delivery might be sufficient to make a speaker successful with an audience. In fact, some people say that good articulation and effective gestures are the major points stressed in a public speaking course. How important do *you* think delivery alone is in public speaking? Is it crucial, or do audiences respond primarily to the speaker's ideas?
2. It is stated in this chapter that "the time to worry about yourself ... is before your presentation," and that once you are actually speaking you should worry about your audience. How might such an attitude help a speaker to control nervousness? Do you agree or disagree with this advice? Why, or why not?
3. It is stated in the chapter that an audience is more likely to "trust your nonverbal communication ... than the words you say." From *your experience,* hearing and seeing public speakers, do you agree or disagree? Be prepared to defend your answer.
4. Some people believe that good posture is necessary to be effective in public speaking, and that speakers with poor posture are successful "in spite of their posture rather than because of it." Explain why you either agree or disagree with this idea.
5. Research suggests that often a regional dialect causes negative reactions from an audience, but sometimes "an honest regional accent can work in your favor." More specifically, *what* accents, under what circumstances, might be detrimental to a speaker? Why? When and why might accents be *helpful* to someone delivering a public message?

PROBES

1. Name a speaker whose style you find effective. What specific aspects of his or her style are most impressive?
2. What are your own delivery problems? What can you do to correct them?
3. What *type* of delivery will you use for your next speech? Why? Under what circumstances might you give the same speech with a different type of delivery? Why?
4. Think of a motion picture or television character you either admire or dislike. What aspects of the person's *delivery* do you think contribute most to your impressions, and why?

5. Who is your favorite comedian? What aspects of the person's *delivery* do you think contribute to his or her humorous effect, and why?
6. Observe and/or listen to the delivery of at least three national or local newscasters or sports announcers. Which do you like; which don't you like? To what degree do any aspects of *delivery* influence your reactions?

NOTES

[1] James E. Connolly, *Public Speaking as Communication* (Minneapolis: Burgess Publishing Co., 1974), p. 4.

[2] Shana Alexander, "Unaccustomed As I Am," in W. W. Wilmot and J. R. Wenburg, eds., *Communication Involvement: Personal Perspectives* (New York: John Wiley & Sons, 1974) p. 313. Also *Life,* May 19, 1967.

[3] John Wilson and Carroll Arnold, *Dimensions of Public Communication* (Boston: Allyn and Bacon, 1976) pp. 201–202.

[4] The nervousness referred to in this section is known as stage fright. Stage fright is experienced by most public speakers. A few speakers suffer from speech anxiety, or "high communication apprehension," which generally requires more attention than can be provided in a public-speaking class. See James C. McCroskey and Lawrence Wheeless, *Introduction to Human Communication* (Boston: Allyn and Bacon, 1976), pp. 89–90. The more specific concept, "stage fright," and how it might be overcome, is discussed in James C. McCroskey, *An Introduction to Rhetorical Communication,* 2nd ed. (Engelwood Cliffs, N.J.: Prentice-Hall, 1972), pp. 251–253.

[5] The consultant's name is Dorothy Sarnoff. The First National Bank of Chicago once paid her $2,000 a day for fourteen days to work with fourteen of their executives, and her prices have probably gone up since then. You can read about her for free, though, in Jerry Bowles's "I Improved My Image," *Esquire,* August 1974.

[6] Research studies have generally indicated that although good delivery may not *by itself* enhance a speaker's effectiveness, unfavorable aspects of delivery *can* hamper audience comprehension, the source's credibility, and in some cases, the persuasive impact of the message. See K. C. Beighley, "An Experimental Study of the Effect of Four Speech Variables on Listener Comprehension," *Speech Monographs,* 19 (1952), pp. 249–258; G. R. Miller and M. R. Hewgill, "The Effect of Variations in Nonfluency on Audience Ratings of Source Credibility," *Quarterly Journal of Speech,* 50 (1964), pp. 36–44; K. K. Sereno and G. J. Hawkins, "The Effects of Variations in Speaker's Nonfluency Upon Audience Ratings of Attitude Toward the Speech Topic and Speaker's Credibility," *Speech Monographs,* 34 (1967), pp. 58–64; and J. C. McCroskey and R. S. Mehrley, "The Effects of Disorganization and Nonfluency on Attitude Change and Source Credibility," *Speech Monographs,* 36 (1969), pp. 13–21.

[7] Some research evidence suggests, in fact, that as much as 93 percent of the "social meaning" (or information about our attitudes) that we communicate is conveyed nonverbally. See Albert Mehrabian and M. Wiener, "Decoding of Inconsistent Communication," *Journal of Personality and Social Psychology,* 6 (1967), p. 109; and Albert Mehrabian and S. R. Ferris, "Inference of Attitudes from Nonverbal Communication in Two Channels," *Journal of Consulting Psychology,* 31 (1967), pp. 248–252.

[8] The effects of similarity (or homophily) and dissimilarity (hetrophily) of

source and receiver are reviewed in Michael Burgoon, *Approaching Speech Communication* (New York: Holt, Rinehart, and Winston, 1974), pp. 36–43.

[9]These studies are reviewed in Lawrence B. Rosenfeld and Jean M. Civikly, *With Words Unspoken* (New York: Holt, Rinehart and Winston, 1976), p. 62. For more on the effects of appearance, see G. Wilson and D. Nias, "Beauty Can't Be Beat," *Psychology Today,* September 1976, p. 8; M. Lefkowitz, R. Blake, and J. Mouton, "Status Factors in Pedestrian Violation of Traffic Signals," *Journal of Abnormal and Social Psychology,* 51 (1955), pp. 704–706; R. Hoult, "Experimental Measurement of Clothing as a Factor in Some Social Ratings of Selected American Men," *American Sociological Review,* 19 (1954), pp. 324–328; and J. Mills and E. Aronson, "Opinion Change as a Function of the Communication Attractiveness and Desire to Influence," *Journal of Personality and Social Psychology,* 1 (1965), pp. 73–77.

[10]The existence of this effect has been shown in several studies summarized in Rosenfeld and Civikly, op. cit., pp. 161–164.

[11]P. C. Ellsworth and J. M. Carlsmith, "Effects of Eye Contact and Verbal Content on Affective Response to a Dyadic Interaction," *Journal of Personality and Social Psychology,* 10 (1968), pp. 15–20.

[12]Research suggests that audience comprehension and satisfaction with the interaction are enhanced when the speaker attends fully to audience feedback. See H. J. Leavitt and R. A. H. Mueller, "Some Effects of Feedback on Communication," *Human Relations,* 4 (1951), pp. 401–410.

[13]Experimental studies have demonstrated that listeners can, and do, develop impressions of communicators on the basis of nonverbal auditory cues. Such impressions involve judgments of status, personality, occupation, and emotion. See for example L. S. Harms, "Listener Judgments of Status Cues in Speech," *Quarterly Journal of Speech,* 47 (1961), pp. 164–168; D. W. Addington, "The Relationship of Selected Vocal Characteristics to Personality Perception," *Speech Monographs,* 35 (1968), pp. 492–503; P. Fay and W. Middleton, "Judgment of Occupation From the Voice as Transmitted Over a Public Address System," *Sociometry,* 3 (1940), pp. 186–191; and J. R. Davitz and L. Davitz, "The Communication of Feelings by Content-Free Speech," *Journal of Communication,* 9 (1959), pp. 6–13.

[14]Howard Giles and Peter F. Powesland, *Speech Style and Social Evaluation* (London: Academic Press, 1975).

[15]Sounds of the South," *Time,* August 2, 1976, p. 16.

[16]Paul A. Volcker, "The Dilemmas of Monetary Policy," *Vital Speeches of the Day,* vol. 42 (January 15, 1976).

[17]Such "tag questions," or "rhetorical interrogatives," are one characteristic of a "restricted" language code, or "low linguistic" diversity. Research has demonstrated that such language behavior results in perceptions of the speaker as high in anxiety and low in socio-economic status and competence. See J. J. Bradac, C. W. Konsky, and R. A. Davies, "Two Studies of the Effects of Linguistic Diversity upon Judgments of Communicator Attributes and Message Effectiveness," *Communication Monographs,* 43 (1976), pp. 70–79; and J. J. Bradac, J. A. Courtright, G. Schmidt, and R. A. Davies, "The Effects of Perceived Status and Linguistic Diversity upon Judgments of Speaker Attributes and Message Effectiveness," *Journal of Psychology,* 93 (1976), pp. 213–220.

[18]Shakespeare, *King Lear.*

[19]Alan H. Monroe and Douglas Ehninger, *Principles and Types of Speech Communication,* 7th ed. (Glenview, Ill.: Scott, Foresman and Co., 1974), p. 142.

THREE

The Basics of Message Strategy

The preceding section concerned some basic "how-to" concepts about message preparation. This section deals with concepts of a higher order, concepts that underlie *what* you say and *why* you say it. Specifically, this section deals with *message strategy,* which is the overall plan of any form of communication. Strategies are designed to carry out specific purposes.

Basically, there are four message strategies that are of interest to the neophyte public speaker. They are audience interest, explanation, persuasion, and humor. Perceptive readers will point out that any message might reflect more than one of these strategies. Those readers would be correct. In fact, the first three strategies are cumulative. You have to maintain audience interest before you can explain, and you have to explain before you can persuade.

The final strategy, humor, has a very specific use in public speaking, so it will be covered last. This section begins with a consideration of the most basic strategy: audience interest.

Audience Interest

This chapter deals with audience interest, which is the result of relating to audience needs. The importance of audience needs derives from a basic prediction about message strategy:

A message that relates to audience needs will be more effective than one that does not. [1]

I. AUDIENCE INTEREST AND AUDIENCE NEEDS
II. PHYSIOLOGICAL NEEDS
III. SAFETY NEEDS
IV. SOCIAL NEEDS
V. ESTEEM NEEDS
VI. SELF-ACTUALIZATION NEEDS

AUDIENCE INTEREST AND AUDIENCE NEEDS

Material to capture audience interest is traditionally used in the introduction of a speech, but you would do well to heed this advice:

> The introduction is the first point at which you can try to capture the attention and interest of the listeners, but you do not "capture" it in the sense that it can be securely caged and then left alone. Instead, you will have to use devices to gain attention at the outset of the message and devices to maintain it throughout.[2]

Audience interest is such a fundamental aspect of message planning that it has already been mentioned frequently in this book. The chapter on language discussed action orientation, specificity, and vividness, all of which are recommended to maintain audience interest. The chapter on delivery makes repeated reference to variety, emphasis, and message involvement, which also come highly recommended as attention devices. Explanatory devices such as analogies and anecdotes, which will be presented in the next chapter, and humorous devices, which are covered in the final chapter, are also recommended.

The purpose of this chapter is to examine why attention devices work. For example, five devices that are recommended to capture audience interest and attention, especially in speech introductions, are

1. A reference to the audience: "It's great to have the opportunity to address a group of America's brightest young scholars . . ."
2. A reference to the occasion: "We are gathered here today, as we are every Tuesday and Thursday at this time, to examine the phenomenon of human communication . . ."
3. A reference to the relationship between the audience and the subject: "My topic, 'Communicating with Plants,' ties right in with our study of human communication. We can gain several insights into our communication with one another by examining our interactions with our little green friends . . ."
4. A reference to something familiar to the audience: "Do you realize that the lilac bush outside our window might be reacting, this very moment, to the joys and anxieties that you are experiencing in this classroom?"
5. A startling statement of fact or opinion: "Yes, there is now scientific evidence that plants appreciate human company, kind words, and classical music."

These attention devices work, but the question is, why do they work? The answer is that they relate to an audience's *needs*. Relating to audience needs is by far more effective than screaming, firing a gun, or blowing a whistle—and far less distracting than any of those

ploys. Once the relationship between your audience and your topic is made clear, that audience should be motivated to listen.

The more you know about your audience, the more specific you can be about relating to their needs. If a large percentage of a college audience is graduating soon, they need to hear about future directions. If a large percentage of that audience commutes to school, they need to know how to keep their cars safe and reliable. If most of them live in dormitories, they need to know how to keep from going crazy. And so on.

Sometimes you might not know as much about your audience as you'd like to. When that happens, the analysis of needs developed by the psychologist A. H. Maslow[3] can be used. In fact, these needs should be kept in mind for all audiences, since they are common to all human beings.

Each of the needs outlined by Maslow is an effective attention device if handled correctly.

PHYSIOLOGICAL NEEDS

Physiological needs are those which enable us to survive. They include our needs for food, drink, and sleep.

We are all concerned with survival. One way to increase audience interest, then, is to relate your topic to your audience's survival or to the improvement of their living conditions. So if you gave a speech on food (eating it, cooking it, or shopping for it) you would be dealing with a basic audience need. In a speech on nutrition in America you could relate to physiological needs by reading from a package of food that contains preservatives and explaining what each one of those preservatives can do to a human body.

SAFETY NEEDS

Safety needs are those which center around security in our environment. Whenever you remind your audience of their safety you are tapping into their need to feel secure. This is one reason why we find crime programs on television so enthralling; crime is a threat to security. Also, whenever you relate your topic to your audience's pocketbook you take advantage of their need to feel secure. The president of the American Medical Association reminded his audience at Oregon State University:

> Your interests as patients are at stake in a complicated— and piping hot—debate over a basically simple question . . . which is: *How* should you pay for medical care?[4]

Thus they were reminded that their medical care was directly related to their financial security.

SOCIAL NEEDS

Social needs include needs for love and affection and the need to belong to worthwhile groups. Everyone needs to feel loved. That explains some of the annoying pets people have. It also explains millions of dollars of advertising that relates just about anything—
shampoo, beer, automobiles—to the ability to be loved. People need
to feel that they belong to worthwhile groups, too. Those groups
might be professional groups, family or friends. Any one of these
groups can be referred to in a speech.

One speaker who recognized his audience's need to belong to a
worthwhile group was General Douglas MacArthur. MacArthur was
fired by President Truman in one of the most dramatic incidents in
American political history. He was invited to explain his side of the
story to a joint session of Congress. He responded with his famous
speech "Old Soldiers Never Die." In it, he happened to mention:

> I stand on this rostrum with a sense of deep humility and
> great pride—humility in the wake of those great American ar-
> chitects of our history who have stood here before me, pride in
> the reflection that this forum of legislative debate represents hu-
> man liberty in the purest form yet devised. Here are centered
> the hopes, and aspirations, and faith of the entire human race.[5]

Social needs explain why it is often effective to include personal
references about an audience in a speech. If you tell an audience why
they, as a group, are important, you help satisfy their need to belong.
If you do it well enough, you might even help satisfy their need for
esteem.

ESTEEM NEEDS

Esteem needs are based on prestige. People have a need to feel that
they are respected. The British humor magazine *Punch* once ran a
parody of how a tough-guy entertainer like Frank Sinatra might
sound speaking before a college audience:

> Hey, you in the third row, what you majoring in, gum
> chewin? Throw the bum out, go on get him out of here before I
> hit him. An' toss the two guys out on either side of him, too, for
> being stupid enough to sit alongside a bum like that. Go on, get
> them out.[6]

A strategy like that would be disastrous. A *good* example of recognizing an audience's need for esteem was demonstrated when the
manager of public affairs for *Playboy* magazine spoke before the
Southern Baptist Convention:

> I am sure we are all aware of the seeming incongruity of a
> representative of *Playboy* magazine speaking to an assemblage

of representatives of the Southern Baptist Convention. I was intrigued by the invitation when it came last fall, though I was not surprised. I am grateful for your genuine and warm hospitality, and I am flattered (although again not surprised) by the implication that I would have something to say that could have meaning to you people. Both *Playboy* and the Baptists have indeed been considering many of the same issues and ethical problems; and even if we have not arrived at the same conclusions, I am impressed and gratified by your openness and willingness to listen to our views.[7]

This speaker told his audience that listening to him was a measure of their prestige. In the next example, another speaker uses a different twist to the same device by telling his audience that their prestige might be threatened. The speaker is a vice president of Shell Oil, and he is speaking to students at the Greater New Orleans Science Fair:

You students here today are the first generation that has grown up entirely in the space age. And the quality and imagination shown in your projects is evidence that our investment in science education has really paid off.

And yet, I must say I also feel a certain degree of anger when I reflect on how society might look at these projects. You have accomplished things which should make us all proud. But there are people today who would have us turn away from science and technology—they see only evil in new scientific advances.[8]

SELF-ACTUALIZATION NEEDS

Finally, self-actualization needs are based on the need to accomplish as much as possible with our lives. Maslow points out that whereas the other needs are deficiency needs (people need them to stay healthy), self-actualization is a growth need (it is satisfied by the improvement of an already healthy person). Whenever you relate your topic to your audience's need for self-improvement, you are tapping into their self-actualization need.

Self-actualization is particularly important in a college classroom, because of the audience's need to grow *intellectually*. College audiences are thirsty for knowledge. That explains, in part, the popularity of "trivia" games on most college campuses. (What *was* the name of Tonto's horse?) Because of this, three devices generally recommended as attention-gaining material are:

1. A historical reference
2. A literary reference
3. A startling statement of fact

Any of these three increase an audience's knowledge, and therefore tap into their self-actualization need. For example, Judson C. Ward, vice president of Emory University, recently used a historical reference in a speech to students. He began this way:

> In the year 1760, the same year that George III ascended the British throne and James Wright was named Governor of His Majesty's Royal Colony of Georgia, a red-headed, freckled-faced, lanky boy of 17 enrolled at the college of William and Mary. That boy was Thomas Jefferson. Although he presented no College Board scores, we know that he was already sufficiently proficient in Greek and Latin to read the classics in the original languages. . . .[9]

Most people would consider information like the color of Jefferson's hair to be trivia, yet that type of information grabs our attention. We need to know new things because of our need for self-actualization.

This is true of literary references, also. An insurance executive once began a speech this way:

> An embittered Voltaire put into the mouth of Candide the question: "If this is the best of all possible worlds, what then are the others?" Two centuries later, the American novelist James Branch Cabell added cynically: "The optimist proclaims that we live in the best of all possible worlds; the pessimist fears this is true."[10]

Literature is a vehicle for intellectual growth. When you quote a masterpiece of prose or poetry, you tap into your audience's need for self-actualization.

A startling statement of fact also increases your audience's knowledge, and therefore helps satisfy their need to grow.

Dr. Thomas Elmendorf, in a speech on television violence, mentioned the following:

> By the time a child is 18 years old, he has spent more hours in front of a television set than he has in school. Over TV he will have witnessed by that time some 18,000 murders and countless highly detailed incidents of robbery, arson, bombings, shootings, beatings, forgery, smuggling and torture—averaging approximately one per minute in the standard television cartoon for children under the age of ten.[11]

This startling statement does more than add to our knowledge; it also affects our security. You can relate to many needs at once. You can also use more than one device. Consider the following introduction to a speech given recently by a professor of philosophy at the University of Michigan:

> Of all that was done in the past
> You eat the fruit
> Either rotten or ripe
>
> (T. S. Eliot)

We are a daring civilization. An adventurous civilization. But in the last analysis, we are a stupid civilization. We are a civilization afflicted with a death wish. We are destroying (not just using, but destroying) natural resources, ecological habitats, the tissue of which society is made. We are destroying, by the increasing number and magnitude of various stresses, individual human beings. We are destroying life at large. The civilization which intentionally or unintentionally does all these things cannot be called either judicious or wise. We are a stupid civilization.[12]

The professor used a literary reference by quoting lines of a poem by T. S. Eliot, and thereby tapped into his audience's self-actualization needs. He enhanced the audience's esteem ("We are a daring civilization") and threatened that esteem ("We are a stupid civilization"). He also tapped into his audience's safety needs ("We are destroying individual human beings").

In short, none of the needs stipulated by Maslow are ever completely satisfied, and you can tap into them by either enhancing or threatening them. Either way, a sensitivity to these needs results in a sensitivity to human interest. And that is what audience interest is all about.

SUMMARY

This chapter dealt with capturing and maintaining audience interest. Audience-interest devices that have been dealt with in previous chapters include action orientation, specificity and vividness of language, and variety, emphasis, and involvement in presentation. Attention devices that will be dealt with in later chapters include explanatory and humorous devices. Devices which are commonly recommended to enhance audience interest include references to the audience, references to the occasion, references to the relationship between the audience and the topic, references to things familiar to the audience, and startling or novel statements of fact or opinion. Attention devices work because they relate in some way to audience needs. *Physiological* needs relate to survival. *Safety* needs relate to financial or physical security. *Social* needs relate to love and belonging. *Esteem* needs relate to prestige. *Self-actualization* needs relate to self-improvement. Self-actualization is especially important in a college audience. The audience's need to improve intellectually makes devices such as historical references and literary references especially effective.

QUESTIONS FOR DISCUSSION

1. It is sometimes suggested that television commercials that are "silly" are effective because they employ a strategy that works. Do you agree with this opinion of the strategy of these commercials? Also, do you agree that such commercials are effective? Why, or why not?

2. Five devices for capturing audience interest and attention are mentioned. In your experiences as a receiver of messages, do these devices work, or do they, at least sometimes, turn you off? Why, or why not?

3. Do you think Maslow's needs are common, *to the same extent*, to *all* human beings? If so, why? If not, how does the importance of these needs vary from person to person?

4. Reread the examples of a speaker appealing to the social and esteem needs of the audience. What is your opinion of such strategies? Do you think they would work, or would audiences react in a suspicious or clearly negative manner? Explain your answer.

5. Can you think of any interest/attention devices that are often used, but not mentioned in this text? If so, are they effective, in your opinion? Why, or why not?

6. The chapter advises against sensational methods of gaining attention, such as screaming, firing a gun, or blowing a whistle, since such tactics might be distracting. Can you think of any circumstances in which sensational tactics (perhaps not as extreme as those mentioned here) might be effective?

PROBES

1. The layout of a supermarket is one example of an everyday message strategy. What other, similar strategies can you observe? For example, think about your favorite bar or restaurant. What message strategies do you think are being employed in its decor, physical layout, lighting, types of seats, entertainment (or lack of it), or its other aspects? To make this task easier you might ask the question, "What type of crowd is this place trying to attract, and is it successful?"

2. Some commercials seem to grab our attention more than others. What advertisements do you, and people you know, attend to? Why do you watch them? Are they appealing to one or more of your needs? Explain your answer.

3. Although they are supposed to be objective, newscasts are probably designed to appeal to audience interests, as well as to present the news. Observe several network or local newscasts. What

attention devices do they appear to be employing? Do you think such devices are successful? Why, or why not?

4. Sports announcers are, or at least try to be, masters at maintaining audience interest. Suppose, for example, you were watching a football game in which Whatsamatta U. was being clobbered 31–3, with ten minutes left. What would some of the better-known announcers (such as Curt Gowdy, or Howard Cosell) say to keep viewers from flipping over to a *Brady Bunch* rerun? Do you think these statements would be effective? If *you* were announcing, what would you say to maintain the viewers' attention?

5. Review your last speech, or one that you have found from another source. What needs (from the Maslow hierarchy) were appealed to in the message? Do you think such appeals would be effective? Why, or why not?

NOTES

[1]A. H. Maslow, *Motivation and Personality*, 2nd ed. (New York: Harper & Row, 1970), pp. 35–47.

[2]Gary Cronkhite, *Communication and Awareness* (Menlo Park, California: Cummings Publishing Co., 1976), p. 333. © 1976 by the Benjamin/Cummings Publishing Company, formerly Cummings Publishing Company.

[3]Maslow, op. cit.

[4]Max H. Parrott, "HMOs versus Fee-For-Service," *Vital Speeches of the Day*, vol. 42 (June 15, 1976).

[5]From *Congressional Record, House* (April 19, 1951), pp. 4123–4125.

[6]Stanley Reynolds, "Professor Blue-Eyes Is Back," *Punch*, November 17, 1976, p. 917.

[7]Anson Mount, speech before Southern Baptist Convention, in Wil A. Linkugel, R. R. Allen, and Richard Johannessen, eds., *Contemporary American Speeches*, 3rd ed. (Belmont, Calif.: Wadsworth, 1973).

[8]C. L. Blackburn, "Progress, Pollution, and Parallel Technologies," *Vital Speeches of the Day*, vol. 42 (May 1, 1976).

[9]Judson C. Ward, Jr., "The Practical Liberal Arts," *Vital Speeches of the Day*, vol. 43 (December 15, 1976).

[10]J. Carroll Batemen, "The Best of All Possible Worlds," *Vital Speeches of the Day*, vol. 34 (December 15, 1967).

[11]Thomas Elmendorf, "Violence on TV," *Vital Speeches of the Day*, vol. 43, October 1, 1976. A larger segment of this speech appears in the next chapter.

[12]Henryk Skolimowski, "The Last Lecture," *Vital Speeches of the Day*, vol. 43 (January 1, 1977).

Explanation

This chapter deals with explanation, which is the process of sharing meaning by supplying more than one perspective on an idea. The importance of explanation is based on another prediction about message strategy:

A message that uses explanatory devices will be clearer than one that does not. [1]

  I. THE IMPORTANCE OF EXPLANATION
 II. EXPLANATORY DEVICES
    A. Statements of Fact
    B. Definitions
    C. Descriptions
    D. Restatement
    E. Analogies
    F. Anecdotes
    G. Examples
    H. Quantification and Statistics
    I. Visual Aids
    J. Questions and Answers
III. SAMPLE SPEECH: "Violence on TV"

THE IMPORTANCE OF EXPLANATION

Those who haven't made a careful study of communication are apt to believe that meaning is transferred from one person to another the same way physical matter is transferred: you just hand it over, and that's that. Unfortunately, it is not that easy. Meaning, unlike matter, always changes form in the process of being transferred. People attach different meanings to words and ideas because of different experiences they have had.[2] Those different experiences make explanatory devices necessary.

Most people will admit that everyone has lived different experiences. Few, however, realize how vastly different our *stores* of experience are. There is evidence that the human brain works like a high-speed tape recorder, storing all our experiences. Some of the most startling experiments to demonstrate the phenomenal recording capacity of the brain were conducted by Dr. Wilder Penfield.[3] Dr. Penfield was a neurosurgeon looking for a cure for epilepsy. He believed that he could control epileptic seizures by subjecting the proper section of the brain to electric impulses. In order to test this theory it was necessary for a patient to remain conscious while exposed portions of the brain were probed with an electric current. Each time the probe was inserted, however, the patient began talking about obscure recollections—things that could not otherwise be remembered—in detail so specific that it supported the idea that everything that has been in our conscious awareness is recorded in detail and stored in the brain, either consciously or subconsciously.

Everything is recorded! The ramifications of that are mind-boggling when you consider research that suggests that around 600,000 different "messages" can be received by the average person *each minute*.[4] One psychologist told the story of a bricklayer who, under hypnosis, "described correctly every bump and grain on the top surface of a brick he had laid in a wall 20 years before."[5] Is it any wonder that each one of us attaches meanings to words and ideas in slightly different ways?[6] How could the word "brick" or a statement such as "Brick is the best type of building material" mean the same thing to you that it does to that bricklayer? The answer is that it cannot. You would need to explain your use of the word "best," for example, to make that statement clear to anyone. Would you mean that brick is best for looks, durability, or ease of installation?

The need for quality explanation becomes more severe as modern people become more saturated with messages that demand their attention. Unfortunately, even as the need for quality explanation becomes evident we are losing our faith in our ability to transmit information clearly. We seem to have developed communication paranoia. We are suspicious of all the intervening variables and breakdowns that might occur between a source and a receiver of communication.

This communication paranoia was demonstrated when many women withdrew their support from the proposed Equal Rights Amendment, even though they were in favor of its basic idea: "Equality of rights under law shall not be denied or abridged on account of sex." *Time* magazine analyzed the reticence of those who withdrew their support as follows:

> . . . the brevity and broad phrasing of the amendment seemed to feed suspicions of hidden meanings. Said (NY) State Senator Karen Burstein, "If someone came away believing there was even a 1-in-100 chance of unisex toilets, then she'd vote against ERA.[7]

With that sort of communication paranoia running around unleashed, it becomes imperative to amplify your ideas in such a way that the receiver can consider those ideas from a different point of view. For example, if you were explaining to someone ignorant of automobile mechanics where a carburetor is located, it would do no good to explain that it is "on top of the intake manifold" or "next to the fuel pump" or "to the right of the distributor." Those explanations are all from the perspective of someone who already understands what a carburetor is and where it is located. For someone ignorant of the design of an internal-combustion engine, you might have to say, "It's that big greasy thing right on top of the engine" or "It's right under the thing that looks like a metal frisbee with 'air filter' written on it."

As you can see, quantity of information is not enough. You must pick information that amplifies *and* changes the perspective of what you are explaining. In other words, you have to give your audience a different way to "look at" the idea. There are no less than ten devices that are used to accomplish this. They are: (1) statements of fact, (2) definitions, (3) descriptions, (4) restatement, (5) analogies, (6) anecdotes, (7) examples, (8) quantification and statistics, (9) visual aids, and (10) questions and answers.

EXPLANATORY DEVICES

Statements of Fact

The first and perhaps most important method of developing ideas is a statement of fact. *A fact is something that can be verified through objective measurement* (the center of Hoop U's basketball team is 7 feet 6 inches tall), *observation* (it has been raining for more than an hour) or *historical documentation* (Richard Nixon resigned in 1974).

Often your first mention of an idea will be a statement of fact. You might go on to explain that fact with another device, or you might let the fact stand alone. Either way, you have to make a conscious decision whether more support is necessary. Whether or not you bolster a fact with further explanation you should ensure that your facts *are* facts and not *inferences* or *value judgments.* You might be able to say, as a statement of fact, that the center of Hoop U's basketball team is 7 feet 6 inches tall. That is something you can measure objectively. But if you added something to that statement that could not be measured objectively, you would be making an *inference*, as in "The center of Hoop U's team hates our center." Human emotions are something that we have to infer. Since we can't get inside someone else's brain, we can't measure internal states. If you added an evaluation to that statement, you would be making a *value judgment:* "The center of Hoop U's basketball team is a bum." Value statements indicate personal tastes and preferences. The more value statements you use the more facts you need to back them up. For the example above, you might need to define the term "bum" or describe the particular behaviors that make the basketball player, in your estimation, a bum.

Definitions

Definitions identify ideas in a brief statement. It is a good idea to give your audience definitions of your key terms, especially if those terms are unfamiliar to them or are being used in a unique way. Do not assume that your audience attaches the same meaning to a key word or phrase that you do. Meanings are in people—not in words.[8] Your definitions should be simple, concise, and stated in such a way that no other terms within the definition need to be defined.

Dictionary definitions are handy, especially for determining the most acceptable meaning for a word, but you should be careful about using them to define your terms in your speech. Your own carefully chosen words are usually more effective than a dictionary definition. For example, someone speaking on the topic of abortion might not want to use Webster's second meaning:

By abortion, I mean "monstrosity."

Dictionaries are written for very general audiences. If you were speaking on the abortion issue and relying on another dictionary definition, you might be struck with:

> By abortion, I mean the expulsion of a nonviable fetus.

That might be an accurate definition, but it also might be too technical for a college audience. It might be clearer to say:

> By abortion, I mean the termination of pregnancy before the twelfth week of gestation.

if that's what you mean.

Another thing wrong with dictionaries is that they might give you a definition that includes the term itself, and that will sometimes make it *seem* as if you are clarifying an idea when you actually aren't:

> By abortion, I mean the induced abortion of a fetus.

To define "abortion" with the word "abortion" does not change the perspective on the idea enough to make it clear.

One last problem with dictionary definitions is that they have a tendency to change more slowly than the reality they represent.[9] You might use the term "female chauvinist sexist" in a speech about women employers who discriminate against men. However, if you looked those terms up in *The Random House College Dictionary*, 1972 edition, you would find that "female" means "woman" (as you might expect), but "chauvinist" means "patriot" and "sexist" means "someone who discriminates against women." Therefore, a "female chauvinist sexist" would be a woman patriot who discriminates against women!

Remember: In order to define something, tell what *you* mean by it. There are two ways to do this. You could formulate a traditional definition or an operational definition. A *traditional definition* places a thing in a class and tells how that thing is different from other things in that class. The classic example of this is proposed by Aristotle: "Man is a featherless biped." Man is therefore defined as belonging to a class (bipeds) but different from that class in that he does not have feathers. (It has been pointed out, however, that kangaroos and plucked chickens might be exceptions to this definition.)

Operational definitions tell you how to experience the thing you are describing. It tells you where you have to go or what you have to do to perceive a thing. For example, operational definitions for "man" might sound something like this:

> You want to know what a man is? Go down to the graduation ceremonies for marine boot camp. Those are men.

or:

> You want to know what a man is? Go to the state school for the retarded, and watch the men who work with those kids

every day with compassion and unfailing patience. Those are men.

Descriptions

A description forms an image of how something would be perceived through the senses. It is a "word picture," a direct rendering of the details that summarize something from *your perspective.* An abortion, for example, could be described as a simple, painless, safe operation, or as the nightmare of being at the mercy of a hack butcher. This is how Dr. Martin Luther King, Jr., in his speech "I Have a Dream," described the plight of the Black American:

> There are those who are asking the devotees of civil rights, "When will you be satisfied?" We can never be satisfied as long as the Negro is the victim of the unspeakable horrors of police brutality. We can never be satisfied as long as our bodies, heavy with the fatigue of travel, cannot gain lodging in the motels of the highways and the hotels of the cities. We cannot be satisfied as long as the Negro's basic mobility is from a smaller ghetto to a larger one. We can never be satisfied as long as our children are stripped of their selfhood and robbed of their dignity by signs stating "for whites only."[10]

Dr. King's description helps us to imagine pain and fatigue, as well as the sight of a sign that says "for whites only." These things can be truly perceived only through the senses, but he manages to give us an image of them by capturing their essence in a few words.

In reading the passage above from "I Have a Dream," you probably noticed the repetition of the phrase "We can never be satisfied." The device being used there is one form of *restatement.*

Restatement

There are two types of restatement: repetition and paraphrasing. *Repetition* is repeating a key idea word for word. By repeating you not only stress that particular idea, you also give your audience some extra time to mull it over and, perhaps, find a new perspective on it for themselves.[11] Sometimes you can emphasize particular words in repeating. If you were speaking on "The Need for Permanent Peace in the Middle East" you might introduce one of your main points like this:

> World peace is dependent upon peace in the Middle East. Allow me to repeat that. *World peace* is dependent upon peace in the Middle East.

In that example, the words "world peace" were emphasized the second time around. But you needn't repeat an idea word for word in order to emphasize it. *Paraphrasing* is repeating an idea in different words. If you wanted to stress the idea given in the example above, you might follow it up with a paraphrase like this:

> That is not an overstatement. Every military power in the world now has a stake in the Middle East, so there is no hope for global peace until the Arabs and the Israelis mend their differences.

One way to repeat through paraphrasing is first to ask a rhetorical question and then to answer it. That way, the audience takes an active part in the message by formulating a mental response. You then reaffirm (or, if necessary, "correct") that mental response for them. For example:

> Is peace in the Middle East important to us? Think about it. There is no hope for world peace without peace between the Israelis and the Arab nations.

Restatement is especially effective when you want to stress the importance of a concept. But sometimes you will need to explain concepts that are unfamiliar to your audience. In a case like that, analogies can be used.

Analogies

Similies and metaphors are short comparisons. A simile is a direct comparison that usually uses "like" or "as," while a metaphor is an implied comparison that does not use "like" or "as." So if you said, "Student unrest is like psoriasis: it flares up, then subsides, but never quite goes away," you would be using a simile. If you used phrases such as "the stomach rumble of student unrest" or "an avalanche of student unrest" you would be using metaphors, because you have implied comparisons between student unrest and gastric noises and snow slides.[12]

An analogy is an extended metaphor, and is generally used to compare or contrast an abstract concept with a more concrete one. Analogies enable us to develop thoughts for a particular audience by comparing our idea with something that is more familiar to that audience.[13] For example, if you had difficulty explaining to a public speaking class composed mostly of music majors why they should "rough" their speeches out loud, you might use this analogy:

> We all realize that great masters are able to compose music in their heads; Beethoven, for example, composed his greatest masterpieces after he was deaf and unable even to hear the instruments play out his ideas. However, beginners have to sit down at a piano or some other instrument and play their pieces as they create them. It is much the same way for beginning public speakers. When composing their speeches, they need to use their instruments—their voices—to hear how their ideas sound.

For an audience of music majors, this analogy might clarify the concept of practicing a speech. For a class of electrical engineers who might not know Beethoven from Bobby Vinton, this analogy might confuse the concept rather than clarify it. Two rules to remember when using analogies, then, are (1) to make them appropriate to your audience, and (2) to make sure they clarify your idea rather than confuse it.

Anecdotes

An anecdote is a brief story with a point, usually based on personal experience. (The word "anecdote" comes from the Greek word meaning "unpublished item"). Narrating an anecdote is often an effective way to develop an idea. Anecdotes can add a lively, personal touch to your explanation. For example, it might be boring if you only used theoretical and hypothetical examples in a speech on the way people attach different meanings to words. You might liven things up with a personal anecdote such as this:

> The other day I met an elderly friend of my parents downtown. I had no idea that her husband had died the week before, so I asked her how he was. She said, "He's gone," and I assumed he had gone someplace for his health. Now, there were a million things I could have said at that point that would give no offense, no matter what the situation. But I picked a bombshell. With a polite smile I asked, "Why didn't you go with him?"

Examples

An example is a specific case used to demonstrate a general idea. You can use either factual or hypothetical examples to develop ideas. The dialogue above is a factual example, but factual examples do not necessarily have to be taken from your personal experience. They can be gathered through any of the kinds of investigation discussed in Chapter 4.

Examples enable you to bring an abstract thought into focus. If you said, "I am a generous person," that statement could be viewed from many different perspectives. You could be "generous" when it is to your advantage to be so, or you could be altruistically generous. So it would help to cite an example of your generosity:

> For example, Bill offered me 25 percent interest if I would loan him enough for a concert ticket and I gave him the dough without blinking an eye.

That example would provide a different perspective on the idea of your generosity than this one:

For example, it looked as though the Widow Jenkins was going to have a dreary Christmas, so I worked over Thanksgiving vacation and sent her what I made.

Often a scientific research study is used as an example. If you wanted to develop the idea that American youth are not well informed about the American economic system, you might say,

For example, a 1973 study by the Joint Council on Economic Education showed that 50 percent of high school students could not distinguish between collectivism and a free-enterprise society, and 50 percent did not know the U.S. economy was based on free enterprise.

Hypothetical examples can be even more powerful than factual examples, since hypothetical examples ask the audience to imagine something—thus causing them to become active participants in the thought. If you were speaking on the subject of euthanasia (mercy killing) you might ask your audience to imagine that someone they loved was suffering and being kept alive by a machine. For most audiences, however, hypothetical examples should be brief. Long hypothetical examples take on the dimensions of a fairy tale and they make the speaker seem condescending.

Quantification and Statistics

Quantification is the use of numbers to clarify a concept. One example of quantification comes from a lecture given recently at Columbia University. The lecturer wanted to develop the idea that inflation lowers the value of paper currency. He used quantification in the following manner:

Some time ago, I found a postcard which I had written to my father on November 23, 1923, while I was attending a boarding school in Germany. The card asked that my father send the bursar "immediately 1.2 trillion marks. If the tuition is not paid by the end of the month, you will have to pay four gold marks."

The two figures—1.2 trillion paper and four gold marks—illustrates the catastrophic fraud of the great German inflation which resulted in a revolutionary change in the economic and above all the social order of the country.[14]

Numbers provide one perspective from which to view ideas. Another perspective is provided when numbers are arranged as statistics. Statistics are numbers that summarize something that is true for a large number of cases. Statistics can be viewed as collections of examples. This is one reason that scientific studies, which are usually based on statistics, are very powerful examples. Statistics of all types are readily available through investigation. You might want to collect your own statistics for a speech on "Attitudes Toward the Legalization of Marijuana." If you surveyed your audience in advance, you might analyze and organize your data as follows:

Class responses to the question "Do you believe marijuana should be legalized?"

		Yes	No	No Opinion
	Total Sample	82%	7%	11%
Sex:	Men	85%	6%	9%
	Women	77%	9%	14%
Age:	18–30	92%	5%	3%
	31–45	74%	19%	7%
	Over 45	42%	53%	5%
Major:	Liberal Arts	83%	11%	6%
	Business	54%	15%	31%

Whether you are citing your own statistics or interpreting someone else's, you should remember the aphorism: "Figures don't lie, but liars can figure."

One particularly effective way for liars to "figure" is through statistics of central tendency, such as "averages." Means, medians, and modes are all different measures of central tendency.

If you polled an "average" class of twenty students concerning their income for a year, you might come up with a list of responses such as this:

1. 0	6. 690	11. 1,200	16. 5,700
2. 0	7. 840	12. 1,400	17. 6,200
3. 0	8. 930	13. 1,600	18. 12,600
4. 530	9. 1,100	14. 5,200	19. 20,400
5. 610	10. 1,150	15. 5,500	20. 55,000

In this class, three students (1–3) have no income, ten of them (4–13) have small incomes from part-time jobs, six (14–19) have full-time jobs within a wide range of salaries, and one (20) has inherited a small fortune. Within this set of responses, the mode (most frequent value) is 0, the median (the point at which 50 percent of the values are greater and 50 percent are less) is 1,200, and the mean (the arithmetic average) is 6,032.50. So an unethical speaker could say that the "average" student in this class has an income of $0, $1,200, or $6,032.50 a year, depending on his or her motive. Consider the effect that each of these figures could have on, say, an audience that was deciding whether or not to increase student aid at your school.

The problem demonstrated by these figures is a common one: the same statistics can often be interpreted in different ways.[15] It is said that there was once a judge who admitted that he had set some guilty men free and hanged some innocent ones, but that he had done well "on the average." There is also an old story about a statistician who drowned in a river that was only 3 feet deep, on the average.

This potential for misuse is aggravated by another characteristic of statistics:

> The most disturbing point is that statistics don't have to come from *anywhere* or mean *anything* to convince the average person 75 percent of the time. Try it sometime. It's a great party game. Into a discussion of the relative safety of compacts and full-size cars, drop a line such as: "Statistics show that 78.3 percent of all fatal accidents involve small cars." How often do you think someone will ask you where that percentage came from or what a "small" car is? Right. Less than 2.7 percent of the time.[16]

Statistics can be excellent thought developers, but because of the way they are often misused you should do three things when you use them:

1. Cite the statistic exactly as it was published or tabulated. Do not manipulate it so it sounds better. Don't be like the person who lost a two-person race and then said, "I came in second. The other runner came in next to last." Keep your statistical reporting honest.

2. Cite the complete source of the statistic, along with any other information that would have a bearing on its validity. Established professional pollsters such as Gallup, Roper, and Harris, as well as most reliable magazines and newspapers, have reputations for accuracy. If you cite them, your audience can be relatively assured that your statistics are reliable. Sometimes the source of the statistic will cause it to be suspect, as in this case:

> A few years ago, a cigarette company reportedly mailed cartons of cigarettes to doctors across the land. Several days after receiving the cartons of cigarettes, the same doctors received a questionnaire to determine what brand of cigarettes they were then smoking. Shortly afterward, advertising for the company that had mailed the samples stated that in a recent poll, seven out of ten doctors reported smoking X (that company's) brand of cigarettes.[17]

3. Reduce the statistic to a concrete idea, if possible. For example, $1 billion, if piled in $100 bills, would be about the same height as a 60-story building! Using concrete images will make your statistic more than "just numbers" when you use it.

If you are going to refer extensively to statistical data, they could be tablulated on a chart and presented to your audience as a visual aid.

Visual Aids

We can absorb more information by sight than we can by hearing. This makes the use of visual aids extremely important in an explanation strategy.[18] Although we speak at around 150 words per min-

ute, it is reasonable to assume that an audience can think four or five times that fast. Visual aids can be used to make that difference work for you rather than against you. For one thing, if your audience has something to stare at that pertains to your topic, they might day-dream about that instead of something unrelated to your topic. Also, they will get back on the track faster if they have a visual aid to focus on when they return from their mental wanderings.

Visual aids can be classified as diagrams, illustrations, or three-dimensionals. Diagrams can include charts (bar charts, pie charts, organizational charts), maps, outlines, and schematics. Illustrations can include photographs, drawings, or other kinds of graphics. Three-dimensionals can include the actual object you are talking about or a model of that object, if it happens to be very small (like a microbe) or very large (like a building).

Diagrams and illustrations can be placed on posterboard, drawn on the blackboard, or projected via overhead or slide projector. Each method has its advantages. When you are deciding which type of visual aid to use, keep a few things in mind:

1. Visual aids must be appropriate to your audience and they must relate directly to your topic.
2. They should not detract in any way from the content of your speech.
3. You should not talk to them instead of your audience.
4. They should clarify rather than confuse.
5. They should be large enough for your entire audience to see them at one time, but portable enough so you can get them out of the way when they no longer pertain to the point you are making.
6. You must be in control of your visual aids at all times.

Two anecdotes illustrate the consequences of improperly used visual aids. The first is supplied by two well-known teachers of speech:

> The student's chosen subject was "The Treatment of Snake Bites." Having introduced his subject, he startled his audience by releasing a white rat from a cardboard canister. The speaker announced the rat's name was Maudie, and whipped out a hypodermic needle. Plunging the needle into Maudie, he explained that he was giving the animal an injection of snake venom. Maudie would expire within a few seconds, he said. Meanwhile, he would explain what steps a human being should take if bitten by a poisonous snake. To clarify these steps the speaker now drew grease-penciled lines and circles on his forearm to indicate where incisions should be made in cases of snake bite. But Maudie was dragging herself about, gasping her last in full view of everyone. Naturally, her troubles drew even the speaker's attention away from his explanations. He inter-

rupted himself to comment: "Oh yes. Bleeding at the mouth—quite natural at this stage."[19]

The spectacle of a dying mouse made that student's visual aid more of a distraction than a clarification. Comedian Alan Sherman tells about a similar experience he had at the University of Illinois:

I walked to the lectern. I hemmed. Then I hawed. I cleared my throat. Then I said:

"I shall give an illustrated lecture on the interior of the human mouth—the teeth, the tongue, the upper palate, the lower palate and other points of interest."

Then, to illustrate my lecture, I stuck my finger in my mouth, as if to point out the various things I was talking about, and for five solid minutes I spoke totally unintelligble gibberish, never removing the finger from my mouth and sometimes inserting my entire fist.[20]

Presentation aids that extend senses other than the sense of sight might be effective under some circumstances. If you were speaking about perfume, skunks, or the effects of a chemical plant on a community, actually producing the appropriate smells might help explain your point. (Notice the word *might*. I refuse to take responsibility for olfactory aids that go haywire.) If you are talking about baking brownies or brewing beer, a little taste probably wouldn't hurt. And you could incorporate something to touch if you are speaking about the texture of a substance or how it feels. In fact, a girl in one of my classes used an audience member as an effective presentation aid in her speech entitled "Girls are Not Just Soft Boys."

Audio aids such as tape recordings and records can supply information that could not be presented any other way (comparing musical styles, for example, or demonstrating noise pollution), but they should be used sparingly. Remember that your presentation already relies heavily on your audience's sense of hearing. It is better to use a visual aid, if possible, than to overwork the audio. Of course, there are audiovisual aids. Anyone who has been subjected to a modern education knows that audiovisuals (which include videotape and sound-on-slide as well as films) are indeed the most common aids. These should be used carefully, though, since research suggests that they allow the audience to receive information passively, thus relieving the audience members of the responsibility of becoming *active particpants* in the presentation.[21] Since professionally prepared audiovisuals are striking, they can be used occasionally to illustrate a point you are making. They should never be used, however, to make the point alone or to develop your thought for you.

No matter what type of presentation aid you are using, you have to be explicit about the point you are making. Consider the story of the football coach who was convinced that his team's poor physical condition was caused by alcohol abuse. The coach set up a demonstration for the team. He took two worms, and dropped one into a glass of water and the other into a glass of beer. The worm that was dropped into the water just swam lazily about, apparently enjoying itself. The worm that was dropped into the beer writhed in agony and died within a few seconds.

"There," said the coach. "Do you see what I'm trying to tell you?"

"We sure do," said the offensive tackle, one of the worst guzzlers on the team. "If we keep drinking, we won't get worms."

No matter how explicit you are in explaining your ideas, there is still the possibility that one or two audience members will become confused. That is why the question-and-answer period was invented.

Questions and Answers

You will have an opportunity to answer audience questions after most speeches. This can be an effective time to complete the explanation process.[22] However, you should keep the following things in mind:

1. Avoid defensive reactions to questions. Even if the questioner seems to be calling you a liar, or stupid, or biased, try to listen to the substance of the question and not to the possible personality attack. You can always let the air out of his or her tires sometime later; don't let one heckler detract from the contact that you have established with the rest of your audience.[23]

For example, this type of question is common: "You said A, but isn't B actually the case?"

There are actually two questions there. On one level, the question is "Isn't B actually the case?" This is the question you should listen to. If you listen too defensively, you will hear the question as, "Aren't you, in fact, a liar?" Responding to that question would be self-defeating.

This should not preclude a defense against a direct attack. If one of your listeners raises a hand and asks, "Aren't you in fact a dirty communist?" you don't have to respond with "Now that you mention it, my political leanings are somewhat to the left, and I don't bathe as often as I should . . ." You are entitled, under those circumstances, to defend yourself. But remember that, unfair though it may be, the question refers to you and cannot be answered by referring to the questioner or by asking another question, such as "Aren't *you* in fact an idiot?" In other words, in answering questions defenses are sometimes justified, but offenses never are.

2. Listen for the *substance* of a question. Try to understand the basic, overall question that is being asked, rather than one or two insignificant details. Some people, when accused of killing two men, three women, four children, and a cow will produce the cow as proof of their innocence. Answer the general question. If you have just

given a speech advocating the legalization of cocaine, someone might ask, "Are the demonstrations that you cited actually valid?" and you might respond:

> I did not cite demonstrations. I cited experiments. In demonstrations, you know what the outcome will be in advance. In experiments, you seek answers to the unknown.

If you did that, not only would you have demonstrated that you missed the point of the question, you also would probably have offended the questioner. Instead, an appropriate response might be:

> Yes, I think they are valid. The experiments that I cited were as carefully controlled as possible. They were conducted by experienced researchers who were well respected in their fields. I believe that the probability that they are valid is extremely good.

3. Respond to the question by showing that you understand it, answering it as briefly as possible, and checking to make sure that your answer was understood.

A psychologist named Carkhuff has devised a method of training counselors that is appropriate to the skills needed to respond to questions after a speech. According to Carkhuff, responses can be separated into five levels according to their quality.[24] For our purposes here, Carkhuff's model will be adapted to three general levels of response:

> Level One: The speaker rejects the question, or answers the wrong question.
> Level Two: The speaker shows that he has received and understood the question.

Level Three: The speaker recognizes the question, answers it as briefly as possible, and verifies comprehension.

A Level One response might be a rejection, such as "You are talking out of turn again," or "Please don't ask questions until I'm done talking," or "That is a ridiculous question and it doesn't deserve a response," or "Bailiff, throw that troublemaker out!" A Level One response doesn't have to be intentionally nasty, though. One of the worst, and most common, Level One responses is usually directed to someone of the opposite sex. It is usually an absent-minded response such as "You have beautiful eyes."

A Level Two response would paraphrase the question: "If I understood your question, you are asking _____ ," or "Let me see if I understand your question. . . ." A Level Two response is important to recognize because it is the lowest possible level of *effective* response. In other words, even if your answer was then incorrect, at least the audience member would know that you were responding to the correct question.

A Level Three response accepts the question and shows that it is understood. It also answers the question briefly, without unnecessary verbiage, and seeks verification that the answer has been understood. For example: "As I understand your question, you want to know _____ . Is that right? Well, I think _____ . Does that answer your question?" This would be a far more effective response than one that supplies too much information:

I told you that already, in the beginning of my speech. Weren't you listening? In order to answer that, I have to start from the beginning. Now you'll remember that I began by saying, "Good afternoon, fellow classmates . . ."

The devices listed above have the potential for more interesting and varied uses than can be completely covered here. However, even this sweeping coverage should give you the idea that explanation is a creative process that requires a certain amount of time and effort. That effort can make the difference between being understood and not being understood.

SAMPLE SPEECH

This sample is not a complete speech. It is the introduction to a speech delivered before a committee of congressional investigators. It does *not* use three common forms of explanation—anecdotes, visual aids, or questions and answers. As you read this introduction, you will see that the speaker makes his ideas clear with other devices, some of which are noted in the comments.

VIOLENCE ON TV[25]
The Effect on Children

The Talk

Mr. Chairman and members of the subcommittee, I am Dr. Thomas Elmendorf. I have been in general practice in California for 28 years and in emergency medicine for the last two in Sacramento, California. I appear here today as a past president of the California Medical Association and as a CMA delegate to the American Medical Association. The medical associations that I represent and I are deeply concerned about the effects of television on the youth of today.

Suppose you sent your child off to the movies for three hours next Sunday. And three hours on Monday and the same number of hours Tuesday, Wednesday, Thursday, Friday and Saturday. That is essentially what is happening to the average child in America today, except it is not the screen in the movie house down the street he sits in front of, it is instead, the television set right in your own home.

According to the Nielsen Index figures for TV viewing, it is estimated that by the time a child graduates from high school he has had 11,000 hours of schooling, as opposed to 15,000 hours of television. I would like to repeat that. By the time a child is 18 years old, he has spent more hours in front of the television set than he has in school. Over TV he will have witnessed by that time some 18,000 murders and countless highly detailed incidents of robbery, arson, bombings, shooting, beatings, forgery, smuggling and torture—averaging approximately one per minute in the standard television cartoon for children under the age of ten. In general, 75 percent of all network dramatic programs contain violence with over seven violent episodes per program hour.

Concurrent with this massive daily dose of violence over our television screens has been a dramatic rise in violence in our society. In 1973, 18,000 young Americans from 15 to 24 years of age, died in motor-vehicle accidents, with one of every six of these fatalities estimated to be due to suicide. In 1973, more than 5,000 were murdered, and an additional 4,000 committed suicide. The death rate for this age group was 19 percent higher in 1973 than in 1960, due entirely to deaths by violence.

The largest rise in deaths by homicide during the past two decades was at the ages of one to four. More than a million American children suffer physical abuse or neglect each year, and at least one in five dies from mistreatment. It is a social problem of epidemic proportions.

Some Comments

Fact.

Statistics.

Analogy.

The Talk

In fact, murder is the fastest growing cause of death in the United States. The annual rate of increase exceeded 100 percent between 1960 and 1974. Our homicide rate is 10 times greater than in the Scandinavian countries. More murders are committed yearly in Manhattan, with a population of one and a half million, than in the entire United Kingdom, with a population of 60 million.

Fact.

Statistics.

The age group most involved, with the greatest number of both victims and arrests, is 20 to 24. In 1972, 17 percent of all homicide victims and 24 percent of all arrests were in this age group. Teenagers from 15 to 19 account for another 9 percent of all murder victims and nearly 19 percent of the arrests. In commenting about such crimes by youths, one author said, "It is as though our society had bred a new genetic strain, the child-murderer, who feels no remorse and is scarcely conscious of his acts."

Rhetorical questions.

What is to blame for these heinous statistics? What are the chances that this trend of rising violence can be controlled and reversed? The probabilities are small unless something is done about the moral and socioeconomic environment in which our young people are growing up today in America. One thing is certain. For a considerable proportion of American children and youth, the "culture of violence" is now both a major health threat and a way of life.

We of the medical profession believe that one of the factors behind this violence is televised violence. Television has become a school of violence and a college for crime.

SUMMARY

This chapter dealt with explanation, and the following explanatory devices:

1. *Statements of fact*, which can be verified through objective measurement, observation, or historical documentation. Statements of fact are different from inferences (which refer to things that cannot be observed, such as internal states) and value judgments (which are based on personal opinion).

2. *Definitions* identify things in a brief, concise statement. Definitions of key terms used in a speech are especially helpful.

3. *Descriptions* create a "word picture" of the thing you are explaining. Descriptions help an audience imagine something that could otherwise be experienced only through their physical senses.

4. *Restatement* includes paraphrasing (restating something in different words) and repetition (restating something with the same words, sometimes with different emphasis).

5. *Analogies* are extended metaphors that enable you to compare an idea with something more familiar to your audience.

6. *Anecdotes*, or stories based on personal experience, help you develop ideas in a way that is lively and personal.

7. *Examples* allow you to develop an abstract idea with a specific case demonstrating that idea. Scientific studies are often used as examples.

8. *Quantification* allows you to use numbers to develop an idea. *Statistics*, which are numbers that are organized to show trends, allow you to summarize something that is true for a large number of cases.

9. *Visual aids* allow you to take advantage of the audience's sense of sight, as well as their sense of hearing, during a speech.

10. *Questions and answers* allow you to complete the explanation process through the use of audience feedback.

These devices work because they provide a different perspective from which an audience can view an idea. The ability to provide a different perspective for ideas is essential in public speaking, as well as in all other forms of communication.

QUESTIONS FOR DISCUSSION

1. Do you agree that many people suffer from "communication paranoia?" If so, on what issues have you experienced this problem, either in yourself or in those with whom you have discussed these issues?

2. What, in your opinion, is the crucial difference between a *fact* and an *inference*? Can you think of any guidelines that might help you, in a given instance, distinguish between the two?

3. Consider all the explanation devices discussed in this chapter. Which techniques do you think are generally most effective? Explain your answer. (When you answer, put yourself in the place of someone who might be listening to a speech on a topic about which you know very little.) Are there any *other* devices not discussed in the text?

PROBES

1. To illustrate the point that "meanings are in people and not in words," try using a fairly common word, but attach an unfamiliar definition to it, preferably the fourth or fifth definition listed in the dictionary. Did your listeners understand your usage? If not, how did they react when you explained it? Did they or did they not feel you used the word "correctly"?

2. Dictionaries often change more slowly than the meanings attached to words. To check this out, list four or five fairly common

words that have recently acquired new or different meanings. (For example, at this writing you might list "pot," "heavy," or "wicked.") Do the latest editions of the dictionaries include these new definitions?

3. Analyze a chapter (any chapter) from this text, or from one of your other texts. What explanation devices are used? Are they used effectively? What additional devices could the author(s) employ?

4. As you prepare your next speech, determine what words are most likely to be unclear to your listeners. Develop what you think to be suitable *traditional* and *operational* definitions for these terms. Why do you think they will be effective?

5. Examine the use of statistics in a speech you have recently heard or in an article you have read in a newspaper or magazine. To what extent does the citation conform to the advice presented in this chapter? Do you feel that the presentation might mislead some listeners or readers? If so, why?

6. Look up a piece of statistical evidence that might be used in your next speech. How might you reduce this information to a clear, concrete idea for the purpose of your speech?

7. This chapter lists six suggestions for the use of visual aids. Think about speeches or lectures you have recently heard in which such aids were employed. What errors in the use of these aids do you observe most frequently? How might the speakers have improved their use of such aids?

8. How well do your teachers follow the advice in this chapter for answering questions? On which of the aspects of effective answering do they succeed and on which are they deficient? Explain your answer.

9. Anticipate a question you might have to answer about your next classroom speech or any other speech you might deliver. Develop an appropriate "level three" response to the question. What might be the nature of responses at the other two levels?

10. The introduction to the Thomas Elmendorf speech, presented at the end of this chapter, employs no anecdotes or visual aids. After reading this selection, can you think of any ways in which these two explanation devices could have been utilized?

NOTES

[1]Otis M. Walter and Robert L. Scott, *Thinking and Speaking*, 3rd ed. (New York: Macmillan, 1973), pp. 35–37.

[2]C. Vick and R. Wood, "Similarity of Past Experience and the Communication of Meaning," *Speech Monographs*, 36 (1969), pp. 159–162.

[3]Those interested in this heady topic can consult Wilder Penfield, *A Critical Study of Human Consciousness and the Human Brain* (Princeton, N.J.: Princeton University Press, 1976).

[4]This estimate is based on a quote from Ralph W. Gerard, "What is Memory?" in Robert A. Daniel, ed., *Contemporary Readings in General Psy-*

chology (Boston: Houghton Mifflin, 1959), p. 95. The actual quote was: "Some tests of perception suggest that each tenth of a second is a single frame of experience for the human brain. In that tenth of a second it can receive perhaps a thousand units of information. ...." Cited in William D. Brooks, *Speech Communication*, 2nd ed. (Dubuque: Wm. C. Brown Co., 1974), p. 33.

[5]*Ibid.*

[6]Recall that studies, cited in Chapter 2, indicate that our attitudes and prior experiences influence how we perceive what we see or hear. These studies are discussed in A. Hastorf, D. Schneider, and J. Polefka, *Person Perception* (Reading, Mass.: Addison-Wesley, 1970), pp. 3–10.

[7]"End of an ERA?" *Time*, November 17, 1975, p. 65.

[8]This slogan was the war cry of a movement called General Semantics that was once widespread and that still influences the thinking of communication theorists. The bible of the General Semantics movement was Alfred Korzybski's *Science and Sanity* (Lancaster, Pa.: Science Press Printing Co., 1933). Unfortunately, that work is practically unreadable. If you are interested, a better treatment is provided in Wendell Johnson's masterwork, *People in Quandaries: The Semantics of Personal Adjustment* (New York: Harper and Row, 1946), or, more recently, Neil Postman's *Crazy Talk, Stupid Talk* (New York: Delacorte Press, 1976).

[9]The potential problems with dictionary definitions, from a *communication* point of view, are discussed more extensively in I. A. Richards, *The Philosophy of Rhetoric* (London: Oxford University Press, 1936).

[10]From James C. McCroskey, *An Introduction to Rhetorical Communication* (Englewood Cliffs, N.J.: Prentice-Hall, 1968), pp. 248–249.

[11]The effects of restatement have been documented in a study by R. Ehrensberger. See "An Experimental Study of the Relative Effects of Certain Forms of Emphasis in Public Speaking," *Speech Monographs*, 12 (1945), pp. 94–111.

[12]Research evidence suggests that listeners can, and do, distinguish between literal and figurative (or metaphorical) usage. See: W. J. Jordan and M. L. McLaughlin, "Figurativeness as an Independent Variable in Communication Research," *Communication Quarterly*, 24 (Fall 1976), pp. 31–37.

[13]The effectiveness of this explanatory device, in terms of a message's persuasiveness, has been documented by experimental research. See J. C. McCroskey and W. H. Coombs, "The Effects of the Use of Analogy on Attitude Change and Source Credibility," *Journal of Communication*, 19 (1969), pp. 333–39.

[14]G. C. Wiegand, "Inflation," *Vital Speeches of the Day*, vol. 43 (June 15, 1976).

[15]If you are interested in a closer examination of how people lie with statistics, you will want to read Darrel Huff, *How to Lie With Statistics* (New York: W. W. Norton and Co., 1954). A more recent treatment of this subject is provided in Stephen K. Campbell, *Flaws and Fallacies in Statistical Thinking* (Englewood Cliffs, N.J.: Prentice-Hall, 1974).

[16]Gary Cronkhite, *Communication and Awareness* (Menlo Park, Calif.: Cummings Publishing Co., 1976), pp. 234–235. © 1976 by the Benjamin/Cummings Publishing Company, formerly Cummings Publishing Company.

[17]Bert E. Bradley, *Fundamentals of Speech Communication: The Credibility of Ideas* (Dubuque: Wm. C. Brown Co., 1974), p. 157.

[18]Studies have indicated that when information is presented solely by *telling*, immediate recall by receivers is 70 percent, and three days later only 10 percent. If a verbal presentation is accompanied by pictures, immediate recall increases to 85 percent, and three days later, 65 percent. This research is discussed in W. Linkugel and D. Berg, *A Time to Speak* (Belmont, Calif.:

Wadsworth, 1970). Visual aids have also been shown to be effective in achieving attitude change. See W. J. Seiler, "The Effects of Visual Materials on Attitudes, Credibility, and Retention," *Speech Monographs*, 38 (1971), pp. 331–334.

[19]John F. Wilson and Carroll C. Arnold, *Public Speaking as a Liberal Art* (Boston: Allyn and Bacon, Inc., 1964), p. 160.

[20]*A Gift of Laughter, The autobiography of Alan Sherman* (New York: Atheneum, 1965), pp. 63–64.

[21]A good discussion of the effects of presenting material through various media is provided in Joseph T. Klapper, *The Effects of Mass Communication* (New York: The Free Press, 1960).

[22]The effectiveness of responding to audience feedback was demonstrated by H. J. Leavitt and R. A. H. Mueller, "Some Effects of Feedback on Communication," *Human Relations*, 4 (1951), pp.401–10.

[23]Hecklers can be helpful. See "A Politician's Guide to Success on the Stump: Hire a Heckler," *Psychology Today*, April 1971.

[24]R. R. Carkhuff, *Helping and Human Relations*, Vol. 1 (New York: Holt, Rinehart and Winston, 1969).

[25]Thomas Elmendorf, Speech before the House Subcommittee on Communications, Los Angeles, Calif. August 17, 1976, *Vital Speeches of the Day*, vol. 43 (October 1, 1976).

10

Persuasion

This chapter deals with persuasion as a message strategy. The importance of a persuasive strategy is based on another prediction:

A message that has carefully chosen persuasive appeals will be more effective than one that does not. [1]

THE ETHICS OF PERSUASION

Persuasion is the act of moving someone, through communication, to a particular belief, attitude, or behavior. Persuasion is considered *ethical* if it conforms to accepted standards. But what *are* the accepted standards today? Whose opinion should you accept for what is good or bad? If your plan is a selfish one, and perhaps not in the best interest of your audience, but you're honest about your motives, is that ethical? If your plan *is* in the best interest of your audience, but you lie to them to get them to accept the plan, is *that* ethical?

It's a thorny question. Eventually, the answer will depend on a set of moral values you decide to live by. For the purposes of this book, however, a simple general definition is sufficient: *Ethical persuasion is defined as communication that does not depend on false or misleading information to induce attitude change in an audience.* Not all persuasion is ethical, even by this simple standard. Sometimes it is difficult to recognize whether persuasion is ethical or not because of different types of persuasive strategies. It is important, therefore, to be able to differentiate between *direct*, *indirect*, and *unethical* persuasion.

Direct Persuasive Strategies

A direct persuasive strategy will not try to disguise the desired audience response in any way. "Buy Burpo—It's Good" is a direct persuasive strategy. Direct persuasion is the best strategy to use with a friendly audience, especially when you are asking for a response that the audience is likely to give you.

> I'm here today to let you know what you can do to take part in the Red Cross blood drive.

> Have you ever wished that students had more rights and power? They can, if they organize effectively. I'm here today to show you how to do just that.

> I'm going to try to convince you today that Polly Ticker is the best candidate for student senate, and that she needs your vote.

A speech that uses a direct persuasive strategy can announce the desired audience response right away, in the introduction of the speech. Then that response can act as the focus of the speech.

Indirect Persuasive Strategies

Indirect persuasion disguises or de-emphasizes the desired audience response in some way. "Wouldn't you really rather have a Burpo?" is based on indirect persuasion, as is any ad that doesn't come right out and ask you to buy the product. Indirect persuasion is not necessarily unethical. Sometimes, in fact, it is necessary for a completely ethical message. When the audience is hostile to either you or your topic you might want to ease into it slowly.[2] You might want to take some time to make your audience feel good about you or the social action you are working for. So if you are speaking in favor of Polly Ticker, but Polly is in favor of an increase in tuition and your audience is not, you might want to talk for a while about the benefits they might derive from that increase.[3] You might even want to change your desired audience response. Rather than trying to get them to rush out and vote for Polly, you might want them to simply read a recent article about Polly in the student newspaper, or attend a speech she is giving later in the day. But one of the things you can't do is begin by saying:

I'm not here to speak in support of Polly Ticker . . .

because that would be a false statement. It is more than indirect, it is unethical.

Unethical Persuasion

Some messages are unethical because they border on deception, like "Enter the Burpo sweepstakes and win a million dollars a week for the rest of your life." That appeal makes it sound as though just entering the sweepstakes makes you an automatic winner, when your chances are actually pretty slim.

Other messages are unethical because they are absolutely false. They purposely seek to mislead the audience. An example of this type of message might be: "Congratulations! You have won a free one-year supply of Burpo, and all you need to pay is the cost of postage and handling!" This strategy is used in door-to-door magazine con games. After people sign for the "free magazines" they wind up paying more for the "postage and handling" than they would for a regular subscription.

Ethical persuasion can be direct or indirect, but it cannot deceive. With that in mind, an examination of persuasive arguments is in order.

PERSUASIVE ARGUMENTS

Persuasive arguments supply your audience with reasons to say yes to a plan. Persuasion is different from coercion. If you hold a gun to someone's head and say, "Adopt this plan or I'll kill you," that's coercion. It is also illegal. It will probably be ineffective, too, because once you take the gun away the plan will probably be dropped.[4]

Persuasive arguments make an audience *want* to adopt your plan. If your "plan" is to borrow a friend's car for the weekend, your friend might want to lend it to you if he or she knows that the car will be returned washed, or vacuumed, or with a full tank of gas. The early Greeks first outlined a set of devices through which reasons can be given convincingly. Aristotle labeled these *ethos*, *logos*, and *pathos*. These correspond roughly to appeals based on credibility, logic, and emotion.

Credibility

Credibility has two main components.[5]

1. Authoritativeness (the person knows what he or she is talking about).
2. Trustworthiness (the person can be believed).

Credibility can be based on either the speaker's own reputation or on the testimony of an expert the audience trusts. If the speaker is an atomic physicist who has studied the safety of a nuclear power plant for many years, an audience would probably consider that speaker a credible source for the topic of safety in nuclear power plants. Chances are that if the audience members were in favor of nuclear power, and this speaker told them that nuclear power was unsafe, they would have something to think about. If the speaker was a student who had never visited an atomic power plant it would be easy for the audience members to discount the student's arguments.[6] If the student quoted the expert or the results of a study the expert ran, that student would borrow some of that expert's credibility. It is important to acquire expert testimony from highly credible sources and then carefully attribute that testimony to the proper source.[7] The student with no background in nuclear power might have done careful research into nuclear power and decided on the basis of that research that nuclear power plants are unsafe. That student might then say:

Nuclear power plants are unsafe.

and expect the audience to believe it. But why should they take the student's word for it? In order to bolster the credibility of the message, the student might say:

According to several books I read, nuclear power plants are unsafe.

But what books are these? They might be works of fiction by a source no more authoritative than the speaker. Worse yet, these books might have been distributed by special-interest groups for propaganda purposes. The best move would be for the speaker to take an extra breath and give a concise, carefully worded statement of the credibility of the outside expert:

> According to Professor A. Thom Kerschmacher, a highly respected nuclear physicist and winner of the Nobel Prize for his work in nuclear safety, nuclear power plants are unsafe.

Establishing your own credibility requires a somewhat different procedure.[8] If you are not already well known to your audience, you might have to answer the question "Why should these people listen to *me*, anyway?" To answer this question you could make a statement about your experience concerning your topic, or how important it is to you, or the amount of research you have done on it. No matter how you establish your credibility, it is important that you be enthusiastic about it. You don't have to jump up and down and scream. "I'm the greatest," but you should be wary of false modesty. As long as what you are saying about yourself is true and reasonable, don't be afraid to lay it on thick. When the chairman of General Motors spoke before a congressional committee on economic planning, he began, after the customary amenities, this way:

> In preparation for this meeting today, my colleagues and I have undertaken a very careful assessment of the proposed legislation and our views with respect thereto. We have thoroughly reviewed the thoughts of many others who have analyzed the proposal.
> We also have reviewed the brief episodes of what might be called economic planning in U.S. history. . . . [9]

Of course, that sounds a bit stuffy for classroom use. A more lively example is the president of Columbia University speaking before an audience of lawyers:

> A national conference of jurists and eminent scholars of the law chosen especially for their competence in considering the philosophical underpinnings of American justice offers no easy forum to an untarnished legal virgin.
> Robert Benchley, when he was a student at Harvard, once tried to answer a difficult examination question on the fishing industry of Nova Scotia by offering his analysis from the point of view of the fish. Perhaps I might bring you a fish-eye's view, or better yet a worm's eye view, of popular dissatisfaction. The most obvious qualification I can offer is that during my eight years of service as a university president, I have been sued repeatedly for engaging in what I have taken to be the simple performance of my duty. . . . [10]

If an audience accepts you and your sources of information as being credible, they are likely to give your logical arguments a fair hearing.

Logical Arguments

TYPES OF REASONING

In their purest form, logical arguments supply an audience with a series of statements that lead to the conclusion the speaker is trying to establish.[11] The most common forms of logical reasoning are *induction* and *deduction*.

Induction.   *Induction* is reasoning from specific evidence to a general conclusion. In induction, we observe that something is true for a specific sample. From this, we reason that it is *generally* true. If you are seeking to prove that your local government is generally corrupt, you might build your case with specific examples: The mayor has been convicted of bribery, the building inspector has resigned after being charged with extortion, the fire chief has been indicted for running the station's dalmation at the track, and the police chief has admitted to keeping his infant nephew on the police department payroll. If you used these specific instances to conclude that most of your local officials were corrupt, you would be using induction.

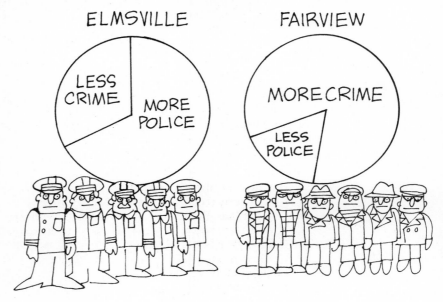

Deduction.   *Deduction* is reasoning from general evidence to a specific conclusion. Deductive reasoning can be demonstrated in syllogisms, which are arguments made up of two premises (a major premise and a minor premise) and a conclusion. For example, the classic syllogism is:

All men are mortal.
Socrates is a man.
Therefore, Socrates is mortal.

The concept of a syllogism is important, since we use shortened forms of this device all the time. If all logical appeals were expressed as complete syllogisms, people could examine their major and minor premises and decide if the conclusions drawn from those premises were valid. Unfortunately this would make most arguments long and tedious, so we generally use *enthymemes* for logical appeals. An enthymeme is a compressed version of a syllogism in which the underlying premises are concealed, as in:

Since Socrates is a man, he's mortal.

Enthymemes become dangerous when they disguise faulty premises. Some of the best examples of this type of enthymeme are provided in the form of arbitrary rules. For example, take the rule enforced by some college-town landlords: "Since Joe Schmidlap is a college student, he will have to pay a damage deposit before he can rent an apartment."

This rule is based on an enthymeme which is based on the following syllogism:

College students wreck apartments.
Joe Schmidlap is a college student.
Therefore, Joe Schmidlap will wreck this apartment.

The conclusion, "Joe Schmidlap will wreck this apartment," is based on an untrue, unstated premise: "College students wreck apartments."

College students often run up against this type of reasoning from landlords and utility companies. Even if they can supply letters of reference from former landlords and receipts for utility bills paid on time, they are still told things like: "I'm sorry, we don't rent to college students. It's a rule we have." or "I'm sorry. We require a $35 deposit to turn on your electricity. It's a rule." or "There's no sense arguing. We don't need to give you a *reason*. It's a rule."

The frustration you feel when you are subjected to illogical rules is the same frustration that an audience will feel when it is subjected to an argument that does not supply valid reasons. To assure that your reasons are valid when you are using induction or deduction, be sure to examine the underlying premises of your argument.

Although induction and deduction are the most common types of logical reasoning, there are other forms. Worthy of mention here are reasoning by sign, causal reasoning, and reasoning by analogy.

Reasoning by Sign.   Sign reasoning is reasoning from specific evidence to a specific conclusion without explaining how the evidence and conclusion are related. The classic example of sign reasoning is, "It is snowing outside, therefore it must be winter." Sign reasoning is used when the argument will be easily accepted by the audience. For example, an audience would probably accept the claim that an increase in bank robberies is a sign that a community is becoming more dangerous to its inhabitants. We wouldn't need to go into a long logical explanation of our reasoning in that case, and the time we save could be used to develop more important aspects of the argument. For example, we might want to go on and claim a particular *cause* for the rash of bank robberies. That would require causal reasoning.

Causal Reasoning.   Causal reasoning, like sign reasoning, is reasoning from one specific to another specific. However, in causal reasoning you go on to prove that something happened or will happen *because* of something else. So if you claimed that the increase in bank robberies in your community was caused by a decrease in police manpower, you would be involved in causal reasoning. In fact, in that case you would be involved in *effect-to-cause reasoning*, since you are arguing about something that has already happened. If you were arguing about something that *will* happen (for example, the probability of future bank robberies because the police have cut the size of their force, or the hours they patrol) you would be using *cause-to-effect reasoning*.

Reasoning by Analogy.   Reasoning by analogy is reasoning from specific evidence to a specific conclusion, by claiming that something is *like* something else. For example, if you were arguing that the methods of law enforcement that curbed bank robbery in a nearby city would also work in your city, you would have to argue that your city is similar to that city in all the respects that are important to your argument, such as number of banks, size of banks, size of police department, and so on. Thus, if you could argue that the two cities are alike except in one respect—for example, the size of their police forces—you could argue that this one difference is what makes the difference in the incidence of bank robbery. If you did so, you would be arguing by analogy.

There are two types of analogy: *literal* and *figurative*. The above analogy of two cities is a literal analogy, because it compares two things that are really (literally) alike. A figurative analogy compares two things that are essentially different. So if you argued that bank robberies are like diseases that must be treated to keep them from spreading, you would be using a figurative analogy.

No matter which type of reasoning you are using (induction, deduction, sign, causation, or analogy) you can check the validity of your arguments through the *Toulmin model*.

THE TOULMIN MODEL

In its most basic form, the Toulmin model calls for every claim to be supported not only with data (evidence)[12], but with a warrant that ties the claim and data together. A warrant, in this sense, is a statement that justifies the use of data for a particular claim. For example, you might say,

> Studying public speaking is a matter of life and death.

That is a claim that even a gullible audience would find difficult to swallow. So you might back the claim up with some hard data:

> Forty-five thousand American men lost their lives in Vietnam.

But then the audience might be really confused. And they would probably be a little frustrated if you left your argument like that. They probably would not want to dismiss what you have to say automatically, but they might have to, unless you supply a warrant, such as this:

> A generation of young people who understood that the Vietnam War was wrong could not communicate that idea to the people in power at the time. It might have been different if those young people had studied public speaking.

Your audience might not agree with your argument if you said that, but at least they could identify your line of reasoning. Better yet, you could identify it yourself, and therefore decide whether or not to use it. The point here is that *every claim you make has to be examined to see if it needs data to back it up, and all the data you use needs to be examined to see if it needs a warrant to justify it in light of the claim.* Sometimes neither the data nor the warrant needs to be stated out loud. For example, a typical college audience would accept the following claim today:

> Cigarette smoking is dangerous to your health.

After all, such an audience would be familiar with the Surgeon General's report and the research leading up to it. The data and the warrant are therefore already known to the audience, and do not have to be stated by the speaker. Yet 20 years ago, before the link between cigarette smoking and respiratory disease was established, some audiences would have found this claim difficult to inhale. That was before the Surgeon General's report and before the findings of cancer research were well known. An audience of that time might have needed data to back up the claim, and a warrant to prove that the data was justified in light of the claim. For example:

CLAIM: SMOKING IS HAZARDOUS TO YOUR HEALTH.

DATA: A STUDY FOUND THAT TWICE AS MANY SMOKERS AS NONSMOKERS DEVELOP LUNG CANCER..

WARRANT: THIS STUDY WAS CAREFULLY CONTROLLED AND OTHER EXPLANATIONS OF THESE FINDINGS ARE UNLIKELY.

DIFFERENT DATA WOULD REQUIRE A DIFFERENT WARRANT: CLAIM: SMOKING IS HAZARDOUS TO YOUR HEALTH.

DATA: LABORATORY STUDIES PROVE THAT RATS HOOKED UP TO A SMOKING MACHINE DEVELOP CANCER

WARRANT: THE RAT'S SMOKING MACHINE REASONABLY SIMULATES A HUMAN SMOKING HABIT..

The Toulmin model is useful to public speakers because they can apply it to each claim they make to see if that claim needs evidence and/or a warrant to back it up. An examination of the different types of claims, data, and warrants will facilitate this use of the model.

Types of Claim.   There are four types of claim: claims of *fact, definition, value,* and *policy*. The type of claim you make will depend on the type of issue you are dealing with. It will also determine the type of evidence you need to back up your claim.

Claims of fact answer the question "Is it true"—in other words, is, was, or will something be so? If you were giving a speech on the assassination of John Kennedy, and you sought to establish that the assassination was the result of a conspiracy, you might have to make the claim "More than one gun was used in the Kennedy assassination." If you did so, you would be asserting a claim of fact, and you would have to use facts to back it up.

Claims of definition answer the question "What is it?" If you were arguing against the reestablishment of the military draft, you might want to advance the claim "The military draft is an infringement of our basic constitutional rights." If you did so, you would have made a claim of definition, and you would have to provide a definition of "constitutional rights" to back it up.

Claims of value answer the question "Is it good or bad?"—in other words, they place an evaluation on something. If you claimed that the military draft was bad, or immoral, or unethical, or if you expressed any other value judgment of it, you would be advancing a claim of value, and you would have to back it up by relating it to values your audience already holds, such as freedom, equality, fair play, and so on.

Claims of policy answer the question "What should be done about it?" If you suggested to your audience that the Kennedy assassination investigation should be reopened, or that the military draft should be re-established, you would be advancing a claim of policy. Since a claim of policy suggests that something should be done (i.e., that some policy should be adopted), you have to back it up with a specific policy (i.e., tell your audience *how* it should be done.)

Types of Data.   There are three types of evidence, or data: *audience belief, speaker assertion,* and *outside authority*.

Audience belief data are based on something your audience already believes to be true. For example, if you were a union organizer at a small-town textile plant, you might know that your audience believes that the owners of their plant will become angry if they (the workers) support the union. Your job, then, would be to use this data to your advantage, and to explain to your audience that the reason the plant owners will be angry is that they will be forced to give the workers added benefits. At the same time, you would have to reassure the workers that they will not lose their jobs if they support the union.

Speaker assertion data is based on something the audience believes you, the speaker, to know. Thus, if you had established yourself as the organizer of several successful union plants, your audience might accept what you say about the proper procedures for unionizing their plant.

Outside authority data is based on something the audience believes an outside expert to know. If your audience didn't know much about unions, and they didn't particularly trust you, you might quote a local civic leader or the president of the American Federation of Labor/Congress of Industrial Organizations. If you did so, you would be using outside authority data.

The success of speaker assertion data and outside authority data depends on how well you build up their credibility, as discussed earlier in this chapter. This "building up of credibility" is one type of warrant.

Types of Warrant. There are three types of warrant: *authoritative*, *substantive*, and *motivational*. Warrants are usually not explicitly stated by the speaker; rather, they are used to "check back" on reasoning.

An *authoritative warrant* is based on the credibility of the source of the evidence. Thus, if you argued that a state clean-air act would improve health, and you cited as evidence that a well-known doctor or the Surgeon General said so, your warrant would be an authoritative one (that is, the doctor or the Surgeon General is a credible source).

A *substantive warrant* is based on one of the logical relationships we have already discussed: induction, deduction, sign, causation, or analogy. Thus, if you were arguing for the establishment of a state clean air act, and you claimed that such an act would work in your state, and you cited as evidence that it worked in a neighboring state, your warrant would be a substantive one based on analogy (that is, your state is *like* the neighboring state).

A *motivational warrant* is based on the desires of your audience; it ties the data into the claim with an assertion about something the audience *wants*. So if you claimed that we should have separate smoking and nonsmoking sections in restaurants, and your evidence for that claim was that smoking and nonsmoking sections would make dining more pleasant, your warrant would be a motivational one (that is, pleasant dining is something your audience *wants* to have).

Before leaving our discussion of the Toulmin model, there are two other components of the model that are worthy of mention: *qualifiers* and *reservations*.

A *qualifier* expresses the degree of probability of the claim. It is often dangerous to state that *all* of anything is true. You might not want to claim that *every* restaurant in your state should have separate smoking and nonsmoking sections; if you claimed instead that *most* restaurants should, "most" would be your qualifier. Most claims are qualified with "probably," "presumably," "75 percent of the time," or some other qualifier.

A *reservation* is a question dealing with a possible flaw in your logic, such as "Do I have enough evidence to back up this claim?" or "Does my conclusion follow from my premises?" Reservations can be expressed in a speech, and then be answered, to strengthen an argument. This is an effective tactic when the reservation is one that your audience is likely to hold already. The more common use of a reservation, however, is in the analysis of your own argument. Your analyses of the possible reservations in your argument will depend on your understanding of *logical fallacies*.[13]

LOGICAL FALLACIES

Scholars have devoted lives and volumes to the description of various types of logical fallacies. The three most common types seem to be (1) insufficient evidence, (2) non sequitur, and (3) evasion of argument. Most fallacies can be included under one of those categories.

The fallacy of insufficient evidence is sometimes difficult to recognize. This is especially true when it is caused by *ignored causes* or *ignored effects*.

Examples of *ignored causes* run rampant through everyday conversations. Take a typical discussion about college sports:

> State U. beat State Tech.
> State Tech creamed State Teachers.
> Therefore, State U. will murder State Teachers.

This argument might ignore previously injured players who are now back in action, or stars who are now injured, or a host of other variables. Logical fallacies based on *ignored effects* are even worse:

> If other nations overcharge for oil that is needed for American consumers, an invasion of those countries is warranted.

That argument ignores undesirable effects of war, such as drafting college students who would rather be studying public speaking, and so on.

You might not recognize that an argument is based on insufficient evidence because the argument *sounds* so reasonable. One cause of this deception is reasoning according to formula, or slogan. Max Black provides an excellent example of this:

> We hear all too often that "the exception proves the rule." Probably not one person in a thousand who dishes up this ancient morsel of wisdom realizes that "prove" is here used in its

older sense of "probe" or "test." What was originally intended was that the exception tests the rule—shows whether the rule is correct or not. The contemporary interpretation, that a rule is confirmed by having an exception, is absurd. This tabloid formula has the advantage of allowing a person to glory in the fact that his general principle does *not* square with the facts.

"It's all right in theory, but it won't do in practice" is another popular way of revelling in logical absurdity. The philosopher Schopenhauer said all that needs to be said about this sophism: "The assertion is based upon an impossibility: what is right in theory *must* work in practice; and if it does not, there is a mistake in theory; something has been overlooked and not allowed for; and consequently, what is wrong in practice is wrong in theory too."[14]

Fallacies of insufficient evidence are caused by not telling enough. *Non-sequitur fallacies* are those in which the conclusion does not relate to (literally, "does not follow from") the evidence. Unreasonable syllogisms sometimes used by landlords and utility companies are non sequiturs based on faulty premises, but non sequiturs based on true premises can be just as dangerous. Take, for example, the non-sequitur fallacy known as *post hoc*, which is short for *post hoc ergo propter hoc*. Translated from the Latin, that means "after this, therefore because of this." This fallacy occurs when it is assumed that an action was caused by something that happened before it.

Post hoc arguments are often applied to politics:

Obviously, Jimmy Carter caused the gas shortage of 1979. It happened, after all, during his administration.

Spurious research is often post hoc:

Nearly all heroin users started with marijuana. Marijuana obviously leads to the use of harder drugs.

Nearly all heroin users started with milk, too, but milk doesn't lead to the use of drugs. At least, not necessarily.

Another type of non sequitur is an *unwarranted extrapolation*, which is a statement that suggests that because something happened before it will happen again, or because something is true for a part it is true for a whole.

State U. has massacred State Teachers every year for the past five years. They'll do it again this year.

Ronald Reagan is a good actor. *Bonzo Goes to College* must be a good movie.

Then there is a *circular argument*, in which the evidence is dependent upon the truth of the argument.

Of course the administration is concerned with student welfare. It says so, right in the college catalog.

Finally, there is the logical fallacy of *evasion of argument*. This type consists of arguments like *ad hominem*. Ad hominem is the fallacy of attacking the person rather than the issue:

Of course Louie thinks cornsilk should be legalized. Louie is an idiot.

The *red-herring* argument evades the issue by concentrating on another issue. This expression derives from the practice of dragging an odoriferous fish across a trail when running away from bloodhounds.

No argument is perfect. If all the evidence were available and it related perfectly to the argument, then there probably wouldn't *be* an argument in the first place. You should recognize the major fallacies, though, and watch for them in your own reasoning. If an audience is able to discount your arguments as illogical, persuasion will probably not occur.

Emotional Appeals

An emotional appeal uses a feeling like love, hate, fear, guilt, anger, loneliness, envy, or pity to entice an audience to change its attitude.[15] An emotional appeal is not necessarily unethical, although it does allow the most room for an unethical speaker to operate. It is not necessarily illogical, either. Emotional appeals are *psychological*, and because of this they can be particularly powerful. Clarence Darrow once pointed out, "You don't have to give reasons to the jury. Make them want to acquit your client and they'll find their own reasons."[16]

It would be a good idea for you to accept half of Darrow's advice. Give your audience reasons *and* make them want to accept your plan. Instead of just giving reasons from expert authorities why nuclear power plants are unsafe, you might also describe a nuclear holocaust or explain the details of radiation illness. On the other hand, if you were arguing in favor of nuclear power, you might describe what life is like without any energy sources—freezing to death and all that. Let's take a look at three emotions on which emotional appeals are sometimes based: *fear, anger,* and *pity.*

FEAR

Appropriate fear appeals are sometimes effective persuaders. Modern advertising—especially the TV variety—commonly appeals to audience fears. In fact, television advertising has done more than its share of originating new fears. The fear of body odor, one of the classics of prime-time advertising, has recently been fragmented into more specific fears like the fear of foot odor (one commercial featured a hapless father driving his entire family from the house by taking off his shoes), the fear of personal-hygiene odor, and the fear of soap odor ("That's just it," explains the reticent young stranger to the girl in the kissing booth. "You *smell* like a deodorant soap.")[17]

Fear appeals can be detrimental if they go too far. A classic study conducted in 1953[18] showed this. In this study, high school students were presented persuasive messages about toothbrushing. In the high fear appeal, the students were shown grotesque pictures of dental diseases, rotting gums and black stumps of teeth. The moderate fear appeal merely mentioned tooth decay in passing, but the researchers found it to be more effective. One writer explains this finding as follows:

> [The researchers] suggested one possibility: the students may have actively repressed the rather disgusting high fear appeal, so it may have had less effect on their toothbrushing habits for that reason. A second reason may have been peer pressure. You can probably imagine how a group of high school students would react to a presentation like that—by laughing it up, right? That message may have become such an object of derision that the students were embarrassed to admit that they had started brushing their teeth more regularly. Remember, this was 1953. Any cat caught with a toothbrush in his hand for the next month probably tried to pretend he was using it to brush up his blue suede shoes or slick back his ducktail haircut. No way he would admit he was using it on his teeth. "You scared of 'pie rea,' man? Here let me see if yer teeth are fallin' out. . . ."[19]

It is all right to tap into audience fears if you do so with compassion and moderation. This is true also for the emotion of anger.

ANGER

If your audience is angry about something, it is a good idea to recognize that anger. If you can show your audience that you are angry about the same thing, it will do two things: (1) It will show that you are similar to them in this way, and therefore increase your persuasiveness,[20] and (2) it will allow you to offer your solution as a cure for whatever is causing that anger. For example, as this is being written, a few miles away a bandwagon full of political hopefuls are telling people how angry they are about the rate of inflation in the United States today. But fear not, the audience is told. There is a way to change this situation: vote for Candidate X.

Appeals based on anger can be successful, but in order to be ethical you have to honestly *feel* the anger. According to our definition of ethics, you can't say you're angry if you're not.

PITY

Pity is the emotion that allows us to feel sorrow for the suffering of others. Pity can be used as an emotional appeal by reminding your audience that someone, somewhere, is suffering.[21] Pity is an especially potent emotion if the sufferer comes from a group that we already feel sympathetic toward, such as children or dumb animals. One very effective anti-abortion message was delivered from the point of view of an unborn fetus, who explained that it was able to feel pain from the beginning of its development. Therefore, to allow abortion to remain legal was to allow this fetus to suffer. The listeners were thus told that a *child* was suffering; and worse yet, that they were partially responsible.

The key to an emotional appeal is sincerity. Most audiences will be able to recognize false emotions and reject the appeals that are based on them.

Emotional appeals, as well as logical reasoning and credibility, are important to keep in mind when planning a persuasive strategy.

PLANNING A PERSUASIVE STRATEGY

Earlier, it was mentioned that the three basic message strategies are cumulative. When you seek to persuade you are still interested in maintaining audience interest by relating to needs. Psychologist James V. McConnell sums it up this way:

> The best "persuader" appears to be whatever best satisfies the deep-felt needs of the audience.[22]

You are still concerned with explanation, too. In fact, a persuasive speech is actually like three different explanation speeches. You have to explain *the problem, the solution, and the part your audience can play in that solution.* Each one of these explanatory tasks requires the same kind of planning that a full "speech to explain" would require.

The Problem

One way to establish a problem is to answer three basic questions. First: *Is there a problem from the audience's point of view?* After all, what seems like a problem to you might not seem like a problem to other people. For example, you might want to show that laws against prostitution are a problem. What would make those laws a problem for your audience? Does the absence of legal prostitution lead to profits for organized crime? Does it lead to disease, or sex crimes, or an overdependence on sex in other (nonprofessional) relationships? What

arguments could you use to establish these things as problems for your audience?

The second question you need to answer is: *How does this problem relate to your audience?* Here you get back to the idea of audience needs. Do the profits of organized crime represent a threat to your audience's safety and security? Could they become infected with a dread social disease? Are their children safe from perverts? Do their relationships with others suffer because of pent-up sexual frustrations that could be given legal channels of release? In other words, you must prove the relationship of your problem to your audience.

The final question is: *Does this problem actually require a change?* For example, if your main argument is that organized criminals benefit from illegal prostitution, your audience might mentally refute that argument by reminding themselves that there are laws against organized crime; therefore, the real problem would be a lack of law enforcement. Also, some problems will go away if you ignore them long enough. How can you prove that your problem doesn't fit into this category?

Basically, then, this first task requires you to figure out why your audience might think that your problem was not a problem for them. You have to impress them with the importance and personal relevance of your problem. For example, let's say that you are proposing a student prison program in which students will do volunteer counseling and tutoring at a nearby prison. Your first step in planning your message would be to analyze why the students would *not* want to take advantage of such a project. If you thought about it, you might come up with reasons like these:

1. They are too busy with activities that are more important to them.
2. They believe that their participation in such a program would not make a difference.
3. They do not feel that the prisoners are their concern anyway.

You now have a guide for establishing the problem. You merely answer those arguments:

1. Show that the program *will* be a valuable experience for them. You could explain what they are likely to learn, or the feeling of fulfillment they are likely to achieve, or how good "Tutor, State U Prison Project" will look on their résumés when it is time to look for a job.
2. Show that their participation *will* make a difference. You can cite prison programs at other universities to prove this point.
3. Show that the prisoners *should* be their concern. You might explain that the more prisoners who return to their community without being rehabilitated, the more dangerous those communities will be.

Thus, there are at least two requirements for the problem you establish:

1. It must relate directly to your audience. If you live in New Jersey, the repeal of the Nebraska state income tax would be an inappropriate problem.
2. It must be a problem that your audience can play some part in correcting. The existence of cancer would be an inappropriate problem, but the lack of funds for cancer research would be appropriate because your audience could contribute money or sign a petition supporting government funding.

You should take both of these requirements into consideration when establishing the problem. Then you will be ready to consider the solution.

The Solution

A solution is a plan proposed to correct a problem. Once again, you might want to answer three questions in order to establish your plan as the answer to the problem. First: *Will the plan work?* If your plan is to legalize prostitution so that prostitutes can be regulated and therefore protected against crime and disease, can you give evidence to suggest that our suspiciously inept bureaucracy is actually capable of such regulation?

A second question is: *Will the plan be practical?* Perhaps the bureaucracy is capable of regulating legalized prostitution. But what would be the cost of such regulation? If the cost is too great, then the plan would not be practical. How can you prove that your plan will not cost more than it is worth?

The final question might be: *What advantages or disadvantages will result from your plan?* This question takes into account that there are costs and rewards besides economic ones. In changing laws against prostitution, there could be costs to our religious beliefs, our national self-concept, and our ability to teach morality to our young. How could you prove that your plan would not create more problems than it would solve?

The Desired Audience Response

This third step is uniquely characteristic of a persuasive strategy. This step, like the first two, should answer three questions. First: *What part can the audience play in putting the plan into action?*[23] It doesn't help much if your audience simply agrees with you but does not do anything to help change the problem. The most brilliant speech is not good enough if your audience leaves thinking, "That kid sure was right. There's a real problem there. Yup, there sure is. I wonder what's for dinner tonight?"

The second question that you might ask is: *How do the audience members go about playing their part?* The behavior that you ask your audience to adopt should be made as simple as possible for them. If you want them to vote in a referendum, tell them when to vote, where to go to vote, and how to go about registering, if necessary. Be very specific in your request. Don't ask them to write their congressman. *You* write the letter (to the congressman who is in charge of the subcommittee that is investigating the problem, perhaps) and ask your audience members to sign it. Don't ask them to start a petition. *You* draw up the petition and have them sign it. Don't ask them to picket. Give them the placards and tell them what time to meet you at the administration building.

Finally, you might want to answer the question: *What are the direct rewards of this response?* Your solution might be of importance to society, but this is just one of the possible rewards that you can offer to your audience for responding the way you want them to. If you think about it, there are probably some direct personal rewards involved also. Is there a chance that the congressman will answer

AUDIENCE RESPONSE

them personally? Will the picket session be fun, as well as meaning-ful? Will there be coffee and doughnuts and interesting people at the polling place? If these direct rewards need to be proved, how would you go about proving them?

The study of persuasion is as complex as the study of human communication. In fact, some people believe the terms "persuasion" and "communication" are synonymous. To reduce persuasion to three steps is a tricky business and even then it is complex. Even then it requires you to do the following things:

  I. Focus the problem.
     A. Analyze the arguments that the audience might have against the importance of the problem.
     B. Answer those arguments.
 II. Focus the solution.
     A. Analyze the arguments the audience might have against the solution.
     B. Answer those arguments.
III. Focus the desired audience behavior.
     A. Analyze the arguments against this behavior.
     B. Answer those arguments.

SAMPLE SPEECH

The following speech was given by one of my students. The student's purpose was to persuade his classmates to sign and carry an organ-donor card. Some comments on his persuasive strategy are noted.

"THE GIFT OF LIFE"[24]

Some Comments

His introduction suggests that this will be a direct persuasive strategy.

He begins with a moderate fear appeal.

His next statement suggests that both he and his information are credible.

He begins establishing the problem by explaining that the kidneys are essential organs.

He explains next that kidney disease is prevalent. This is basically a logical argument.

He diverges from the focus of his speech slightly . . .

The Talk

If any of you needed a kidney or other vital organ to live, would you be able to get one? Would you know where to begin searching for information which would lead to obtaining this needed organ?

These are questions many of us have never even considered. Yet, each year, in America alone, many people died with kidney disease because donated kidneys were not available. Now wouldn't it be nice—no, *fantastic*—to have a major role in curbing some of this tragic and needless dying? You can do just that. I'd like to show you how, today.

In researching and preparing for this speech, I had the opportunity to conduct an interview with the state secretary for the Kidney Foundation, Mrs. Florence Murray, at her home. She related some basic background information about kidneys, kidney disease, and kidney donation, and I would like to relay this information on to you.

Kidneys are vital to human life. They are the "twin organs" that perform the following vital life-maintaining functions:
1. They clean waste materials and excess fluids from the blood.
2. They filter the blood, retaining some compounds while excreting others.
3. They help regulate blood pressure and red blood cell count.

The human body cannot function without kidneys, and kidney disease is the fourth leading health problem in this country today. Over 8,000,000 Americans suffer from some type of kidney disease. Approximately 60,000 people die of it each year. In addition, over 4,000 children between the ages of 1 to 6 are stricken annually with "childhood nephrosis," which is simply medical jargon for kidney disease.

Perhaps your first question might be—what is being done to combat this disease? The national Kidney Foundation has many objectives, including the following:

1. It offers advice and assistance on important topics like kidney disease detection (warning signals), diagnosis (tests, X-rays, and so on), and drugs needed to treat this disease.
2. It provides assistance in obtaining artificial kidney machines, which are also called dialysis machines.

Some Comments

... but pulls himself out with the final point.

3. But most important, it coordinates the kidney donation and transplantation program, whereby donors may give one kidney while living or two kidneys posthumously in order to save another person's life.

Having finished his explanation of the problem, he offers a solution.

Since the first kidney transplant back in 1954, over 5,000 of these operations have been performed. Thanks to improved medical techniques, better blood testing, and new tissue-typing processes, doctors are now reducing the risk of organ rejection. If rejection does occur, the patient can go back on dialysis to await a second, third or even a fourth transplant, until one is successful.

(Here he picks up one of the cards as an illustration.)

To accelerate organ donations, the Kidney Foundation is also responsible for the widespread distribution of these uniform donor cards.

These cards enable you to donate a vital organ after your death.

In order to illustrate how this program works, let me use as an example one of our neighbors, whose life was recently saved by a transplant.

He offers some evidence that the solution is a good one. This is basically an emotional appeal.

I refer to a 16-year-old New Hampshire boy, John Warner, Jr., whose body had already rejected his father's kidney transplant. Now, a second transplant was essential to save the boy, whose parents could not afford the costly dialysis machine—$150 per treatment, three treatments per week. Luckily, on December 9th of this year, a matching tissue donor posthumously gave his kidney to Johnny and the transplantation was performed and determined a success. The original transplant from his father came three years earlier and the boy had waited since then for a matching kidney. Now, thanks to this wonderful donation, no further wait was necessary.

Instances like these really touch us when we stop to realize that the next victim could be someone close to us.

He misses a transition here which is a little confusing.

I had the opportunity to speak with Dr. Steinmuller, a well-known New Hampshire nephrologist and head of the "organ-retrieval team" whose job it is to go out and retrieve the organs that donors have pledged.

He builds up credibility for his next point.

Dr. Steinmuller told me that skeptics always have excuses for not giving a vital organ, and he asked me to say a few words about some of those excuses:

Some
Comments
He answers
some of the
arguments that
the audience
might have.

The Talk

1. The first excuse is usually a lack of knowledge about the donation procedures. People do not know where to go, or whom to contact. This is a problem I hope to solve for you with this speech.

2. Apathy and lack of time. Some people are indifferent to the needs of others—they just do not care or they claim to be too busy to waste time on such endeavors. Actually, there is little or no time involved, and I know from personal experience that you are not apathetic people.

3. Inconvenience. Some people fear a delay in funeral and burial arrangements. However, since the operation has to be performed immediately after death, no delay is ever caused in funeral arrangements.

4. Usefulness. Some people assume that their gift will not be used. So far, however, the overwhelming problem has been a lack of donors—not recipients.

He provides his
own arguments
in favor of the
action he wants
them to take.

Consider now two reasons why each of us should give of ourselves in this worthwhile way:

1. The gift of life itself. The act of giving this organ will very probably save someone's life in the future. Isn't that a nice thought—to think that you had a part in saving another human's life?

2. Personal pride and satisfaction. How can anyone be more proud or satisfied with himself than when he has contributed to an effort which saves lives? No emotions can compare with those associated with a generous donation for the sake of others.

He answers a
final argument.

Perhaps one last question in your mind might be: If I sign up at this time, can I change my mind later? The answer to this question is yes. Since the only way authorities will know you are a donor is by the donor card in your possession, you could simply tear up the card at any time and no one will be the wiser.

Now that all of you are more informed about this vital and worthy program, I would like to conclude my speech by setting the example—signing the first donor card myself. Then, I will circulate the other cards to each of you.

He asks for
a specific
response, and
he makes it as
easy as possible.

Please search your innermost being and conclude that such a gift would be an unselfish and generous sacrifice on your part, and then sign the donor card. Thank you very much.

SUMMARY

This chapter dealt with persuasion, which is the act of moving someone, through communication, to a particular belief, attitude, or behavior. Persuasion as discussed here refers to ethical persuasion, which does not use false or misleading information. Ethical persuasion can be either direct (with the speaker's purpose completely undisguised) or indirect (with the speaker's purpose disguised or de-emphasized early in the speech).

Persuasive communication supplies an audience with reasons to say yes to a plan. These reasons can derive from credibility, logical reasoning, and/or emotional appeals.

Credibility is based on the authoritativeness and trustworthiness of the speaker or an outside expert the speaker quotes.

Logical reasoning is based on induction (reasoning from specifics to a generality), deduction (reasoning from generalities to a specific), sign (reasoning that one specific is indicative of another specific), causation (reasoning that something happened or will happen because of something else), or analogy (reasoning that something is like something else). Logical fallacies are arguments that sound reasonable but actually are not. Basic fallacies include insufficient evidence, non sequitur, and evasion of argument.

Emotional appeals give the audience reasons to *want* to adopt the plan. Emotional appeals are based on feelings such as fear, anger and pity.

Credibility, logical reasoning, and emotional appeals are used by a speaker to do three things: (1) to establish a problem, (2) to establish a solution to that problem, and (3) to establish a desired audience behavior. These three tasks are the basics of a persuasive strategy.

QUESTIONS FOR DISCUSSION

1. What in your opinion constitutes ethical persuasion? Do any of the techniques presented in the chapter seem *unethical* to you? If so, why do you think so?
2. The chapter distinguishes between "direct" and "indirect" persuasive strategies. Do you agree with the advice as to when each type should be used? (For instance, have you ever been offended by a direct strategy because you thought it was too much of a "hard sell"?) Why or why not?
3. From your experience, do you feel that listeners or readers usually demand *warrants* before they accept claims supported by data, or are the data often accepted at face value? Cite examples to support your answer.

4. From your experiences hearing or reading persuasive messages about social or political issues, how well do you think the advice for planning a persuasive strategy (explain the problem, the solution, and the part the audience can play) is followed? If you feel such advice is *not* heeded what steps or components of the process are most often ignored or slighted?

5. Study the sample speech at the end of the chapter. Do you feel that from your point of view the speaker explained the problem, the solution, and the audience's role in the solution adequately? Can you suggest any changes that might have improved his presentation?

PROBES

1. Examine several advertisements from television, magazines, newspapers, billboards, and so on. Which type of persuasive strategy do you believe is used most often, "direct" or "indirect"? Do you feel the strategies are used effectively? Why or why not?

2. The chapter points out that one common shortcoming in the use of logical appeals is "disguised faulty premises." In your experiences with landlords, banks, loan companies, registrars, deans, and other people, what "disguised faulty premises" and "illogical rules" have you encountered? Explain why you think the logic is faulty.

3. Read several newspaper editorials or political speeches, or examine some television commercials. What unwarranted claims do you find? What warrant(s) would you demand before accepting the claims?

4. In your experiences in informal conversation, or with formal public messages, what arguments do you encounter that are based on "ignored causes" or "ignored effects"? Specifically, *what* causes or effects are ignored in these arguments?

5. Non sequiturs are common fallacies in logic. What examples of non sequiturs can you cite from arguments you have heard over political, sports, or social issues, or from advertisements? What types of non sequiturs do you perceive, and how could you refute them?

6. Consider the topic you have selected for your next speech. List four or five emotional appeals that could be employed. Which of these appeals do you feel are unethical and why? Which appeals might be successful when you speak to your classmates? Why?

7. (a) Think about the topic for your next speech. List three audience needs that you might emphasize to make the listeners believe a problem exists. Which appeal do you think would be the most effective and why?

(b) List three or four actions that you might ask of your audience in support of your solution. Which act seems to best conform to the suggestions offered in the text, and why?

8. In your next speech you may want your audience to support a program or project. For your topic, follow the suggestions in this chapter. List all the reasons you can think of why the audience will *not* accept the arguments, list an answer you might present.

NOTES

[1]Winston L. Brembeck and William S. Howell, *Persuasion: A Means of Social Influence* (Englewood Cliffs, N.J.: Prentice-Hall, 1976).

[2]Some research findings suggest that audiences may perceive a direct strategy as a threat to their "freedom" to form their own opinions. When this occurs, persuasion is hampered. See J. W. Brehm, *A Theory of Psychological Reactance* (New York: Academic Press, 1966). There also exists considerable evidence to suggest that announcing an intent to persuade in the introduction reduces a message's effectiveness. Sample studies on this include J. Allyn and L. Festinger, "The Effectiveness of Unanticipated Persuasive Communications," *Journal of Abnormal and Social Psychology*, 62 (1961), pp. 35–40; C. A. Kiesler and S. B. Kiesler, "Role of Forewarning in Persuasive Communications," *Journal of Abnormal and Social Psychology*, 18 (1971), pp. 210–221.

[3]At least one survey study indicates that beginning with points acceptable to the audience is an effective strategy. See J. C. McCroskey and S. V. O. Prichard, "Selective Exposure and Lyndon B. Johnson's January, 1966, State of the Union Address," *Journal of Broadcasting*, 11 (1967), pp. 331–337.

[4]A more extensive discussion of the relationship between persuasion and coercion is provided in Herb Simons, "Persuasion in Social Conflicts," *Speech Monographs*, November 1972, pp. 227–247.

[5]Source credibility is an important variable in communication research, and it has received a lot of attention. Other characteristics of credibility have been discovered in later investigations: J. C. McCroskey, T. Jensen, and C. Todd, "The Generalizability of Source Credibility Scales for Public Figures," Paper Presented at Speech Communication Association Convention, Chicago, Ill., December, 1972; and R. Applbaum and K. Anatol, "The Factor Structure of Source Credibility as a Function of the Speaking Situation," *Speech Monographs*, 39 (1972), pp. 216–222. The various aspects of credibility are summarized in Michael Burgoon, *Approaching Speech/Communication.* (New York: Holt, Rinehart and Winston, 1974); and James C. McCroskey, *An Introduction to Rhetorical Communication*, 2nd ed. (Englewood Cliffs, N.J.: Prentice-Hall, 1972).

[6]Many studies, too numerous to list here, have demonstrated that high source credibility enhances persuasion. The major studies are discussed by K. Andersen and T. Clevenger, "A Summary of Experimental Research in Ethos," *Speech Monographs*, 30 (1963), pp. 49–78.

[7]Research indicates that quoting expert testimony increases the effectiveness of a message, *especially* when the source is initially low in credibility, *and* the audience is *extremely* opposed to the speaker's position. See J. C. McCroskey, "A Summary of Experimental Research on the Effects of Evidence in Persuasive Communication," *Quarterly Journal of Speech*, 55 (1969), pp. 227–233; and, T. B. Harte, "The Effects of Evidence in Persuasive Communi-

cation," *Central States Speech Journal*, 27 (1976), pp. 42–46.

[8]A speaker *can* increase his or her credibility very early in a speech. See, for example, R. Brooks and T. Scheidel, "Speech as Process: A Case Study," *Speech Monographs*, 35 (1968), pp. 1–7. The determinants of a speaker's credibility are summarized in J. C. McCroskey, *An Introduction to Rhetorical Communication*, 2nd ed. (Englewood Cliffs, N.J.: Prentice-Hall, 1972).

[9]Thomas A. Murphy, "There are Clear Limits to the Growth of Government," *Vital Speeches of the Day*, vol. 42 (January 1, 1976).

[10]William J. McGill, "Peacemaking in an Adversary Society," *Vital Speeches of the Day*, vol. 42 (April 15, 1976).

[11]Although the use of logical arguments is advisable, the speaker should be cautioned that logic, *by itself*, may not be sufficient. Listeners sometimes tend to engage in "wishful thinking," that is, arguments are evaluated according to what they *want* to believe. Evidence for this tendency is reported by W. J. McGuire, "A Syllogistic Analysis of Cognitive Relationships," in C. I. Hovland and M. J. Rosenberg, eds., *Attitude Organization and Change* New Haven, Conn.; Yale University Press, 1960), pp. 65–111.

[12]S. E. Toulmin, *The Uses of Argument* (New York: Cambridge University Press, 1964). A more recent and expansive discussion of this model appears in Stephen Toulmin, Richard Rieke, and Allan Janik, *An Introduction to Reasoning* (New York: Macmillan, 1979).

[13]You are *especially* likely to encounter trouble with logical fallacies if your audience is not yet in agreement with your position, *and* if they have been informed about the nature of faulty reasoning. See R. Wood, J.J. Bradac, S. Barnhart, and E. Kraft, "The Effect of Learning about Techniques of Propaganda on Subsequent Reaction to Propagandistic Communications," *Speech Teacher*, 19 (1970), pp. 49–53.

[14]Max Black, "Fallacies," in Jerry M. Anderson and Paul J. Dovre, eds., *Readings in Argumentation* (Boston: Allyn and Bacon, Inc., 1968), pp. 301–311.

[15]It has been frequently demonstrated that a speaker is more effective if his or her proposition is related to the audiences' feelings. See M. Rosenberg, "An Analysis of Affective-Cognitive Consistency," in C. Hovland and M. Rosenberg, eds., *Attitude Organization and Change* (New Haven: Yale University Press, 1960), pp. 15–64. Similar studies are reviewed in C. A. Insko, *Theories of Attitude Change* (New York: Appleton-Century-Crofts, 1967).

[16]Quoted in John Hasling, *The Audience, The Message, The Speaker*, 2nd ed. (New York: McGraw-Hill, 1976), p. 79.

[17]A more thorough examination of message strategies used in TV commercials appears in *New Times*, December 1975.

[18]Irving L. Janis and Seymour Feshbach, "Effects of Fear-Arousing Communications," *Journal of Abnormal and Social Psychology*, 48 (1953), pp. 78–92. Numerous additional experiments have also indicated that high fear appeals may be ineffective in *some* circumstances. An insightful discussion of this research can be found in G. Cronkhite, *Persuasion: Speech and Behavioral Change* (Indianapolis: Bobbs-Merrill, 1969).

[19]Gary Cronkhite, *Communication and Awareness* (Menlo Park, Calif.: Cummings Publishing Co., 1976), pp. 212–213. © 1976 by the Benjamin/Cummings Publishing Company, formerly Cummings Publishing Company.

[20]The relationship between similarity and persuasiveness is developed in Ellen Berscheid and Elaine C. Walster, *Interpersonal Attraction* (Reading, Mass.: Addison-Wesley, 1969).

[21]Appeals to audience sympathy can be ineffective if overdone. People apparently like to believe in a "just world," or that we get what we deserve. Hence, there is a tendency to reject and/or blame those who suffer. See M. J. Lerner and C. Simmons, "Observer's Reaction to the 'Innocent Victim': Compassion or Rejection," *Journal of Personality and Social Psychology*, 4 (1966), pp. 203–210; M. J. Lerner and G. Matthews, "Reactions to Suffering of Others Under Conditions of Indirect Responsibility," *Journal of Personality and Social Psychology*, 5 (1967), pp. 319-325; and C. Jones and E. Aronson, "Attribution of Fault to a Rape Victim as a Function of Respectability of the Victim," *Journal of Personality and Social Psychology*, 26 (1973), pp. 415–419.

[22]James V. McConnell, *Understanding Human Behavior* (New York: Holt, Rinehart and Winston, 1974), p. 820.

[23]Research indicates that specific recommendations for audience action can increase the amount of attitude change obtained. See, for example, P. R. Biddle, "An Experimental Study of Ethos and Appeal for Overt Behavior in Persuasion," Doctoral Dissertation, University of Illinois, 1966; and H. Leventhal, R. Singer, and S. Jones, "Effects of Fear and Specificity of Recommendation upon Attitudes and Behavior," *Journal of Personality and Social Psychology*, 2 (1965), pp. 20–29.

[24]Reproduced from a manuscript of a speech given by Phillip L. Doughtie, University of New Hampshire, Merrimack Valley Branch, December 14, 1976.

Humor

This chapter derives from a final prediction about message strategy:

> *Some messages can be made more effective by being made humorous.* [1]

HUMOR

Understanding humor as a message strategy requires an understanding of entertainment. Entertainment derives from the Latin word *tenir*, meaning "to hold." Entertainment is anything that holds your audience's attention by making your message pleasant for them to listen to. Successful entertainment requires careful audience analysis. If you have ever seen an entertainer who was more interested in his message than in his audience, you what I mean by that. There's a little bistro near my home where relatively unknown folk singers are given a chance to perform. The other night a young singer got up on the makeshift stage there and began tuning his guitar. He had a difficult time because of the noise of the crowd. Finally he was ready, and he said into the microphone, "I'd like to start off with a song I wrote," but then he paused. There was no decrease in the crowd noise. So he said a little louder, "Could I have your attention please? I wrote this song and the lyrics are really important." The noise level stayed about the same. Finally the singer screamed out, *"Shut up, will you? How can I sing in all this noise?"*

His voice had that trembling, breaking quality that we associate with potential mass murderers. There was absolute silence for a moment, but then the noise started up again. The new noise was caused mostly by people in the audience asking each other, "What's with this guy? Who does he think he is?" The noise increased and the singer, after threatening his audience once or twice more, stomped off the stage, knocking over the microphone on his way.

The poor guy. He didn't understand an important truth about public communication: *It is the source's responsibility to entertain the receiver.* Respect has to be earned, and one symptom of that respect is attention. If the singer had understood that, he would have simply made his set as pleasant as possible. Audiences will pay attention to things they find pleasurable. That's why humor was invented. People will do almost anything to keep from missing a joke. They'll even pay attention.

Research suggests that humor is not appropriate for all messages (more on appropriateness below), but it does make a *dull* message more interesting, and therefore more effective.[2]

REQUIREMENTS FOR HUMOROUS ENTERTAINMENT

It is easiest to discuss humorous entertainment by borrowing examples from professional comedians as well as professional speakers. But a word of caution is appropriate here. The goal of this discussion is not to make you a professional entertainer. The hours are terrible.

Professionals are used as examples only because it pays to learn from the best.

You can learn a lot about humor by examining messages that are designed primarily to entertain. The most important features of this type of message are: (1) *levity*, (2) *originality*, and (3) *appropriateness*.

Levity

Levity is the quality of being light. "Funny" is not the key word in humor. "Light" is the key word. A speech to entertain is one that doesn't take itself altogether seriously. It deals with the serious in an absurd manner or with the absurd in a serious manner.

For example, marital strife, poverty, and religion are serious topics; but who can help but laugh when Flip Wilson tells his story about the wife of the poor minister who comes home with her third new dress of the week? "The devil made me buy this dress," she screeches. "He pulled a gun, and he threatened me, and he made me sign your name to a check . . ."[3] It is difficult to keep a straight face when that many frightening subjects are shown to be absurd.

Speakers often use levity to capture audience interest in a serious topic. Sam Nunn, the U.S. Senator from Georgia, recently spoke to the New York Militia Association on "Gearing Up to Deter Combat in Europe." Before he began his comments on this deadly-serious topic he managed to make light of both the Civil War and the Inauguration of President Carter:

> Few Southerners since the war of Northern Aggression—I believe you still call it the Civil War—have been accorded such gracious hospitality so far north of the Mason-Dixon line. Even the absence of mint juleps and boiled peanuts at this conference is an understandable indiscretion. Come January 20th [1977], we shall exact our revenge for this and other Yankee slights such as reconstruction and Sherman's march through Georgia. As one of my southern colleagues in the Senate recently observed: "We've finally got an opportunity to get a man in the White House without an accent."[4]

Senator Nunn then went on to relate "the recent unpleasantness known as the Civil War"[5] to his topic, and when he did he took his audience's attention with him.

Originality

Routines like Flip Wilson's "The devil made me do it" have become classics. Classic jokes, however, are not the most effective tactics for an amateur speaker seeking to entertain. For example, take Henny

Youngman—please.[6] It is funny when he says, "My grandson complains about headaches all the time. I tell him, Larry, when you get out of bed, feet first. . . ."[7] But that might not be funny if you said it. Anecdotes of your own about strange experiences, strange people, or unique insights into everyday occurrences are the best ingredients for a speech to entertain. "Original" in this sense does not mean "brand new." It means "firsthand" or "derived from the source." Take Bill Cosby's anecdote "Hofstra":

> The truth of the matter is that it didn't take much to play for Temple at the time that I was playing because we had lost twenty-seven games in a row, and we played against real weak teams . . . they all killed us. Especially Hofstra. Hofstra beat us 900 to nothing. In their street clothes. They wiped us out. Vassar wouldn't even play us, that's how bad we were. . . . So I'm going to give you some insight about what happens in a loser's locker room.
> We were gonna play against Hofstra . . . and when you play for a team like Temple you got nothing to do except pace up and down in the locker room and say, "Boy, I sure do hope I don't get hurt. I almost made a tackle last week. I must have been crazy. . . ."
> I played on the second team, which was actually the nut squad. These are the guys who can play, but they're afraid. They don't want to go out there. So they do nutty things, like put their helmet on sideways, look out through the ear hole; some guys got on scuba outfits, no shoes, and an ice skate. . . .[8]

Actually, the unpleasant feeling of facing overwhelming odds is one that we all encounter from time to time. It's a relief—and funny—to see that feeling burlesqued in this manner. But Cosby's story is funny because it is original. It is him. He hasn't borrowed it. But he hasn't just made it up, either. He's probably been telling the story, in some form, since his high school days. Each time he tells it he recognizes some new twist or phrase or facial expression that makes people laugh more, and he incorporates it into the anecdote. The anecdote becomes part of him. It just wouldn't be as effective for anyone else. There are two lessons here: (1) Original anecdotes are funny because they are best suited to the speaker, and (2) original anecdotes are funny because they aren't original in the sense of being "brand new." They are tested, tried, and true. When a comedian does a "bit" he knows it is funny. Comedians test their humor in all their interactions, and they don't get up in front of an audience with an unproved product. This second lesson is probably the most important one. Test out your anecdotes first.

Appropriateness

Humor must be appropriate to the audience, the speakers, and the occasion. One should be very careful telling Polish jokes to the Kasimir-Pulaski Social Group, or drunk jokes at an Alcoholics Anonymous meeting. George Carlin's takeoff on the news, for example, might not be funny to an audience in a war-torn country:

> . . . And to kind of wind up the news tonight we'll take a look at the *News Hostilities Scoreboard*—find out how we're treating each other around the world. According to the scoreboard we got four civil wars going on right now, two brush-fire wars, four vest-pocket wars, 9 wars of liberation, 2 police actions, 16 revolutions, 35 rebellions, 58 border clashes, 21 terrorist bombings, 36 retaliatory raids, 400 guerrilla operations, 95 commando strikes, 612 acts of sabotage, 237 cease-fire violations, 44 surprise attacks, 6 outside aggressions, 6 internal upheavals, 3 protective-reaction strikes, 10 counter insurgencies, 21 violent disturbances, 30 warlike acts, 906 hostile incidents, 10 arms races, 18 deliberate provocations, 61 threats to security, 9 dangerous escalations, 2 military confrontations, 6 belligerent moves, 17 reprisals, 3 powder kegs, 2 tinder boxes, and an ul-ti-i-ma-a-a-tum.[9]

Consider one more example. Consider how appropriate Woody Allen's "lecture" on "The Origin of Slang" would be for an audience of students studying any facet of human communication:

> How many of you have ever wondered where certain slang expressions come from? Like "She's the cat's pajamas," or "to take it on the lam." Neither have I. And yet for those who are interested in this sort of thing I have provided a brief guide to a few of the more interesting origins.

Unfortunately, time did not permit consulting any of the established works on the subject, and I was forced to either obtain the information from friends or fill in certain gaps by using my own common sense.

Take, for instance, the expression "to eat humble pie." During the reign of Louis the Fat, the culinary arts flourished in France to a degree unequaled anywhere. So obese was the French monarch that he had to be lowered onto the throne with a winch and packed into the seat itself with a large spatula. A typical dinner (according to DeRochet) consisted of a thin crepe appetizer, some parsley, an ox, and custard. Food became the court obsession, and no other subject could be discussed under penalty of death. Members of a decadent aristocracy consumed incredible meals and even dressed as foods. DeRochet tells us that M. Monsant showed up at the coronation as a wiener, and Etienne Tisserant received papal dispensation to wed his favorite codfish. Desserts grew until the minister of justice suffocated trying to eat a seven-foot "Jumbo Pie." Jumbo pie soon became *jumble* pie and "to eat a jumble pie" referred to any kind of humiliating act. When the Spanish seamen heard the word *jumble,* they pronounced it "humble," although many preferred to say nothing and simply grin.[10]

SOME TECHNIQUES OF HUMOR

There are many techniques of humor (short of just falling down) that you can use to make your own experiences or insights entertaining. Some basic techniques are discussed below.

Overstatement

Overstatement (exaggeration) is one of the most effective humorous techniques. You could begin a speech something like this:

In order to prepare today's speech I read 27 books, interviewed 36 experts, ran 14 carefully controlled experiments, and surveyed the entire population of Tanganyika. I worked on the speech for over a year, taking only short breaks for sustenance and catnaps. During that time I have lost considerable weight as well as my entire life's savings, and my wife has run off with a stevedore from San Diego. I am proud to tell you, though, that it was all worth it, for today I am fully prepared to explain to you *Why Ice Floats.* . . .

A speaker recently overstated the condition of Washington, D.C., this way:

As municipalities go—Washington is going. . . . It has been said that Washington has more people out of work than any

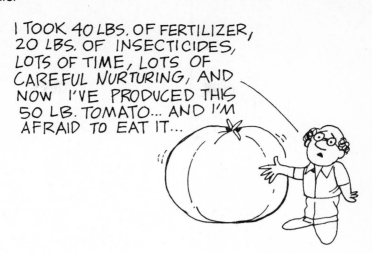

I TOOK 40 LBS. OF FERTILIZER, 20 LBS. OF INSECTICIDES, LOTS OF TIME, LOTS OF CAREFUL NURTURING, AND NOW I'VE PRODUCED THIS 50 LB. TOMATO... AND I'M AFRAID TO EAT IT...

other city in the country, but fortunately most of them are employed by the federal government. A recent survey showed that 10 percent of the population was on welfare, 30 percent on unemployment, and the rest on tranquilizers.[11]

Understatement

Understatement (representing something as less than what it is) is another common humorous technique:

I had a difficult time investigating this topic. I tried researching it at _____ [12] library, but it was closed. Someone had checked out the book.

The chairman of the board of Exxon Corporation used secondhand understatement recently in a speech before the Economic Club of Detroit:

I promise to be brief. I'm told that Mrs. Frankfurter used to complain about the lengthy speeches the Justice made. "There are two things wrong with Felix's speeches," she once said. "One is that he always strays from the subject. The second is that he always returns to it." Well, I'll try to stick to the point, at least.[13]

The fact is, any library has more than one book, and Justice Frankfurter was a better speaker than Mrs. Frankfurter would have us believe. However, understatement was used to make both examples funny.

Incongruities

Incongruities (statements that are out of place or inconsistent) can also be used to inject humor into a speech. Herbert S. Richey, the chairman of the board of directors of the United States Chamber of Commerce, recently began a speech with an incongruity:

> Thank you for that most generous introduction. I'd like to have a copy, if one is available . . . so I can show it to my wife occasionally.[14]

Elreta Alexander, a district court judge, used the same type of humor in her address at a high school commencement. After thanking her audience for a warm welcome, she said:

> Viewing you in your radiance, I am impelled to respond as did a witness in court after I repeatedly admonished him to look at the jury as he testified. I finally ordered, "Mr. Witness, will you please address the jury!" He nodded, turned to the jury and said, "Howdy."
> Howdy, all you beautiful people. Your presence is encouraging.[15]

Thomas A. Vanderslice, an executive of General Electric Company, recently borrowed an incongruity from Casey Stengel:

> I am told that Casey Stengel, on reaching one of his supernumerary birthdays, was asked, looking back on his long life in baseball, what would he have done differently.
> The "Old Perfesser" thought a bit, and said: "If I'd have known I was going to live so long, I'd have taken better care of myself."[16]

Incongruities, like any other form of humor, must relate directly to your topic to be effective in a speech. For example, Vanderslice followed his anecdote about Casey Stengel with a smooth transition into his topic:

> My remarks today are dedicated to the proposition that this country, and our form of government, will be around for a while yet, and we'd better take good care of what we have.[17]

Word Plays

A play on words allows you to create humor by manipulating language. One way to do this is to place an unexpected ending on a familiar expression:

> Where there's a will, there's a lawsuit.

Another way is to change a word or two in a familiar expression:

> You can lead a man to college, but you can't make him think.

You can also rearrange words in some nonsensical way:

> I showed that wiseguy; I hit him right in the fist with my eye.

A *pun* is a special type of play on words. It uses a word or expression to emphasize different meanings (such as when you introduce a dentist as a man who looks down in the mouth) or uses a word that sounds like another word (a girl's best friend is her mutter.).

Puns should be handled carefully in a speech. They are usually clever rather than funny. They "fool" people rather than entertain. They make people groan, rather than laugh. Because of this, they are a high risk. For example, the punch line of the following anecdote relies entirely on the effect of five puns strung together mercilessly at the end:

> There was once a scientist who won a million-dollar government grant to see what would happen when a mammal mated with its own tenth-generation offspring. The first step in this research was to find a mammal that could survive ten generations and still be interested in mating. The scientist had heard of a type of porpoise that lived in a lake in central Africa. The porpoise reportedly lived for so long that the natives called it "the whale that will not die." The scientist went to Africa, where he was told that the immortal whale was considered sacred and that he would have to wear an equally sacred myna bird on his shoulder to ward off evil spirits. He hired a native guide for the 500-mile trek into the wilderness. When he had almost reached his destination he found his path blocked by a dead lion. The native guide warned the scientist not to step over the animal, since it belonged to the state. The scientist stepped over it anyway, and was immediately arrested for *transporting a myna across state lions for immortal porpoises.*

Some audiences might be angry with you if you took that much time for a pun. People have a tendency to think that puns are the lowest form of humor, unless they think of them first. Still, puns can be used sparingly for humorous effect as long as they do not interfere with your message.

Satire

Satire (humor based on the exposure of human vice or folly) is considered a much higher form of humor.[18] One example of this technique is Lily Tomlin's characterization of "Ernestine of the Telephone Company." Ernestine, harassing customers between snorts and "ringie-dingies," exposes the impersonal treatment we sometimes receive from public utility companies. When Ernestine tells one customer that the phone company has been recording his phone conversations because he owes them $23.64, she responds to his protests, "Privileged information? (snort) . . . Oh, that's so cute. No, no, no, you're dealing with the telephone company. . . . We are omnipotent."[19] Later, Ernestine declares to another customer, "When you anger me you anger the phone company and all the power necessary to tie up your lines for the next 50 years!"[20]

Satire was used recently by the U.S. Commissioner of Food and Drugs to begin his speech on government control of drug information:

> Those of you who read columnist George Will may have recently seen his list of the three least credible sentences in the English language.
>
> They are: First, "Your check is in the mail."
>
> Second, "Of *course* I'll respect you just as much in the morning."
>
> And finally, "I'm from the government and I'm here to help you."

Lee Loevinger used satire when discussing the Watergate scandal:

> You may recall that a while back a fellow named Rexford or Robert or Richard Nixon, or something like that, used to stay at the White House when he was in Washington as he traveled between California and Florida. One day when he was out of town, somebody started a rumor that he had taken the original copy of the U.S. Constitution. Nobody around Washington had used it for quite a while so they couldn't tell at first whether it was missing. However, a couple of Washington *Post* reporters printed a rumor that Nixon was going to trade the Constitution for the Magna Carta which he liked better than the Constitution. This got Congress excited because it was trying to make its own deal with the British for the Magna Carta. As a result, Congress voted to terminate Nixon as caretaker at the White House and hire Jerry Ford.
>
> After all this, it turned out that Nixon was trying to sell the Constitution to the New York *Times* for a million dollars. The *Times* was seriously considering the deal because it was running low on stolen government documents to publish. However, the *Times* finally turned the deal down because the editors decided that nobody was interested in reading the Constitution these days anyway.[21]

Thus were investigative reporting, executive privilege, and public apathy all satirized in two short spoken paragraphs. It should be apparent from reading that passage that satire, as much as any other type of humor, has to be handled carefully. It has to be appropriate to the speaker, the audience, and the occasion.

No matter what type of humor you use, you should follow three rules during your presentation:

1. Do not, under any circumstances, *try* to be funny. Some of the best humor is accidental. Be light, be original, and be appropriate, but let the "funny" take care of itself.
2. If you do get a laugh, don't step on it. Wait until it has hit its

peak and is beginning to subside before you resume speaking.
3. If you don't get a laugh, keep going as though nothing had happened.

SAMPLE SPEECH

The need to infuse humor into even formal speeches is well accepted. The head speech writer for Gerald Ford, during his presidency, was a comedy writer named Bob Orben. Another political leader, Adlai Stevenson, was known for his ability to inject humor into a speech. When he conceded defeat in the 1952 presidential election, he said he felt like a little boy who had stubbed his toe in the dark: "It hurts too much to laugh," he said at the time, "but I'm too old to cry."[22] He was soon making others laugh, though, as shown in his next speech before the Gridiron Club of Chicago.

Adlai Stevenson
A FUNNY THING HAPPENED TO ME
ON THE WAY TO THE WHITE HOUSE*

Some Comments	The Speech
A play on words, featuring a surprise ending to the familiar, "A funny thing happened to me on the way here tonight."	A funny thing happened to me on the way to the White House!
(Dwight Eisenhower.) Understatement A play on words; the usual expression is "snatching victory from the jaws of defeat."	The fact was, of course, that the General was so far ahead we never even saw him. I was happy to hear that I had even placed second. But no one will say, I trust, that I snatched defeat from the jaws of victory.
(Thomas E. Dewey of New York.) A play on words	Which reminds me that four years ago, occupying the seat I occupy tonight, was another great governor—excuse me, the governor of another great state—some say the second greatest state in the Union. What just happened to me had just happened to him. In fact, it had just happened to him for the second time.

*Reprinted by permission of Harold Ober Associates, Inc. All rights reserved.

Some Comments

The Speech

Satire: Dewey had campaigned vigorously for Eisenhower, and had been offered a Cabinet post by him. A play on words: changing words in a familiar statement.

But did he despair? He did not. He said to himself—if I may take a newspaperman's license and tell you what a man says to himself—he said: "If I cannot be President myself, I can at least make somebody else President." Which, blast his merry heart, he proceeded to do. Look at him now. He's as contented as the cat that swallowed the canary, or should I say, the Cabinet.

Satire: Stevenson had been accused repeatedly of being too much of an intellectual.

At that Gridiron dinner just four years ago, the newly elected governor of Illinois sat down there with you common people—which reminds me that I rather enjoy talking over your heads—at last! I was happy and carefree and had nothing to worry about; nothing except the organization of a new administration to clean up the state of Illinois after the long years of the usual Republican misrule.

Understatement.

Overstatement.

Incongruity.

I, a Democrat, had just been elected governor by the largest majority ever received in Republican Illinois. And here I am, four years later, just defeated by the largest majority ever received in Democratic America.

I had not planned it that way. I had wished to continue as governor of Illinois, there to erect a shining temple of administrative purity and political probity. But the gods decreed otherwise—after meeting in the Chicago Stockyards. Mindful of the Chinese maiden's philosophical acceptance of unwanted and aggressive attentions, I concluded to accept my fate gallantly and joyfully.

Site of the 1952 Democratic Convention.

Now I content myself that it is all for the best. After all, didn't Socrates say that the duty of a man of real principle is to stay out of politics? So you see I'm delighted that the sovereign people have put an even higher value on my principles than I did.

Understatement.

I am happy that almost 27 million voted for me. I was a little baffled by the emergence of that word "egghead" to describe the more intelligensiac members of that lunatic fringe who thought I was going to win. I am happy to note you have refrained from saying of the eggheads that the yolk was on them.

Overstatement.

Pun.

Some Comments	The Speech
Overstatement	I enjoyed the campaign—in spots. There were times, I confess, when I was afraid I wouldn't die, times when I felt I wouldn't do it to a dog. Let me add, by the way, that, like every red-blooded American patriot, I own a dog. It was not a campaign contribution. And I think the General would say to me that there are times when he wishes he was in my shoes—you see, I had them fixed.
Satire, referring to Nixon's 1952 Checkers Address. A widely circulated photograph of Stevenson showed him with a hole in his shoe. His supporters made his trademark. A play on words; Reference to a popular song "Bewitched, Bothered and Bewildered."	As to my future. Well, there are those like the man who changed the sign on his car after the election from "Switched to Stevenson" to "Switched, Bothered and Bewildered," who feel that I should devote my classic talents to the welfare of mankind by frequent talking.
	Then there is another smaller group who insist that God and/or the election has appointed me the scourge of the Republican Party. And finally there is the much smaller group that feels that it is not wholly unworthy or improper to earn a living. My sons are numbered in the latter group.
Understatement. Play on words.	But despite anything that you may have read or written, there are some plans of action that I have definitely rejected. I have declined an invitation to become president of the National Association of Gagwriters. And I will not go into vaudeville. It is equally definite that I will not become manager of the Washington Senators—I mean Clark Griffith's, not Mr. Taft's.
Satire.	I have great faith in the people. As to their wisdom, well, Coca-Cola still outsells champagne. They may make mistakes. They do sometimes. But given time they correct their mistakes—at two- or four-year intervals.
Satire.	I have faith in the people—and in their chosen leaders: men of high purpose, good will and humble hearts, men quite prepared to stand aside when the time comes and allow even more humble men to take over.

SUMMARY

This chapter dealt with humor. Being humorous is one way to make a dull presentation more interesting.

Humorous entertainment has three requirements: (1) It should be "light," although not necessarily "funny"; (2) it should be original, although not necessarily "brand new"; and (3) it should be appropriate to both you and your audience. There are many techniques for humor, including overstatement (exaggeration), understatement (representing something as less than what it is), incongruities (statements that are out of place or inconsistent), word plays (manipulated language), and satire (pointing out vice or folly).

QUESTIONS for DISCUSSION

1. Humor can, at least in some cases, be effective in a speech. The problem is, what will an audience consider humorous? Do you agree with the definition of humor as "a sudden perception of incongruity accompanied by a sense of well-being"? Explain your answer making use of examples.
2. The chapter advises you not to *try* to be funny, but to "let the 'funny' take care of itself." What is your interpretation of this statement? Do you agree or disagree with this advice? Why or why not?
3. Humor is a device that can be used when a speaker is trying to capture audience attention on a serious topic. Do you agree that such a tactic can be effective, or is humor sometimes counterproductive? Cite examples to support your answer.

PROBES

1. Suppose you were the master of ceremonies for a banquet in your home town, and that you have the money and the influence to invite any famous comedian. Considering the audience and the occasion, which humorists would you want to speak? Why? Which people would you not consider as entertainers? Why?
2. Consider the comics who make you laugh the most. In what ways do they exhibit the characteristics of effective humor (levity, originality, and appropriateness) mentioned in this chapter? Cite examples. Are there other aspects of their humor, not mentioned in the text, that you find noteworthy?
3. Anecdotes that are original are usually the most effective. Think about the topic for your next speech. Based upon your own experiences, acquaintances, or insights, what anecdotes might be original for *you?* What anecdotes do you think are too unoriginal to use?
4. To understand further the idea that anecdotes must be original to the speaker, think about two comedians you enjoy, and consider the nature of their humor. Which anecdotes suitable for one of these people would be inappropriate for the other? (For example, what elements of George Carlin's humor would not be appropriate for Bill Cosby?) Explain your answer.

5. As you examine the topic for your next speech, decide which techniques of humor would be appropriate and effective for your classroom audience. What techniques might be appropriate for a different audience such as the Rotary Club? Explain your reasons for any differences you cite.

NOTES

[1]Dorothy Markiewicz, "Effects of Humor on Persuasion," *Sociometry,* 37, 3 (September 1974), pp. 407–422.

[2]Ibid.

[3]Flip Wilson, "The Devil Made Me Buy This Dress," Little David Records, Los Angeles, Calif.

[4]Sam Nunn, "Gearing up to Deter Combat in Europe; the Long and the Short of It," *Vital Speeches of the Day,* vol. 42 (November 1, 1976).

[5]Ibid.

[6]For those of you born too late, this clever phrase refers to Youngman's most classic line: "Take my wife—please." Like most humor, if you have to explain it, it's not funny.

[7]"Take My Wife—Please," *Newsweek,* February 2, 1976, p. 75.

[8]Bill Cosby, "More of the Best of Bill Cosby," Warner Bros. Records., Inc., Burbank, Calif. By permission of Bill Cosby.

[9]George Carlin, "An Evening with Wally Londo Featuring Bill Slaszo," Little David Records, Los Angeles, Calif., 1975. By permission of George Carlin. Carlin recites his scoreboard in the rapid staccato of a play-by-play sports announcer, up until the final three items, which are sung to the tune of the last line of "The Twelve Days of Christmas."

[10]Woody Allen, *Without Features* (New York: Random House, 1975), pp. 206–207. By permission of Random House Inc.

[11]Lee Loevinger, "Is There Intelligent Life in Washington?" *Vital Speeches of the Day,* vol. 43 (January 1, 1977).

[12]Fill in the name of your school's library when you read this.

[13]C. C. Garvin, Jr., "Recognizing Today's Realities: Where is the U.S. Energy Policy?" *Vital Speeches of the Day,* vol. 43 (December 1, 1976).

[14]Herbert S. Richey, "The Theologians of Freedom," *Vital Speeces of the Day,* vol. 43 (December 1, 1976).

[15]Elreta Alexander, "Reflections for a Graduate," *Vital Speeches of the Day,* vol. 42 (August 1, 1976).

[16]Thomas A. Vanderslice, "The Vital Need for Technology and Jobs," *Vital Speeches of the Day,* vol. 43 (December 15, 1976).

[17]Ibid.

[18]Experimental evidence into the effects of satire is somewhat inconsistent. There is some evidence to suggest that if an audience is initially favorable to a speaker's position, both the message and the speaker will be evaluated more favorably when satire is employed. See L. Powell, "Satire and Speech Trait Evaluation," *Western Journal of Speech Communication,* 41 (Spring 1977), pp. 117–125. The speaker should be cautioned, however, that if listeners tend to be neutral or in opposition, satire is either at best ineffective, or at worst, counterproductive. See D. Berlo and H. Kumata, "The Investigator: The Impact of a Satirical Radio Drama," *Journalism Quarterly,* 33 (1956), pp. 287–298; C. R. Gruner, "An Experimental Study of Satire as Persuasion," *Speech Monographs,* 32 (1956), pp. 149–153; and N. Vidmar and M. Ro-

keach, "Archie Bunker's Bigotry: A Study in Selective Perception and Exposure," *Journal of Communication,* 24 (1974), pp. 36–47.

[19]Ellen Cohn, "Lily Tomlin: Not Just a Funny Girl," *New York Times Magazine,* June 6, 1976, p. 91.

[20]Ibid.

[21]Lee Loevinger, "Is There Intelligent Life in Washington?" *Vital Speeches of the Day,* vol 43 (January 1, 1977).

[22]"Good Loser," *Time,* November 10, 1952, p. 25.

FOUR

Small Group Communication

Many public speaking classes involve one or more group assignments. Sometimes these are group research projects, and other times group presentations or group discussions. Even if your class does not include such an assignment, you may still be involved in group-type work in the criticism and discussion of classroom speeches. This final section provides a brief overview of some of the concepts that are essential to small group communication.

12

Small Group Communication

This chapter is based on a final prediction:

Group work will tend to be more productive when group members are aware of the underlying dynamics of group interaction.

SMALL GROUP COMMUNICATION

In Florida recently, a group of boys collected some neighborhood pets—cats and small dogs, mostly—and fed them to an alligator in a nearby swamp. Later, after their misdeed was discovered, the boys insisted that they didn't know *why* they had done it, but each was pretty sure that he would not have done it if he had been alone.

About the same time, a movie producer, a director, and two writers were locked up in a motel outside Los Angeles. They had been brainstorming for three straight days. Piles of crumpled paper and half-eaten room-service sandwiches were everywhere. But at the end of three days, they emerged with a script that they felt was destined to become a motion-picture classic. Each knew that he or she could not have done it alone.

In Senate chambers in Washington, D.C., and in corporate headquarters in New York City, similar groups meet every day. They do so to take advantage of the phenomenon of *group process*,[1] which allows people sometimes to accomplish more by working together than the same number of people could accomplish working alone.[2]

GROUPS IN SOCIETY

Because of the potential effectiveness of group work, we have come to live in a group-oriented society. Groups are everywhere. We work, play, solve problems, and make presentations in groups. Something special happens when people interact in a group. Sometimes this is a good thing, and sometimes it is a bad thing; the difference usually depends upon the quality of communication within the group. One ethical, skillful person can sway a lynch mob, and one boy who knows right from wrong can save neighborhood pets from an alligator, if they communicate well enough.

The skills that you use in preparing and presenting a group assignment are skills that will prove useful throughout your life.

CREATIVITY IN GROUPS

One reason that group work is so popular is that it is known to enhance individual creativity. In fact, so many groups meet for the purpose of enhancing creativity that hard-core advocates of group process insist that "there is no such thing as a creative individual. There are only creative groups."[3] I won't go that far, but I will admit that a group can be a stimulating setting for creativity. That is the basis for group brainstorming, which was mentioned in Chapter 4. And even when groups are formed for reasons other than stimulating creativity, they are still most effective when they allow creativity to operate. This is because all groups are involved in some way with *problem-solving*. The problem might be some great social malaise or it might be simply sharing information or practicing group interaction. All of these are problems that might require creative solutions. When groups *don't* need to be creative, they are usually involved in a task that could be handled just as well by one or more individuals working alone.[4] (Such tasks would include those that require high-quality technical expertise and those for which there is only one "correct" answer.)

GROUP PHASES

In Chapter 3 it was mentioned that creativity is a process with four phases: *preparation, incubation, illumination,* and *verification*. These phases become very distinct in group interaction, in which they are called the *orientation, conflict, emergence,* and *reinforcement* stages.[5]

Orientation

This is the "preparation" stage of group creativity. In the orientation stage the group members get acquainted and agree upon such things as group goals and methods. It is essential that all members of the group understand its purpose and the way it will operate. In a public speaking class, a group's purpose might be to prepare and present a discussion on inflation. During the orientation phase, the procedure that will be used to fulfill this purpose will be hammered out: how long each person will speak, what they will speak on, and so on. Also, the rules of the group—when, where, and how often it will meet, who will accept which responsibilities, and so on—will be made clear.

Conflict

This is the stage in which opinions are expressed and debated. In an effective conflict stage, members will listen to each other's ideas, and those ideas will stimulate them on to new ideas. Thus the "conflict" stage of group process is the "incubation" stage of group creativity.

In the example above, in which a group meets to prepare and present a discussion on the topic of inflation, each group member would bring in completed research on inflation and share it with the rest of the group. Each member would expand his or her understanding of his own material by relating it to the material his fellow members present.

Emergence

This is the phase in which understanding, decision, and agreement begin to emerge. In other words, this is when the creative group will experience "illumination."

In the example above, the group members would begin to see how their individual presentations fit together. They would begin to organize their talks so they flow smoothly with transitions from one member's presentation to the next, with an overall introduction and conclusion that ties everything together. Themes, main ideas, and insights surface during group "illumination."

Reinforcement

This is the phase in which the group agrees upon what it has accomplished and "verifies" its creative illumination. In the example above, "verification" would probably be accomplished as the group practices its final presentation. It is at this time that the "rough edges" of the presentation will be smoothed over.

These stages appear in groups that meet for any type of problem-solving, as well as the preparation of a discussion. No matter what the purpose of the group, creativity should be encouraged by giving each of these phases time to operate. We often cut the orientation phase short because it seems wasteful. "All right," we say, "let's cut the small talk and get down to work." We sometimes cut the conflict stage short because it seems unfriendly to express and defend ideas. "Let's not fight," we say, assuming that conflict is always detrimental (which it is not). We sometimes rush to the emergence phase out of a desire to finish the task, and we sometimes just touch on reinforcement—that is, after the first solution emerges we jump on it and say, "That's good, let's do it," without considering other options.

To encourage group creativity I would suggest the following, as time permits. Stay in the orientation phase until all group members seem comfortable with one another and agree on group goals. Then, stay in the conflict phase as long as innovative ideas are being expressed and defended. When the ideas become redundant, summarize them and push on for emergence or illumination. When the final product emerges from the group work, stay in the reinforcement phase until all members seem comfortable with that product and with their part in carrying it out. Don't be afraid to back-pedal into an earlier phase, if necessary. These are not lock-step phases, and each group will experience its own variations.

GROUP ROLES

The suggestions above on encouraging group creativity are not only for the designated "group leader." All members of a group will take on various roles that will help move that group toward the completion of its goals. Different theorists list different group roles,[6] but for our purposes here we could say that they boil down to three: *starting* roles, *continuity* roles, and *quality-control* roles. Each of these roles is further broken down according to two different processes that occur within a group: the *task process* and the *social process*. The task process is the series of steps that lead to the fulfillment of the group's work, and the social process involves how the members feel—their feelings of satisfaction with the group and with their own performance within it.

The roles that the group members take on are not exclusive. One member might perform several roles within a group, and from time to time those roles might change. Also, several members might perform the same role simultaneously. No matter how they evolve, all task and social roles are necessary to the progress of the group.

Process Starters

Process starters might be *task* starters or *social climate* starters. Task starters may give, or ask someone else to give, the facts, ideas, or opinions that are necessary to start working on the task. They may propose goals or make suggestions on how to proceed. They are the first to focus the group into the task at hand.

Social process starters help make the individual members comfortable. They will encourage people to participate, and attempt to build team spirit. They might ease tension during the orientation phase by joking or just by being open and friendly. An effective social process starter will often propose an entertaining approach to the group work.

Process Continuity

Task continuity people keep the ball rolling. They are the people who stimulate the group when energy is low, summarize related ideas and major points, and diagnose problems the group encounters in reaching its goals. They coordinate ideas and suggestions by showing similarities and relationships among ideas. Above all else, they suggest ways to keep going.

Social continuity people are tension relievers. They will help members communicate their feelings, and they help resolve conflict by promoting open discussion. If all else fails, they might joke or make light of a dysfunctional conflict (discussed below) to move the group beyond it. Social continuity people believe in keeping the group going by keeping the members happy.

Quality Control

Quality control people help the group work *efficiently* toward its goals. They are less concerned with forward movement (the continuity person's concern) than with the *direction* (that is, quality) of that movement.

Task quality control people evaluate ideas and compare them with group goals. They test the practicality of ideas. They evaluate alternative solutions, and they apply them to real situations.

Social quality control people observe and evaluate the emotional climate of the group. They ask members how they feel about the progress of the group, and they observe nonverbal indications of boredom and/or dissatisfaction (such as yawns, vacant stares, and impatient finger-drumming). They identify these problems when they see them, and they will deal with them even if it means taking a break from task-oriented work.

Group Roles as Distributed Leadership

Group roles are often referred to as *distributed leadership* roles, because they emerge when leadership is shared. Shared leadership increases member commitment and satisfaction. In some cases, it increases group output. It is therefore considered a good thing to have.

There are two ways to share leadership. One is to have no designated leader, and the other is to have a designated leader who is willing to share responsibility. Since most groups have designated leaders (that is, leaders chosen by the group or by an outside authority), it is a good idea to examine traditional styles and responsibilities of group leadership.

TRADITIONAL LEADERSHIP STYLES

Authoritarian Leadership

Traditionally, three leadership styles are identified. The first is authoritarian leadership, which is the "I'm the boss so do as I say" style. The authoritarian leader is concerned mostly with efficiency—getting the job done as quickly and with as little wasted effort as possible—and therefore seeks compliance rather than commitment from the other group members.

Laissez-Faire Leadership

The second leadership style is the permissive or laissez-faire style of leadership. This type of leader does not guide the group in any way.

The laissez-faire leader sometimes relinquishes leadership responsibility in favor of being "just another member" or, even more passively, just an observer of the group. This encourages spontaneity among group members, but often leads to disorganized and confusing group meetings.

Democratic Leadership

The third style is known as democratic leadership. The democratic leader encourages all members to contribute and interact, while at the same time guiding them toward the group goal. At its best, democratic leadership will be just as efficient as authoritarian leadership and will stimulate spontaneity just as well as laissez-faire leadership. Because of this, it is considered the preferred type of leadership in most speech classes; still, you should recognize that the other styles have their place. Military units are still most comfortable with authoritarian leadership, and therapy groups that attempt to have members "come out of their shells" are most effective when handled by a laissez-faire leader.

TRADITIONAL LEADERSHIP FUNCTIONS

Designated leaders are well advised to share leadership responsibility in the group. Still, by accepting the title of "leader" they accept the responsibility of making sure that certain things get done. These things include the following:

Traffic Control

Traditionally, the leader takes on the responsibility of regulating *who* talks, *when*, and for *how long*. Part of traffic control involves encouraging participation from all members; therefore, if one member tends to monopolize the group's time, the leader is expected to tactfully inhibit that member in some way. (The leader might say, "That's a good idea, Fred, and your anecdote about summer camp certainly proves it. But let's see what some of the others think.") And if another member doesn't contribute in any way, the leader is expected to bring that member out. Sometimes this requires a sensitivity to nonverbal cues. Members who want to speak might not say so, specifically. They might just look puzzled or exasperated. At such times those members should be specifically invited to speak. ("Did you have a question, George?" or "Martha, did you want to add something to that?")

Sometimes traffic control is enhanced by the physical arrangement of the group. People sitting across from each other, for example, will tend to interact more. And people physically isolated from the group—such as two members in the back of the room, alone—will tend to form a "clique group" and interact with themselves rather than with the rest of the group. A circle is considered the ideal physical arrangement for group interaction.

Conflict Resolution

When conflict becomes *dysfunctional*, the leader is expected to help the group move beyond it. Some conflicts are functional; arguments over ideas and opinions that are leading to increased understanding, for example, are good. But other conflicts stifle group activity. For example, if two group members begin arguing over who did the most work in the last group they both belonged to, the leader might have to step in and say, "Let's not dwell on past history. This is a new group, and a new opportunity for success."

Record and Review Progress

The leader stresses progress toward goals, and periodically reviews that progress. ("So far we've accomplished _____ , _____ , and _____ . According to the goals we've agreed upon, we still have to accomplish _____ .")

Establish and Maintain an Agenda

The leader organizes an agenda, which is a plan of group activities. Enough needs to be said about agendas that they deserve their own section.

THE AGENDA

Establishing the Agenda

To make sure that a group moves toward its goals, an agenda should be planned out in advance. For example, if you have an assignment to give a group presentation, your agenda for your first group meeting might look something like this:

1. Introduce group members
   A. Areas of interest
   B. Areas of expertise
2. Establish group goals
   A. Requirements for assignment
   B. Norms for the group (how often we'll meet, time limits for meetings, and so on)
3. Choose topic for presentation
4. Discuss topic
   A. Division of topic
   B. Division of labor for group members
5. Explore avenues of research
   A. Library research
   B. Interviews
   C. Surveys/experimentation

Organizing the Agenda

As can be seen in the example above, an agenda is organized according to the principles of outlining (division, coordination, and order) as discussed in Chapter 5. All the necessary activity is divided, grouped, and ordered for effect. We often do that naturally. If you ever planned a party with a group of friends, you will remember facing a list of problems such as this:

Who gets the beer?
Who gets the tap?
Who gets the ice?
Who gets the potato chips?
What band should we get?
Should we, in fact, get a band?

When should we have this party?
Where should we have it?
How many people should we invite?
How should we distribute invitations?
Should we have any other food?
Should we have any other drinks?
What about other entertainment?
Who pays for all this stuff?
How much will it be?
Is it worth all this trouble?

And so on.

Chances are that if your party ever got off the planning board it was because someone organized that list according to the principles of division, coordination, and order. If they did, the result probably would have been an agenda that looked like this:

I. The basics
   A. When—date and time
   B. Where—place to be held
   C. Who—do we invite
   D. How—to pay for it
II. Refreshments
   A. Beer
   B. Tap
   C. Ice
   D. Munchies
      1. Chips
      2. Dip
   E. Other
III. Entertainment
   A. Band
   B. Other

With an arrangement like that, you can take care of one problem at a time and be done with it.

The Standard Agenda

Different group situations will require different agendas. One list of activities, however, is based on John Dewey's process of reflective thinking and is known as a *standard agenda*.[7] This agenda can be used as a model for many types of problem-solving groups. It looks like this:

1. Definition of problem. Included under this step might be the identification of the group's goals: "This group will present a discussion of American foreign aid and how it might be made an effective part of our foreign policy."

2. Analysis of the problem. The background, causes, and effects of the problem are discussed. The problem might be broken up into subproblems at this stage. Criteria for solutions are determined. For example, the group might determine that their suggestions for the improvement of foreign aid must be practical in light of our recent relationships and subsequent foreign policy problems with the following countries: Iran, Nicaragua, Mexico, and Cuba.

3. Proposing solutions. For the example above, group members might suggest that American foreign aid should be made contingent upon free elections, constitutional reforms, human rights, clean government, and the willingness of countries to repay debts to the International Monetary Fund.

4. Testing solutions against criteria for solutions. The group's suggestions would be tested against their practicality in dealing with Iran, Nicaragua, Mexico, and Cuba.

5. Selection of final solutions. Those solutions that pass the test of your criteria will be the ones you present in your final presentation.

Hidden Agendas

Organizing group work around stated agendas helps keep *hidden agendas* from interfering with group efficiency. Hidden agendas are plans, usually based on individual needs, that are not discussed openly. Examples of hidden agendas include one member's plan for revenge against another member. You can't always stop hidden agendas, but you can operate efficiently in spite of them if you have a stated agenda to keep the group on the track.

MAKING GROUP PRESENTATIONS

The preceding discussion refers to groups that are working to get something done, such as problem-solving or the preparation of a group presentation. These groups generally meet in private, but when their work is complete their final presentation is made publicly. A specific format is helpful in a public presentation. The most common formats are *formal* and *informal panel discussions*, either one of which could be followed by an *audience forum*.[8]

The Informal Panel Discussion

In an informal panel discussion, the participants are prepared to be knowledgeable on their topic, but they do not make formal presentations. The atmosphere of an informal panel discussion encourages interaction and spontaneity; participants often interrupt each other and exchange heated comments. They are often on a first-name basis with one another, so they might joke occasionally also. In spite of the informality, this type of panel will often meet to discuss serious matters, such as community planning.

After a panel discussion the audience may be invited to ask questions and make comments to the panelists. At that point the panel discussion becomes a *forum*.

The suggested procedure for an informal panel discussion is as follows:

1. The chairperson introduces the topic and the panel members.
2. The chairperson then poses a question to one of the panel members.
3. All members discuss the question informally.
4. The chairperson "controls traffic," making sure that each panelist is given a chance to complete his or her thought before the next panelist begins speaking, asking specific questions when the interaction seems to falter.
5. The chairperson clarifies, summarizes, restates, or paraphrases ideas if necessary.
6. At the end of the allotted time, the chairperson summarizes the discussion.
7. If a forum is scheduled, the audience is invited to ask questions or comment. The chairperson controls the audience "traffic," also.

The Formal Panel Discussion

A formal panel discussion is one in which each participant gives a prepared presentation. The suggested procedure for a formal panel is as follows:

1. The chairperson introduces the topic and the panel members in the order in which they will speak.
2. The members then make their formal presentations. Although they may refer to each other, they do not interact during the presentations.
3. The chairperson generally supplies transitions from one participant to the next. However, in one variation the members supply the transitions themselves as part of their conclu-

sions. This variation, if prepared carefully, can result in an exceptionally smooth presentation.
4. The chairperson, or the final speaker, summarizes the discussion. If scheduled, the forum is then begun.

SUMMARY

We live in a society in which group work is popular because of its efficiency in problem-solving and its stimulation of creativity.

A group will go through a series of phases in which orientation, conflict, emergence, and reinforcement occur. These phases correspond closely to the phases of creativity. Creativity is encouraged when enough time is allotted to each of these phases.

Members in a group perform various functions, or roles. These roles could be either task-oriented or social-process-oriented, and include process starting (getting the ball rolling) continuity (keeping the ball rolling), and quality control (making sure it is rolled in the right direction). These are sometimes referred to as distributed leadership roles because they are most functional when leadership is shared.

Traditional leadership styles include authoritarian leadership (I'm-the-boss-so-do-as-I-say), laissez-faire leadership (permissive), and democratic leadership (in which everyone participates and the leader supplies guidance). Traditional leadership responsibilities include traffic control, conflict resolution, recording and reviewing progress, and establishing and maintaining an agenda.

The agenda is a list of group activities, arranged according to the principles of division, coordination, and order. The standard agenda is used for problem-solving and lists the following activities: definition of problem, analysis of problem, proposing solutions, testing solutions against criteria for solutions, and the selection of the final solution. Stated agendas help thwart hidden (that is, undiscussed, personal) agendas.

An understanding of underlying dynamics such as these helps make group work more productive.

The most common formats for group presentations are formal and informal panel discussions, either one of which could be followed by an audience forum.

QUESTIONS FOR DISCUSSION

1. Groups are very prevalent in our society. What groups have you been involved in? Do you consider them successful groups? Why or why not?
2. It is stated in this chapter that "all groups are problem-solving groups." Do you agree or disagree with this statement? Why?

3. It is also stated that one or more of the four stages of group process (orientation, conflict, emergence, and reinforcement) is often cut short. In your experience with groups, which phase is cut short most often? What is the effect of cutting that phase short?

4. Different leadership styles might be most effective in different situations. Name one group situation in which each of the leadership styles (authoritarian, laissez-faire, or democratic) might be most effective.

PROBES

1. Divide into groups of three to five, with an observer for each group member. As the group procedes with any task, keep a record of the comments made by its members. Identify the comments as being related to task or social process: starter, continuity, or quality control role; and note the disposition, settlement, or effect of the comment. Each observer should note the comments of the group member observed on a graph such as this:

Suggestions	Task	Social	Starter, continuity or quality control	Disposition
"Let's start off by telling what we all did last summer."		X	Starter	Ignored
"Let's take a break."		X	Quality Control	Considered, rejected
"Let's use a standard agenda to attack this problem."	X		Starter	Considered, accepted

Use the graph as the basis for a discussion on group roles. If time permits, repeat the exercise with observers as group participants.

2. Keep a similar record of the effect of nonverbal behavior, showing the behavior and the disposition of that behavior on a graph such as this:

Behavior	Disposition
Fidgeting; quizzical expression	Ignored
Drumming loudly on desk top with fingers	Other members look annoyed; no one asks for the reason for this behavior.
Clearing throat; raising hand	Other members become silent so participant may speak.

NOTES

[1]"Group process," for our purposes here, is synonymous with the terms "group dynamics," "group interaction," and "group discussion." Different theorists, however, may distinguish between these terms for their own purposes.

[2]This is known as the *assembly effect*. See B. Aubrey Fisher, *Small Group Decision Making* (New York: McGraw Hill, 1974), pp. 40–41.

[3]David W. Johnson and Frank P. Johnson, *Joining Together: Group Theory and Group Skills* (Englewood Cliffs, N.J.: Prentice-Hall, 1975), p. 161.

[4]Lawrence B. Rosenfeld, *Human Interaction in the Small Group Setting* (Columbus, Ohio: Charles E. Merrill Publishing Co., 1973), pp. 88–92, discusses the difference between individual and group tasks. Also, see the abridgment of this text in Brent D. Peterson, Gerald M. Goldhaber, and R. Wayne Pace, *Communication Probes*, 2nd ed. (Palo Alto, Calif.: SRA, 1977), p. 179.

[5]B. Aubrey Fisher, "Decision Emergence: Phases in Group Decision-Making," *Speech Monographs*, 37 (1970), pp. 53–66.

[6]For a list of 20 of these roles, see Johnson and Johnson, op. cit., pp. 26–27.

[7]John Dewey, *How We Think* (Boston: Heath and Co., 1910).

[8]Six variations of these methods of group presentations are outlined in Ronald L. Applbaum, Edward M. Bodaken, Kenneth K. Sereno, and Karl W. Anatol, *The Process of Group Communication* (Palo Alto, Calif.: Science Research Associates, 1974), pp. 249–274.

Appendix

Speakers on Speaking

This appendix provides seven model speeches for analysis and discussion. It also gives seven professional speakers (two speech writers, two corporate executives, and three college professors) the opportunity to expound on their ideas concerning public speaking and communication. There is a diversity of viewpoints and speaking styles represented here, but generally these professionals agree on the fundamentals. The speeches in this appendix demonstrate how they put those fundamentals to work.

Each of the speeches is followed by a few questions for discussion.

This speech is by Max D. Isaacson, the Vice President in charge of
Administration at Macmillan Oil Company. He gave his speech before a
seminar on speech improvement, "Speechcraft," that was held at Des
Moines City Hall in Des Moines, Iowa on February 1, 1980. We can assume
that his audience included a wide cross-sample of society, including
business managers, sales people, college students, and others who were
interested in improving their speechmaking skills. Mr. Isaacson focuses his
speech on two important aspects of public speaking: speech anxiety and
self improvement.

Public Speaking
and Other
Coronary Threats

The Value of Self
Improvement

MAX D. ISAACSON

1   In my job and at other functions, quite often I'm called on to speak
and my wife says that I get up so often that I'm living proof of the old
adage that hot air always rises. But I have something a little more sub-
stantial than hot air to talk about today.

2   I'm glad you are here because that tells me you've had the ded-
ication and the interest in this important speechcraft course. I can tell
you from personal experience that the ability to express oneself well
in public is certainly valuable in my business and in every walk of life
that I know of.

3   In addition to my interest in public speaking, I'm happy to be
here for another reason. Since I'm on the staff of an oil company, I'm
happy to be invited *anywhere* where there is a cordial reception . . .
that's a pleasant accomplishment.

4   Speaking of accomplishments, your chairman asked me to
speak on "Accomplishments Through Speechcraft." A more appropri-

Reprinted by permission of *Vital Speeches of the Day*, March 15, 1980, pp. 351–352.

ate title might be: "PUBLIC SPEAKING AND OTHER CORONARY THREATS!" because in public speaking, many are called but few want to get up. You know and I know that it can be scary indeed to get up to address a group. But listen to these statements:

5   Daniel Webster said:

> "If all my possessions were taken from me with one exception, I would choose to keep the power of speech, for by it I would soon regain all the rest [of my possessions]."

Sigmund Freud observed:

> "Words call forth emotions and are universally the means by which we influence our fellow creatures ... by words, one of us can give to another the greatest happiness or bring about utter despair."

6   The eminent Dale Carnegie said:

> "Every activity of our lives is communication of a sort, but it is through speech that man asserts his distinctiveness ... that he best expresses his own individuality, his essence."

7   Someone else has observed, and I certainly agree, that "self-confidence has *always* been the first secret of success." Of the known phobias—and there is a long list of them—the fear of public speaking consistently ranks at the top in public surveys. It's even more feared than death. But why should intelligent people fear public speaking?

8   Most of us have at least average intelligence and when we look around us—at co-workers, bosses, politicians—we know that our level of knowledge is as great or greater than theirs, but the thing that so often separates us is our *inability* to feel confident when expressing ourselves ... we fear to speak up.

9   It's true that we make ourselves vulnerable when we speak up ... vulnerable to criticism. It's usually easier and more comfortable to stay out of the spotlight and to languish in the comfort of the non-speaker's role, to avoid the risk of feeling inferior.

10   But I've always been fond of quoting Eleanor Roosevelt on the subject of self-confidence and it was she who said: "No one can make *you* feel inferior without *your* consent." Think about that for a moment. "No one can make you feel inferior without your consent." Isn't that a remarkable statement?

11   And here are some remarkable figures to prove that man is his own worst enemy. MORE PERSONS KILL THEMSELVES EACH YEAR THAN MURDER OTHERS. There are 25,000 suicides annually in the U.S. and 18,000 homicides. Suicide is the severest form of self-hatred. But a milder form of self-hatred is the inferiority complex many of us secretly harbor.

12   One of my kids recently told me a riddle. He said, "Dad, do you know what the largest room in the world is?" "The largest room ... ?"

I replied that I did not. He answered, "THE ROOM FOR IMPROVE-MENT!" That's why I believe in speechcraft, because it's a valuable means for improvement. It offers what most of us need to become better public speakers.

13   Isn't it incredible that there is so little emphasis throughout our educational and business training on this needed skill of oral communication? I've found that in high school, college, military service, graduate school and in business, any emphasis on oral communication HAS BEEN CONSPICUOUS BY ITS ABSENCE. And yet, you and I communicate orally more than in any other way when dealing with people.

14   Some time ago I attended a conference whose main speaker was a nationally-known management expert and he said that we are not in the oil business, the insurance business, the government service business, the manufacturing business ... rather WE ARE IN THE *PEOPLE* BUSINESS! It behooves us to do whatever we can to improve our communications among people in all walks of life in order to improve human relations.

15   Where will you go from here? What will you do with the valuable experience you've gained at these speechcraft sessions? Unfortunately, most persons stop their training after the formal speechcraft course has ended. They apparently are satisfied with their progress or don't want to make the effort to continue. But can you imagine a pianist stopping after 10 lessons and saying, "I've arrived—and I'm now accomplished!"? Public speaking takes on-going practice so I would encourage you to stick with it through regular Toastmaster training.

16   I'm convinced you'll do better on the job, in your community organizations and in your house of worship. One of my biggest thrills was that of becoming a certified lay speaker in the United Methodist Church—just one of the many ways that experience in public speaking can be applied for personal fulfillment and self-realization.

17   Let me close with a thought that I've shared with graduating high school seniors and other groups concerning the value of self-improvement. It goes like this:

God said, "Build a better world,"
And I said, "How?"
The world is such a cold, dark place and so complicated now;
And I so young and useless, there's nothing I can do,
But God in all his wisdom said, "Just build a better you."

QUESTIONS FOR DISCUSSION

1. Mr. Isaacson is a business executive speaking to a diverse group of seminar students. We can assume that his audience will feel a

certain amount of distance from him. How does he attempt to bridge that difference and establish "good will" in his introduction?

2. Mr. Isaacson bolsters his own credibility with quotations from Daniel Webster, Sigmund Freud and Dale Carnegie. Given his audience, do you think these were appropriate sources?

3. To make his conclusion memorable Mr. Isaacson ends his speech with a short poem. Do you think this was an effective tactic?

This speech was given by Charles A. Boyle, a professional speech writer. Mr. Boyle discusses the importance of face-to-face public speaking in an age of mass media, and he stresses the importance of preparation in speech writing. Mr. Boyle presented his speech before the Mercer Island Rotary Club in Seattle, Washington on June 25, 1975. The Rotary Club is a national organization devoted to civic service. At the time of this speech, the club's membership was exclusively male, made up of businessmen from the community who met once a week and listened to an invited speaker.

A Few Words About Speeches

Rhetoric Is Action

CHARLES A. BOYLE

1   When I first went into business, my goal was to simply write speeches for other people and let it go at that. However, I found out rather quickly that many of my clients were not taking advantage of all the opportunities that giving a speech can generate ... such as press coverage and printed copies distributed to various people and publications. And so I began offering advice in these allied areas.

2   As a result, when I had my new brochures and business cards printed, I changed them from Confidential Speech Service to Charles A. Boyle, Writer/Consultant. But, I'm not as impressed by the term consultant as much anymore as I once was.

3   Lately, when I see the word consultant on a title or letterhead, I'm amused because it reminds me of the two old maids who live in my neighborhood. They have a big, black tomcat and they call him Sylvester.

4   It used to be that every night about ten o'clock, Sylvester would

Reprinted by permission of *Vital Speeches of the Day*, September 1, 1975, pp. 682–685.

raise a fuss to get out of the house. And when they couldn't stand it anymore, the ladies would turn him loose to roam the neighborhood.

5   Of course, they wouldn't see him again until the next morning when he'd get hungry.

6   Well, it bothered those two old maids to realize that Sylvester was having all that fun . . . so they decided to do something about it and they took him down to the veterinarian where they had Sylvester fixed, figuring that would solve their problem.

7   The net result is that Sylvester still makes his evening calls . . . but now he goes around as a consultant.

8   I stole that story from Mick Delaney . . . a friend of mine who is a professional speaker. But I'm not a professional speaker . . . I never get paid for giving a talk. I'm a professional writer and get paid for writing talks for other people to give. And everything I write is stolen from somebody. I want you to understand however, that it's not plagiarism.

9   Plagiarism is when you take stuff from *one* writer . . . when you take it from a lot of writers, it's called research.

10   In the course of my research for this talk I stumbled across some of the history of Johann Von Goethe.

11   I always thought of Goethe (if I ever thought of him at all) as simply the author of Faust and one of history's greatest writers.

12   But Goethe was more than a writer . . . he was a politician and, in a friendly meaning of the word, a bureaucrat. Early in his career he held many civil offices and, with his extraordinary intelligence, was able to develop a keen understanding and deep insight of the people known as the general public.

13   Goethe believed . . . and said . . . "The public wishes itself to be managed like a woman: One must say nothing to it except what it likes to hear."*

14   This could be done in Goethe's day, but if we use the popular ways of reaching the public in 1975 it's nearly impossible. To paraphrase Lincoln, we can tell some of the public what it wants to hear all of the time, but not all of the public what it wants to hear even some of the time.

15   The reason for this inability to please everybody with our words is that we try to reach the public simultaneously, instantly and indiscriminately through the mass media. And since we are aware of the vast range of differing opinions in the radio, television and newspaper audience, we begin thinking in defensive terms before we open our mouths rather than aggressive advocacy of our cause.

16   For we know that a large percentage of those listening will be in sharp disagreement with us . . . no matter what we say.

17   Consequently, in an effort not to be too offensive to a large por-

*See "Questions for Discussion."

tion of that audience in a TV commercial, or when we speak in the presence of reporters, whenever we say black is black or white is white, we most likely qualify it by acknowledging every shade of gray.

18   Goethe didn't have this problem ... there was no mass media in his day.

19   When he spoke to the people of Frankfurt gathered in small audiences, he didn't have to dilute his remarks in fear of offending the people of Berlin or Munich. He knew the desires and needs of his audience in Frankfurt and spoke to them alone ... not to them and the people of Berlin at the same time.

20   A leading public relations counsel and author, Phillip Lesley of Chicago, put it this way ... "the more closely a communication is beamed to a specific audience, the more likely it is to be received and accepted ... each communication activity must reach SPECIFIC publics in ways that can gain THEIR interest and motivate THEIR support."

21   It's pretty hard to motivate the public while vacillating and apologizing.

22   But that's what's done too often by business and political leaders trying to tell their story through the mass media alone, because they KNOW they are not reaching a specific public ... they're hitting the whole spectrum of thought and opinion and pull their punches accordingly.

23   Whether deserved or not, business and government are under massive attack with no holds barred. And their defense, through the mass media, is soft-sell.

24   It's about all they can do in a 30-second radio or TV spot whether that 30 seconds is in the form of news or a commercial.

25   Lately, some industries began to realize that those 30-second announcements ... *alone* ... are not enough. More of the story has to be told and it takes longer than 30 seconds to do it.

26   Here's an example—

In the April 11, 1974 edition of the *Wall Street Journal*, the headline read ...

"BIG OIL COMPANIES HIT LUNCHEON TRAIL TO BATTLE BAD IMAGE."

27   According to the Journal story, many oil companies are creating speakers bureaus or are expanding the ones they already have.

28   A. D. Gill, who heads Gulf Oil Corporation's Vital Source speakers bureau, says their program has been expanded from 200 speech-giving employees to 350. Gill says Gulf reached about 400 audiences in 1973 and one thousand audiences in 1974.

29   In the past year or so, the oil companies have probably been the most visible targets of the "anti's." But the power companies, lumber industry and phone companies are ships in the same convoy

coming under attack. To some degree, most of these industries realize that a pretty ad alone cannot tell their story effectively and gain support from the general public. And the general public, incidentally, really isn't totally committed to one side or the other—but it does lack information from both sides of an issue.

30   As I mentioned, the oil companies ... and some others ... have discovered that speaking to live audiences, where there is time to say more than what can be said in a minute or less and where there is an opportunity for face-to-face questions and answers, can be a very effective way of getting a message across.

31   There is a rub, however. Too many speeches are done badly.

32   And, with typical American free enterprise initiative ... or what's left of it ... a number of firms have cropped up recently to teach the fundamentals of speech-making to company executives.

33   One of these firms is Carl Terzian Associates of Los Angeles.

34   Terzian personally receives two thousand requests a year to give speeches and responds to about 200-250 of them.

35   Just to give you an example of how much money or trouble some executives will pay for coaching, Terzian had one client ... a vice-president of a firm in Portland ... who had Terzian meet him once a month. Terzian would fly to Portland, meet his client at the airport where they had lunch, coach him for an hour in a conference room, get back on a plane and return to Los Angeles.

36   Terzian told me ... and it's been published in California Business magazine ... that on an average day in Los Angeles there are 25 thousand audiences meeting. In New York, it's 40 thousand a day ranging all the way from PTA's and high school assemblies to conventions, garden clubs and service clubs. And they all want a speaker.

37   When I first decided to go into my own business about 2 years ago, I wondered how many speeches were being given in the Seattle area. Using the Rotary Club was a barometer ... 20 clubs in the Seattle area meeting 52 weeks a year for about one thousand speeches at Rotary clubs alone ... I figured that at least 5 or 6 thousand speeches were being given in Seattle each year. It's probably more like 1 or 2 thousand a day. Or more.

38   The audiences are there and always have been.

39   Speeches are a great way to reach the public ... and the best way to reach and tell a story to specific publics.

40   But only if the speeches are done effectively.

41   The trouble is, too many speeches are deadly.

42   How many times have you heard the phrase ... "I have to go and listen to a speech?"

43   What a negative reaction to speeches that is!

44   And yet, almost every great thought of mankind was first expressed in a speech.

45   Aristotle, Socrates and Cicero gave speeches that were taken

down in shorthand by slaves and then written in longhand and—in the case of Cicero—sold to the public.

46   Shakespeare wrote plays which were mostly speeches.

47   Or even today, how many people can remember the words John Kennedy wrote in his book, "Profiles in Courage?"

48   How many people can forget what he said in his inauguration speech ... "Ask not what your country can do for you, but what you can do for your country."

49   Which, incidentally, was first said in a speech about 300 years ago by Frederick the Great of Prussia.

50   I ask you ... can you quote from the books of Winston Churchill? Can you forget his phrase ... "the iron curtain" ... given in a speech at Columbia, Missouri?

51   Newton Minow may be a name the public cannot remember. But the public remembers what he called television in a speech ... a vast wasteland.

52   From Washington's farewell to Lincoln's Gettysburg Address ... to Roosevelt's "we have nothing to fear" to Churchill's blood, sweat and tears, the list of memorable speeches is endless.

53   Good speeches are *printed* and *quoted* and *remembered*.

54   The audiences can be far greater than those present at the time they are given.

55   But none of those great speeches was given spontaneously.

56   None of those great men got up before an audience, hemming and hawing, stumbling and searching for words ... trying to put thoughts into continuity at the same time they were speaking.

57   They put their thoughts in order on paper *BEFORE* they spoke.

58   Whether you agree with their words or not, good speakers ... while on the platform ... never give you the uncomfortable feeling that you have to help them out. You won't see them groping around for words while you squirm and say to yourself ... "come on, I know the word you're looking for ... say it."

59   Mark Twain said ... "it usually takes more than 3 weeks to prepare a *good, impromptu* speech."

60   But the sin of most people called on to give a speech is that they direct their efforts in proportion to the size of the audience.

61   For instance, if a businessman was given the opportunity to speak to the 500-member downtown Rotary Club, he would probably be willing to pay a fee for help in coming up with a good speech.

62   But if that same businessman was asked to speak to a small Rotary Club in some suburb, he might not be too anxious to go to any expense over it.

63   Yet, with one good speech he could give it to 15 small Rotary Clubs, not only reaching a bigger audience than the downtown club, but some of the people doing make-ups at the smaller clubs.

64   I had one client last year who gave the same speech 30 times to 30 different groups in a period of one month. He was giving that

speech every day or evening ... sometimes twice a day. He not only reached two thousand people in person, but parts of his speech were quoted in the two big daily papers the first time he gave it and in the neighborhood weeklies the rest of the month.

65   I'm happy to say he was promoting a certain cause and it was successful.

66   Giving a speech is sort of like being on the stage. I suppose there's a little bit of the ham in all of us and, if we perform well, favorable attention will be directed our way.

67   I'm sure you've all heard of movie actors who want to be in Broadway plays ... they want to see and feel the reaction of the audience.

68   Even Lloyd Cooney, who's on television every day, still likes to give speeches where he can be in touch with his audience.

69   And he always reads his speeches.

70   But speakers and potential speakers are told time and time again that they should never ... never, use a script or read a speech.

71   That's ridiculous ... unless you happen to be a professional speaker. And you'd be amazed at how many professional speakers use scripts ... it just looks like they aren't.

72   When's the last time you ever saw a president or a governor give a speech without a script? And if it was on television and they didn't have a script in front of them ... you can bet it was on the teleprompter.

73   Even Lincoln wrote the Gettysburg Address ... not once, but five times. Parts of it were used in other speeches for years before he spoke those immortal words in Pennsylvania. And when he gave it, he had the script in his hand, in spite of the fact that it was only about two minutes long.

74   Businessmen and political leaders should always use a script. After all, once they utter the words ... they can't be erased. And by talking from the top of your head, even if you've mentally outlined your talk or are using notes, the wrong words have a way of slipping out inadvertently and the right word is too often forgotten at the moment. This can't happen if a script is followed faithfully.

75   The trouble with most speech writers, however, is that they write material that's great to read at your leisure. That's a written speech ... pretty to the eye of the silent reader. But someone has to stand up and SPEAK that speech. The good speech writer knows that and writes for an oral presentation ... for the EAR.

76   There's a great deal of difference between material that is written to be read and material written to be heard.

77   Another, anti-script argument is that some people think it's an insult to an audience to read a speech. I think it's a compliment ... by putting your thoughts down in the form of a script, you are, in effect, saying that you care enough for your audience's time to spend hours ... not talking and rambling ... but researching and writing. And peo-

ple who are experts in their field usually have enough knowledge and information about their field to talk for hours. The trick is to boil it down to the time frame allotted and still make the essential points.

78   Winston Churchill was asked on at least one occasion how much he would charge to give a half-hour speech. He said ... $2,500 dollars. The people who asked him thought that was kind of high, so they asked how much it would cost for a 15 minute speech. Churchill replied ... $5,000. Twice as much for half the time. He ... as most of us ... found it harder to say something in fewer words.

79   As for the person who hires a professional to put his knowledge into a concise presentation, if the audience should guess or know that someone else wrote the speech, the person that hired the writer is telling the audience that he cares enough about them to spend some money to give them the best talk he can.

80   One of the things I always try to do myself, and depending on the type of audience, advise my clients to do, is never go to the bitter end of the allotted time with a prepared talk, but leave some time for questions and answers. That's what I'm about to do now. But I can't resist slipping in at least one bit of philosophy which may be appropriate to our times.

81   In recent years the word rhetoric has been demeaned. Perhaps you've heard people say, in effect, no more rhetoric ... let's have some action.

82   Well—rhetoric *is* action. Plato said, "Rhetoric is the art of ruling men's minds." And, of course, once you've ruled their minds, you rule all of them. I think it's time businessmen ... who are men of action ... start sharpening their skills of rhetoric. Lord knows, the people tearing down business have been using it.

83   I think businessmen should be blowing their own horn more often, for — as W. S. Gilbert put it — "If you wish in the world to advance — your merits you're bound to enhance; you must stir it and stump it, and blow your own trumpet, or trust me, you haven't a chance."

QUESTIONS FOR DISCUSSION

1. Although Mr. Boyle's audience was almost exclusively men, many experts would consider the following quotation to be inappropriate: "The public wishes itself to be managed like a woman: One must say nothing to it except what it likes to hear." Do you feel this quotation was appropriate? Why or why not?

2. Mr. Boyle obviously prefers manuscript speeches. In building his case for this type of speech, he mentions none of its disadvantages. Do you find his one-sided argument on this point appropriate and effective?

3. What traits would you expect of an audience at a Rotary Club meeting? How does Mr. Boyle adapt his message to this audience?

This speech was given by Waldo W. Braden, a professor of speech at Louisiana State University. Professor Braden stresses that a speech should be aesthetically pleasing—"eloquent"—as well as effective. As he is quick to point out, this viewpoint is often ignored. Professor Braden's speech was delivered to students and faculty at the Third Annual Communication Week at the University of Texas, Austin, on March 8, 1972.

Eloquence as a Creative Art

The Very Best

WALDO W. BRADEN

1   Eloquence once was a favorite word in the vocabularies of those who discussed speakers and public address. Hence, the best speeches were collected under such titles as *American Eloquence, Selected British Eloquence,* and more recently *Modern Eloquence.* Emerson wrote two essays on the subject, using the word in his *Journal* in at least one hundred contexts. He associated the quality with the speaking of Daniel Webster, Edward Everett, Edmund Burke, and Wendell Phillip. The philosopher-poet scattered throughout his reflections such observations as these

"Eloquence is the art of speaking what you mean and are."

"The secret of eloquence is to realize all you say. Do not give us counters of base coin, but every word a real value."

"The eloquent man is he who is no beautiful speaker, but who is inwardly and desperately drunk with a certain belief."

2   But preferences have changed since Emerson's time. Seemingly no one today wants to be called an orator and almost no one talks

Reprinted by permission of the author and *Vital Speeches of the Day,* April 15, 1972, pp. 398–401.

about eloquence; consequently, this fine word—once so rich in connotation and inspiration—has slipped into disuse. A check of leading public speaking textbooks will not reveal a single chapter heading or even a paragraph explaining the concept; or not even a listing in an index.

3   In preparing for this talk I encountered *the word* in the titles of two, not too recent, popular books. In 1952 Theodore R. McKelden, while he was governor of Maryland, and John C. Krantz, Professor of Pharmacology at the University of Maryland, assembled a text entitled *The Art of Eloquence,* a how-to-do-it book with speech models.

4   Kenneth McFarland, a popular lecturer, who according to his publisher is "one of the world's best speakers," authored a book entitled *Eloquence in Public Speaking.* In its promotion, the publisher said

> Now at last you can have Kenneth McFarland as your personal mentor . . . quickly acquire from him all the tricks and techniques of 'going over big' with an audience on any speaking occasion. Yes, whether it's an hour-long formal address, or a brief extemporaneous talk, you'll come through with flying colors every time.

5   After reading that statement, I knew that McFarland and Emerson had little in common; but I sought out a copy because the claim was one that I could not brush aside. But I was not surprised to confirm that McFarland did not view eloquence in the sense of a creative art.

6   The ancient Greek and Roman writers on rhetoric had much to say about eloquence. They made it the ideal toward which to strive; it represented the refinement of the art. In discussing Winston Churchill, former Lord Justice Birkett contrasts the orators of ancient times with the speakers of today. Concerning the classical orators, he said

> The orators of ancient times felt themselves to be engaged in a task of their best worth and value. They were 'shaping works for all the future' and 'offering themselves to be examined by all-testing Envy and Time,' as one of the ancient writers said when defending and praising the scrupulous care taken by Demosthenes. Today the care and attention given to the art of public speaking has sensibly declined. It is not to be expected, of course, that men and women in these modern days should bestow upon the art of public speaking the infinite pains that were taken in the ancient world. . . . Men and women in this busy age have little time to strive for perfection in the form of what they say.

7   Unfortunately, what Birkett observed is too true on many occasions. Public address has changed from a creative art to a utilitarian one. Too often the busy executive, the harried government official, the hard-fisted labor organizer, and the super salesman think that they must produce; show results in an immediate overt way. Motivated by

utilitarian goals, these modern communicators demand the practical approach or what McFarland calls "a magic shortcut to success." In too much of a hurry to bother about refinements in their rhetorical methods, they resort to "the tricks of going over big," and equate their success in terms of sold shoes, stirred laughter, and converted sinners.

8   Eloquence as a creative art has been replaced largely by the standard of effectiveness or a shift from concern over method to a preoccupation about results. William Norwood Brigance, one of our most influential American speech teachers of the century, reflects on this change when he says that the speaker of today is "less of an oracle than formerly and more of a plain man talking." What does this statement mean? Instead of giving the impression of careful preparation and polish, the "plain man talking" places a premium upon informality, telling his audience that he is not "giving a speech,"—"just talking" or "making a few remarks," or perhaps "thinking out loud." Above all he wants to give the impression of sincerity and spontaneous retort. He wishes to have his listeners believe that he is thinking on his feet, that what he is saying has just suddenly and unexpectedly been stimulated by the intensity of the moment. At times a speaker seems ashamed to admit that he has carefully prepared. Hoping to suggest that he is just a common man, he strives not to seem rehearsed, well educated, or even too polished. In fact, he may go to the extreme of justifying careless preparation, poor reading, or halting delivery because he wants to exhibit modes of behavior similar to that of his listeners.

9   Each year I probably read or scan two or three hundred speeches in the process of selecting fifteen to twenty speeches for the volume *Representative American Speeches* which I edit. I can testify that the task is laborious, for it involves covering three or four national newspapers, *Vital Speeches,* the *Congressional Record,* and sundry periodicals. In addition, I frequently call upon my colleagues and other friends for help.

10   In my search I think that I see the signs of the times, the results of placing over-emphasis upon the utilitarian goals and ignoring the creative ones. Let me suggest some tentative observations about the public address of today.

11   First, many of the speeches indicate that they are hurriedly done. They are filled with sweeping generalizations, unoriginal examples, commonplace and trite language. They obviously are the products of faceless ghosts who have no pride or interest in authorship or speakership.

12   Second, many of the speeches show little stamp of the speaker's personality or of his unique insights. They are factory efforts that could be used by anyone who could read.

13   Third, the speeches are impersonal and innocuous. They are designed to appeal to large numbers without insulting or alienating any

particular segment of the audience. They are not intended to elicit feedback or stir up opposition.

14   Fourth, a given speaker may have a set presentation which he alters little as he moves rapidly from place to place. Feeble attempts at audience adjustment are inserted in an opening paragraph, which may hastely mention the specific place, a local personality, or the speaker's reason for coming.

15   Fifth, many speeches show little genuine concern for the listeners. The speaker, a public figure or government official, comes when he is beckoned to report on his agency or its activities. He hopes to make a favorable impression without too much effort and without opposition.

16   Have we carried the emphasis upon "the plain man speaking" and upon getting results to the place that we are cheapening or destroying the art? Does our present preoccupation about results encourage tricks, distortion, manipulation, and other Madison Avenue techniques? In my view the "plain man" when he is too plain may care little about or ignore soundness of thought, perfection of method, or moral responsibility. Instead, he is determined to win at any cost. Bothered by these trends, Karl Wallace argues that putting too much stress upon effectiveness "unnecessarily tempts the honest and sincere man." He says:

> If we give much weight to the immediate success of a speech, we encourage temptation. To glorify the end is to invite the use of any means which will work. The end can be used, for example, to sanction distortion and suppression of materials and arguments.... The end, moreover, can be readily called upon to justify the misleading manoeuvres, the innuendoes, and the short-cut tricks of the propagandists. The advertiser, in his zeal to sell, is constantly tempted to promise more than he can deliver. In brief, to exalt the end is often to be indifferent about means....
>
> We associate with 'success' such values as popular prestige and personal ambition. We thus give a premium to the man with a compulsive drive, to him who must win at any cost; and we handicap the man who places the welfare of others above his personal gain.... Finally, the worst evil which follows from an indifference to means is that we make easy the intent of the dishonest, insincere speaker. It is easy to assert high-sounding purposes; it is difficult for the listener to assess the sincerity of these assertions. In short, as Mahatma Gandhi often told us, 'Evil means, even for a good end, produce evil results.'

17   Before continuing, let me suggest some dimensions for eloquence as a creative art. It should be obvious from what I have already said that to me the word is more than a mere synonym for public speaking, that is, in the sense that McFarland probably used the word in his title.

18   Second, the term should suggest more than stylistic qualities associated with apt and fluent diction, with inflammatory and flamboy-

ant passages, or with what is called "empty rhetoric" or mere oratory in a derogatory sense.

19   I think of eloquence in an expanded sense, as an ideal toward which to strive, as the total art of what Cicero called the complete orator; that is, "the supreme power in speaking."

20   The great Roman encompassed the dimension of the concept of his ideal. "But in an orator," he explained, "we must demand the subtlety of the logician, the thoughts of the philosopher, a diction almost poetic, a lawyer's memory, a tragedian's voice, and the bearing almost of the consummate actor. Accordingly, no rarer thing than a finished orator can be discovered among . . . men. Extending this view, Emerson suggests that "eloquence . . . is the best speech of the best soul. It may well stand as the exponent of all that is grand and immortal in the mind." William Jennings Bryan, who won fame for his speaking, defined eloquence as "the speech of one who knows what he is talking about and means what he says—it is thought on fire."

21   It has often been noted that great speeches rank "with great poetry or great music as an expression of the spirit of man. Such eloquence does indeed 'set fire to reason and stimulate man to noble action.' " Here in these thoughts from Cicero, Emerson and Bryan, is an ideal, broad enough in its demands, to keep the speaker pointing toward the perfection of his art. It is a creative goal, instead of a utilitarian one.

22   Does the concept of eloquence have any significance today? Is it as out-of-date as the chariot or the crossbow? Have speed and technology rendered it obsolete? It is true that we cannot expect that "the men and women in these days should bestow upon the art of public speaking the infinite pains that were taken in the ancient world." Public figures today must devote themselves to the tasks at hand. The business executive must attend his board meetings, watch his production reports, and review his financial statements. The reformers cannot stray too far from the slums or pollution or corruption. The political aspirant who jets from meeting to meeting, covering eight to ten states in a day with seven to fifteen appearances, does not have time to produce a polished speech for each audience.

23   On these occasions the speaker can do little more than "just talk," "make a few remarks," or "think aloud." These staged affairs can be and should be no more than ephemeral because the speakers are generally interested only in exposure: being seen by great numbers and in promoting an image. And once the votes are counted the politicians will admit that their efforts were "just campaign oratory."

24   Our complex and difficult affairs often seem to require more than spot commercials, sales talks, and campaign oratory. Could the present so-called credibility gap that exists between the people and their leaders somehow be related to the lack of eloquence? Another thought: Does the type of communication that our leaders use upon

us indicate what a low opinion they have of our intelligence and our ability to discern what is worthwhile and what is false?

25   Especially from the point of view of pedagogy, I think we should give more prominence to eloquence as a creative art. We need to point students toward something more than cheap success and focus their attention upon wholesome motives and method as well as to the end desired. The student of public address should want to work for excellence not easily satisfied and should develop pride in his art. I would hope that the young speaker might have something of Winston Churchill's spirit in his speaking. Earl Winterton, long time associate of the great Englishman, speaks of how Churchill, steeped in the atmosphere and traditions of the House of Commons, prepared "his speeches with great care" because he very properly believed that the House had "a right to expect" that he should "give of his best." To impose upon himself an equally high standard means that the speaker will set eloquence foremost in his preparation.

26   The rhetorical critics of this century have argued that a speech cannot be judged by the standards of permanence and beauty, that it is necessarily planned for a specific occasion and a specific audience, and that once it is delivered, its purpose has been achieved and it may not be meaningful on any other occasion. But I fail to see why permanence and beauty as goals need always to be completely separated from that of effectiveness. How are the two mutually exclusive? Why can't an effective speech strive for qualities that come from long and serious thought, that represent the expression of deep and powerful feelings, that strive to stir meaning and inspiration in future readers, and that in the end will give it rank "with great poetry or great music as an expression of the spirit of man." Why shouldn't a man take pride in his speaking, pride enough to polish it, pride enough not to permit a ghost writer to write it for him, pride enough to hope that it will fare well with future critics? I think that I find the qualities of permanence and beauty in the speaking of Lincoln, in the war oratory of Winston Churchill and in some of the addresses of Franklin D. Roosevelt.

27   I cannot read Lincoln's Second Inaugural or Gettysburg addresses without recalling Lord Curzon's famous statement, "It set one to inquiring with nothing slight of wonder "How knoweth this man his letters ...?'" In truth on these and other occasions the Illinois lawyer exemplified eloquence as a creative art, for he spoke with great sincerity and earnestness; he expressed the essence of the democratic spirit and of the will of the nation to test whether a nation so conceived and so dedicated could long endure.

28   Probably the greatest orator of this century is Winston Churchill. To use Emerson's words the great English prime minister was "inwardly and desperately drunk with a certain belief." He knew that the spirit and determination of Englishmen to resist rested upon his ability to stir them in the face of terrible destruction and disheartening reports from

the battle fields. He knew that he was uttering words to be measured "by all-testing Envy and Time." We often hear the observation that "one picture is worth ten thousand words." But of course we must ask, what pictures and what words. What picture could speak as eloquently as Churchill when he faced the opposition in the narrow-walled Commons? In a speech that he made in 1940 he reviewed the first year of the war and surveyed what he called "the dark, wide field." In the midst of a statement about Great Britain's defences, Churchill said

> The gratitude of every home in our island, in our Empire, and indeed throughout the world, ... goes out to the British airmen who, undaunted by odds, unwearied in their constant challenge and mortal danger, are turning the tide of the world war by their prowess and their devotion. Never in the field of human conflict was so much owed by so many to so few. ...

Again, after Dunkirk, when England feared a disaster of the most grievous kind, Churchill stirred his colleagues in Commons with this statement:

> ... we shall not flag or fail. We shall go on to the end, we shall fight in France, we shall fight on the seas and oceans, we shall fight with growing confidence and growing strength in the air, we shall defend our island, whatever the cost may be; we shall fight on the beaches, we shall fight on the landing grounds, we shall fight in the fields and in the streets, we shall fight in the hills; we shall never surrender. ...

29   I think it can be argued that Churchill through his eloquence contributed to the Englishmen's determination to fight on. That statement is one that we cannot forget. It will be repeated wherever free men are threatened. It is eloquent.

30   What does eloquence as creative art entail? Let me briefly summarize:

31   First the speaker "inwardly and desperately" believes in his cause.

32   Second the speaker set for himself a demanding goal that will stretch his inventive capacities in their achievement.

33   Third the speaker has respect for the intellectual integrity of his listeners. He is moved by the belief that his listeners have a right to hear his deep thoughts and sincere convictions.

34   Fourth the speaker realizes his social responsibility; he leads, but he does not exploit.

35   Fifth, eloquence as a creative art demands that the speaker express his thoughts appropriately, but also with a grandeur approaching the qualities of music and poetry.

36   Sixth the speaker must exercise a powerful delivery that adds depth and character to what is said.

37   Seventh the speaker strives for a lasting impression upon his lis-

teners—both those who hear him and those who may later read him. Eloquence as a creative art is the delivered essence of the democratic spirit.

38   In summary let me emphasize the difference between eloquence as a creative art and the present emphasis upon results. The first gives more attention to goals, preparations and method; it demands of the speaker his very best; the second seeks to gain ends with little attention to means.

QUESTIONS FOR DISCUSSION

1. In the speech before this one in this appendix, Charles Boyle claimed, "... the person who hires a professional to put his knowledge into a concise presentation ... is telling the audience that he cares enough about them to spend some money to give them the best talk he can." Obviously Professor Braden feels differently, since he asks, "Why shouldn't a man take pride in his speaking ... pride enough not to permit a ghost writer to write it for him?" Where do you stand on this issue?
2. On what other points do Mr. Boyle and Professor Braden seem to disagree? For example, do they seem to feel differently about the importance of the "effect" of the speech?
3. Professor Braden's speech deals mostly with the concept of eloquence. In your opinion, has he defined this term sufficiently?

This speech is by Ross Smyth, the Communications Projects Manager of Air Canada. Mr. Smyth's speech, which gives some practical advice on the use of humor in public speaking, was delivered before the Montreal Westward Rotary Club on July 25, 1974.

Humour (or Humor) in Public Speaking

Be Brief, Be Gay, Be Gone

ROSS SMYTH

1   Seeing Wally Doyle in the audience reminds me that, when I was a member of the Montreal Junior Board of Trade's public speaking class over 20 years ago, Wally was one of the instructors. If this presentation falls flat, you can blame him!

2   The subject of humour is a difficult one at the best of times. And what's really funny in the world today anyhow? We have had about 50 wars since World War II. The armaments race continues unabated, and military expenditures are soaring. We have energy problems and a high rate of inflation. A lot of us are up-tight about a language bill before the Quebec legislature.* Around the world several hundred million human beings are living at the starvation level, and we are fairly indifferent. Scientists are warning us that the oceans are gradually becoming polluted, threatening the oxygen supply we need for life. So what is there to be funny about?

*At the time of this speech Quebec was considering making French the official language of the provence.

Reprinted by permission of *Vital Speeches of the Day*, September 1, 1974, pp. 690–693.

271

3   On the other hand, to go through life without exercising our sense of humour would be a drab experience. To enjoy a useful and happy life, we need a proper balance—and therefore I believe a speaker with the ability to entertain and to amuse is providing a humanitarian service for us.

4   Any person who has to give a speech—and that includes almost every business or professional person at one time or another—should insert a little humour or levity into it.

5   "Now, wait a minute," you'll say to me, "I can't match Bob Hope, Wayne and Shuster, or Rich Little—so what's the use in trying."

6   You don't have to compete with these full-time professional humorists. Let's look at it this way. If you give a factual statistic-laden 30 minute speech about your profession or business, it is likely to be boringly dull—and may even put the audience to sleep—UNLESS you have developed the ability to insert a little anecdote or a little story every few minutes that will advance or support the theme of your talk. This will provide a refreshing change of pace keeping your audience alert and interested in your subject. Isn't this your goal? To be successful, you don't have to make them roll in the aisles with laughter. A simple, smile-producing anecdote will provide that change of pace to facilitate better audience comprehension of the more serious parts of your presentation.

7   Let's now look at a few rules and guidelines about the use of humour and anecdotes in public speeches.

8   Over 30 years ago there was an expression bandied about by delayed air travellers: "If you have time to spare, go by air." The origin of the expression can be traced back to the mid-1930's when Imperial Airways, BOAC's predecessor, were pioneering air service from England to Australia with large but very slow airliners having limited range.

9   One of the very first flights took off from Croydon Airport near London and flew to northern France where it was delayed extensively due to bad weather.

10   When it arrived in the south of France, one of the motors had failed and it was necessary to wait for another engine to be shipped by sea from England.

11   There were further lengthy delays along the route in Rome, Cairo, the Middle East, etc., until finally the flight had progressed as far as Singapore.

12   At this point a lady passenger asked the manager in Singapore if he thought the flight would arrive in Australia in the next few weeks because she was expecting a baby shortly.

13   "My dear lady," he replied, "you should never have commenced your trip in that condition."

14   She replied, "I didn't."

15   This story has a very effective punch line. If forgotten or varied, it

could ruin the anecdote. My advice—write the punch line into your notes. You'll probably never need to look at it—but the knowledge that it's there will give you the necessary confidence to put it across well.

16   Shortly after World War II, the converted Lancaster bomber carrying 10 passengers was among the aircraft used to establish transatlantic commercial service—and even then there was bar service available to the passengers.

17   One passenger informed the purser that he was a connoisseur of drinks and could identify any on board. Having a large stock on board, the purser made a wager with the passenger, and served him sample after sample, each one of which was identified correctly. Having exhausted all brands, the purser in resignation finally brought the man a plain glass of water.

18   He tasted it, coughed, made a horrible face and said: "You have me stumped—I don't know what it is—but I can tell you one thing—it won't *sell!*"

19   Speaking of *selling,* the airline industry has a major *sales* challenge today in filling the 365 seats in every large 747 jumbo jet. The last word in the anecdote, "sell," has thus been related to a talk on the promotion of one of my favorite topics, air travel.

20   Let's return to the 1940's and a World War II setting.

21   A Canadian airman was shot down over occupied France and he was trying to escape the pursuing Germans. He came to a religious establishment and asked for permission to disguise as a nun. The Mother Superior consented reluctantly. The Germans were thrown off the trail.

22   A week later, well fed and rested, the airman was walking in the garden of the convent on a beautiful spring day. He saw a young nun, rather attractive, leaning over planting flowers.

23   Losing his better judgment, he patted her on the derriere. Then he heard a deep voice say: "Don't be a silly ass! I've been here since Dunkirk."

24   When selecting a story, it is necessary to consider its appropriateness for the particular audience. If this anecdote were related to a high school graduating class, many might miss the significance of the historic reference. On the other hand, most of you are very familiar with World War II.

25   "Pat" Patrault, one of Canada's aviation pioneers, was chief mechanic at Toronto for many years for Trans-Canada Air Lines, now Air Canada.

26   During one of his business trips to Montreal, his new fedora blew away in a wind storm. He put in a claim for it on his expense account which was rejected in due course by the accounting department in Winnipeg.

27   "Pat" had his secretary type out another expense account to

which he added a personal notation: "The hat is still here but try to find it."

28   This type of true anecdote, of course, is appreciated by any sales or business oriented audience.

29   They say truth is stranger than fiction—and certainly funnier. If you have any problems with your head office, here's one that goes back nearly fifteen years when flight in jet transports was an exhilarating and novel experience.

30   A bishop who had flown in only small airplanes close to the earth's surface was making his first jet flight. He was a little apprehensive and, immediately after takeoff, ordered a double whiskey.

31   Then the captain's voice came over the public address system: "Good evening, ladies and gentlemen, we are on course climbing to an altitude of 39,000 feet."

32   The bishop suddenly mumbled the altitude out loud: "39,000 feet!" and he buzzed nervously for the stewardess.

33   "My dear, you better cancel that whiskey and make it a weak lemonade. We're getting awfully close to my headquarters!"

34   This anecdote could be related to any directives, decisions or problems with a corporate headquarters or head office.

35   In 1949 Air Canada inaugurated its service from Canada to Barbados in the West Indies, and a friend of mine went there for his honeymoon on one of the first flights. A few months ago and some 25 years later, this happy couple returned for a second honeymoon on the exotic Caribbean island.

36   "How was it?", I asked my friend.

37   "Oh fine," he replied, "only this time *I* cried in the bathroom!" I don't know whether to consider that type of story a commercial or not.

38   On their days off members of the aviation fraternity have been known to have some pretty good parties, particularly in the younger days of the industry. As a result of one such wild spree in New York, one of the revellers fell out of the third story window and ended up badly injured in the hospital. When he became conscious, he had no recollection of what happened.

39   One of his partying friends visited him and recalled vaguely the sequence of events.

40   "There you were standing on the window sill claiming that you were going to fly across the street to the apartment building on the other side."

41   "Some friend you are! Why didn't you stop me?" he asked.

42   "Stop you? Hell, I was betting you'd make it!"

43   This brings up the subject of alcohol and nerves. Embryo public speakers often have asked me if one or two stiff ones are advisable to calm their nerves in advance of a public address. It is difficult to respond because individuals vary so much.

44   I used to have a rule that, when there was a reception in advance, I would take as many drinks as the average person in the

group, and thus remain on the same communications wavelength. This worked well until I encountered a two-hour reception. But let's return to sobriety.

45   Air Canada and Aeroflot inaugurated the first scheduled air service between North America and the Soviet Union in 1966. Shortly thereafter a Russian visitor was touring a large industrial plant in Ontario and stopped to speak to one of the men on the assembly line.

46   "Tell me," he said. "Are you a capitalist or a communist?"

47   The man replied: "Reckon I'm a capitalist."

48   "Why is that?" asked the Russian.

49   "Well, I look at it this way. I leave here at the end of my shift and there's the boss, waiting on the parking lot in his limousine. "Hello there," he says. "How about a drink?" So I get in the car and we have several drinks. Then he says: "What about coming to my place for dinner?" So we go to his place, have a few more drinks and he says: "Look it's late, why don't you stay here for the night?" So I stay the night and he drives me back to the plant in the morning. That's the sort of treatment which makes me a capitalist."

50   The Russian was astounded. "Has that actually happened to you?" he demanded.

51   "Well, not exactly," replied the man, "but it happened to my sister!"

52   This story may be an example of the use of timing in the punch line—or it may be considered as a sugar-coated commercial for Air Canada and its pioneering role in building air service from North America to the Soviet Union.

53   Ten years ago in London, England, a pioneer BBC broadcaster told of sitting next to the great Winston Churchill as he gave a splendid oration to a small group. The broadcaster noted that what appeared to be notes in Churchill's hand was only an ordinary laundry slip, and he commented on this later in private to the great statesman.

54   "I know," said Sir Winston, "but it gave confidence to my audience."

55   In preparing your own speeches, it is good strategy to include an anecdote or story about a personality who is well known to your audience.

56   In speaking to the Winnipeg Rotary Club, I arrived a little early for the meeting and was greeted by an attractive lady who asked "What are you doing here?"

57   She looked a little familiar. I thought perhaps I had met her at a convention two years earlier.

58   "I'm out here to give a speech to the Rotary Club," I replied.

59   "Do you do this often," she asked.

60   "Quite often," I said.

61   "Are you nervous before you talk," she demanded.

62   "I don't think so," I replied.

63   She retorted, "Then what are you doing in the ladies' washroom?"

64   And this leads me to the subject of nervousness. Most of us are nervous about telling stories in a speech. When we find a good one appropriate to the theme of a talk, we should first practice it five or six times on our wife, friends, children or even the family dog. If we still like the anecdote, it can be filed away in our memory. The good storyteller develops a good memory and hopes others haven't.

65   We should supplement our memory by opening up a file for stories. If you steal one good story, that is plagiarism. If you steal one hundred however, that is research!

66   Perhaps a less preferable method to collecting your own is to refer to joke books. I recently picked up a book at Halifax airport on Newfoundland or "Newfy" jokes, compiled by a Nova Scotian. One of the cartoons was memorable. It showed the old Newfy at a pretty wild drinking party in Halifax, N.S. He was talking on the phone to one of his friends and he said: "What, you can't come to the party, you've got a case of diarrhea? Bring it along, these Nova Scotians will drink anything!"

67   This story illustrates an important point. It was published by a Nova Scotian and makes Nova Scotians the butt of the joke. In using humour in a speech, you may be treading on sensitive toes if the audience is the butt of the joke. Better it be yourself or your own organization or profession if it is a solid one that "can take a joke." As a general rule, racial and religious jokes should be kept out of public speeches.

68   Many years ago I attended my first out-of-town convention as a Jaycee officer. We worked hard all day, and played hard all night. When I returned home to my wife, she would have nothing to do with me for several days. Then, I discovered a telegram I had sent her from the convention. It said, "Having a wonderful time stop wish you were her."

69   Speaking of telegrams, it's poor technique to telegram or signal in advance that you are going to tell a story in a speech. Work it in gradually to take your audience by surprise.

70   There is a danger, of course, that if you become such a good storyteller, people will think you are never serious. I do not have this problem and would therefore like to end on a serious note, having recently returned from the Rotary International convention in Minneapolis. We in the Montreal area have a great challenge in June, when our city will host this annual conference with an anticipated attendance of 18,000. It is an opportunity to convey to the public that we are not an "eat, greet, grunt and groan" club, as all service clubs were described when I was a brash young Jaycee officer. It is an opportunity to convey that we are a very serious and worthwhile movement, in tune with the times and working on both community and global problems.

71   May I suggest three broad goals for Rotary throughout the world.

72   First, let us renew the spirit of Rotary through promoting the concept of *world citizenship*. In other words, let us put the interest of human beings and the human race ahead of conflicting national and group interests. If this philosophy were being followed in Northern Ireland or Cyprus today, their problems would be quickly resolved. Perhaps as we sing our national anthems at the end of our meetings, we should be planning an anthem promoting the brotherhood of all mankind.

73   Secondly, we could adopt a major worldwide program on a long-term basis, say 5 or 10 years, that could occupy us at the local, district and international level—aimed at solving one of the major global problems of mankind today. Why not tackle the elimination of hunger and starvation on the planet?

74   Several hundred millions of people are living at or near the starvation level today when man has the resources, the technology and the human skills to do something much more effective about it. In the 750,000 members in 150 lands and territories in the Rotary world, we have the expertise which could be mobilized into more effective group action. Let's unite in a major Rotary worldwide project tackling a major worldwide problem.

75   Thirdly, I suggest we urge our senior officers to extend the Rotary movement to become truly worldwide. Must the Iron Curtain continue to exist for Rotary Clubs? Extension to communist countries is a difficult but not impossible objective. Its achievement would be significant in advancing the fourth object of Rotary, the promotion of better world understanding.

76   As I now glance at the hour, I am reminded of a poem:
"The coffee's cold, the sherbet wanes,
The speech drones on and on . . .
Oh Speaker, heed the ancient rule:
Be brief. Be gay. Be gone!"

QUESTIONS FOR DISCUSSION

1. Ross Smyth is a Canadian, speaking to a group of other Canadians. Would his speech have to be changed in any way if he was giving it in your community?
2. Is there any vocabulary used in this speech that might have a slightly different meaning to an audience in your community?
3. Most of Mr. Smyth's examples deal with his main interest: airlines and airplanes. Are these examples appropriate for an audience with interests different from his? Why or why not?
4. Most of this speech is humorous, but toward the end Mr. Smyth injects a few serious points. Do you think this was an effective strategy?

More practical advice is presented in this speech by Professor Jerry Tarver of the University of Richmond. Professor Tarver discusses the use of language in speech writing. His speech was delivered to a group of professional speech writers in Hartford, Connecticut on February 21, 1979.

Can't Nobody Here Use This Language?

Function and Quality in Choosing Words

JERRY TARVER

1   I learned last May you have to be careful in speaking to a group of professional communicators. After I conducted a writer's workshop at the Toronto Conference of the International Association of Business Communicators, Janine Lichacz wrote asking me to speak here tonight and used the communication techniques I had recommended. She even included a footnote citing my lecture. I am susceptible to good communication—and to flattery—so I am pleased to be with you to discuss your topic for the evening, the use of language in the art of speech writing.

2   I suppose we must begin by shaking our heads woefully over the sad state of language today, whether in formal speeches, casual conversation, or in writing. Most of us in this room no doubt agree with the generally negative tone of *Time Magazine's* year-end assessment of 1978 which claims "our language has been besieged by vulgarities." But to preserve our sanity as professionals in communication,

Reprinted by permission of the author and *Vital Speeches of the Day*, May 1, 1979, pp. 420–423.

most of us would probably join *Time* in optimistically expecting English somehow to survive and even to prosper.

3   On the negative side, if I may use a vulgarity to criticize vulgarify, I am often moved in my own profession to paraphrase Casey Stengel and ask, "can't nobody here use this language?"

4   To generalize about the language ability of students, I would say far too many of them can't express themselves well, and they don't seem to care. The most significant hollow verbalization among students today is not "y'know." It is "needless to say."

5   I have a respectful appreciation of the rules of the classical rhetoricians, and on occasion I have discussed in class the stylistic device of antithesis. One of my students, quite unconsciously I am sure, gave the technique a try in a speech on physical fitness and said, "A well rounded body makes for a well rounded mind." We've come a long way down from *mens sana in corpore sano.*

6   Faculty members are often worse. Some time back I attended a conference on setting standards for language competence in Virginia's schools. In one presentation a professor from a distinguished university repeatedly used the expression "scribal language." I finally turned to someone to ask what the devil that meant and was told the term was a fancy synonym for 'writing'. I wrote a letter to the professor suggesting a requirement for a report on competence in language should be competence in language. He did not take it well.

7   One of my colleagues wrote a lengthy document on the proper use of classrooms and stated forthrightly, "It is necessary to employ characteristics of uniqueness where uniqueness is held to be important. The idea of flexibility should be placed in a balanced way with other particular instructional and design needs to achieve a maximized learning atmosphere. In some instances, degrees of flexibility may have to give way to other equally creative and significant dimensions of a classroom environment."

8   I happen to know what that means, and I will be happy to provide a translation at twenty cents a word. If you want the answer, send your dollar to me at the University of Richmond.

9   A certain church group which supports many colleges throughout the South regularly sends me a publication which purports to be educational. Leaders of this group use up a goodly portion of the alphabet with the impressive degrees they attach to their names and employ this publication to increase the size of the audience for their various pronouncements. The quality of the writing is so gloriously and innocently bad that the entire magazine could easily pass as a satire written by a clever member of a high school debating team. One of the speeches from a couple of months ago contained the striking statement, "Drifting causes a loss of direction." That was one of the major points in the speech which incidently was delivered at the inauguration of a college president.

10   On the positive side, *Time* finds our language "enriched by vigorous phrases and terms" from such sources as CB radio and situation comedies. The major bright spots I see are the writing in advertising and on the bathroom wall. Let me quickly add that the *worst* writing also appears in these two places. Some of the most crude and senseless tripe I have encountered has appeared in ads or graffiti. But when they are good, they are very, very good. Both the ad writer and the graffiti artist must work within a small compass. They must be concise. To the point. And each is moved, urgently moved, to communicate. Unfortunately for the motivation of the advertiser, I am one of those people who can enjoy the sizzle and forgo the steak. I don't smoke cigars, and I don't even remember the brand involved, but who can forget the classical commercial in which Edie Adams used to urge, "Why don't you pick one up and smoke it sometime?" I admit I don't have a Texaco credit card, but little I read of modern academic poetry moves me as much as the soothing jingle, "You can trust your car to the man who wears the star."

11   My favorite graffiti is the plaintive sort. A poor soul eloquently crying out to be understood. In the men's room just down from my office, someone in apparent anguish wrote with painstaking care in the grout between the tiles, "What in the hell am I doing here?" Weeks passed before someone undertook a reply. Whether done in a spirit of helpfulness or malice, I cannot say, but finally in different handwriting, there appeared, "If this is an existential question, contact Dr. Hall in the Philosophy Department. If this is a theological question, contact Dr. Alley in the Religion Department. If this is a biological question, take a look."

12   Years ago I saw a quotation printed on a little gummed paper strip which had been attached to the wall of a men's room off the New Jersey Turnpike. It offered a simple Biblical text and had apparently come to the attention of a tired truck driver. The quotation asked the question, "If God be for us, who can be against us?" No doubt in despair, the truck driver had replied underneath, "The dispatcher."

13   How can we capture the vitality of the best of graffiti and advertising in our own writing and speaking? Perhaps some of you would agree with a sociologist friend of mine, Dr. James Sartain. Whenever Jim is offered a chance to improve his teaching, he says, "I already know how to teach better than I do." I suspect this is true for most of us. So, we may not be discovering tonight as much as reminding.

14   But there could be some ground for controversy. Let me first of all attempt to play down the current emphasis on correctness. Grammar—much like spelling—is one of the manual skills of expression. Almost any fool can learn to make a subject agree with a verb according to the standard rules of English.

15   I think the pseudo-objectivity of correctness attracts many followers. But grammatical systems are, after all, themselves arbitrary. We

could change the rules if we wanted to. Our failure to alter our grammar to include a sexless pronoun can hardly be blamed on the sanctity of the rules. If you wish to attack the sentence, "He done done it," you can't attack it by claiming it does not follow a rigid set of rules. It just doesn't follow the system most widely taught.

16   I'm not suggesting you break rules at random. Just don't be too proud of yourself for not using "very unique" or "hopefully, it will rain." And remember George Orwell's advice that you should break any rule rather than "say anything outright barbarous."

17   I suggest to write and speak our best we need, first, a grasp of the function of language and, second, a sensitivity to the quality of our words.

18   My desk dictionary includes among its definitions of the word *function*, "The action for which a . . . thing is specially fitted or used or for which a thing exists." The concept of function reminds us that words act upon people.

19   Let me give you an example of a piece of communication which illustrates function. You may recall in *Catch 22*, Lt. Milo Minderbinder at one point instituted an elaborate procedure for going through the chow line. It involved signing a loyalty oath, reciting the pledge of allegiance and singing "The Star-Spangled Banner." But the entire system was destroyed one day when Major de Coverly returned from a trip and cut through the red tape with two words: "Gimme eat."

20   That simple, and quite ungrammatical, phrase shows language in action. Words at work. Expression that eliminates the unnecessary and gets down to cases.

21   A grasp of function causes a writer to think of results. Impact. Effect. Audience becomes important. Who will read or listen? Why? Function calls for the communicator to examine the reason for the existence of a given communication and to choose words that will be a means of expression and not an end.

22   Next, as I said, we must be sensitive to quality. I know of no objective way to determine quality. But I agree with Robert Pirsig who insists in *Zen and the Art of Motorcycle Maintenance* that most people intuitively know quality in language when they encounter it.

23   Most of us have written material we knew was merely adequate. No errors. All the intended ideas in place. No complaints from the boss or the editor. But deep down inside we knew we had done a pedestrian job.

24   I use a chill bump test for quality. For poor writing or speaking I get one type of chill bumps. For good language, a better brand of chill bumps. For most of the mediocre stuff in between, no chill bumps at all.

25   Quality does not mean fancy. When General McAuliffe reportedly answered a Nazi surrender ultimatum with the words "nuts," his

language had no less quality than the declaration of the Indian Chief Joseph, "From where the sun now stands, I will fight no more forever." Either of my examples would probably not fare well in a classroom exercise in English composition. But anyone who objected to the use of such language in that situation would be guilty of ignoring the concept of function.

26   Only after we agree that we must be concerned about function and quality can we properly turn our attention to rules. I offer the following ten guidelines for the speech writer. Some of the guidelines apply primarily to the language of speeches; some apply to almost any kind of writing. I do not consider my list exhaustive, and I should point out that the items on it are not mutually exclusive.

27   *GUIDELINE NUMBER ONE.* Be simple. Tend toward conversational language. Earlier this month I conducted speaker training for a corporation which distributed a speech manuscript containing such expressions as "difficult to ascertain" and "management audits attest." There's nothing wrong with these phrases in print, but I wouldn't say ascertain or attest out loud in front of the Rotary Club. "Find out" and "show" would sound more natural.

28   *GUIDELINE NUMBER TWO.* Be expansive. Speeches use more words per square thought than well-written essays or reports. The next time you get a speech writing assignment, see if you can't talk your boss into throwing out two-thirds of the content and expanding the remainder into a fully developed expression of a limited topic. I realize gobbledygook is wordy, but I assume none of us will be writing gobbledygook. And I don't know of anyone who has suggested that Martin Luther King's "I Have a Dream" speech suffered from excessive repetition.

29   *GUIDELINE NUMBER THREE.* Be concrete. Specific terms limit a listener's chances to misunderstand. Back in November, Combined Communications Corporation President, Karl Eller, gave a speech out in Phoenix in which he used a glass of milk to describe our free enterprise system. He said, "Some farmer bred and raised the cow. Some farmer owned and tended the land it grazed on. He bought special feed from someone. Some farmer milked the cow or cows and sold the milk to someone else who processed it, pasteurized it and packaged it. He sold it to a wholesaler who sold it to a retailer. And all along the line the product was either made better or its distribution was simplified and narrowed, and a lot of people had jobs. Wealth was created." I've quoted less than a fifth of Eller's description. I'm convinced nobody left his speech confused.

30   *GUIDELINE NUMBER FOUR.* Be vivid. Appeal to the senses. President Carter's speech writers attempted to paint a word picture in the state of the union address when they wrote of the power of nuclear weapons "towering over all this volatile changing world, like a thundercloud in a summery sky." I am reminded of Mark Twain's distinction

between the lightning and the lightning bug. The Carter image fails to stir the imagination. But vivid language can be effective.

31   In demonstrating the point that his company's nuclear plants are safe, Ontario Hydro Board Chairman Robert Taylor told members of the Kiwanis Club of Ottawa, "You could sit naked, if you had a mind to, at the boundary fence around the Pickering nuclear station for a year, drink the water and eat the fish from nearby Lake Ontario, and you would pick up a total of five units of radiation. That's less than you would get from natural sources such as rocks, good air and cosmic rays. A single chest x-ray would give you eight times that exposure."

32   *GUIDELINE NUMBER FIVE.* Be personal. Use the personal pronoun. Don't be afraid of making a speaker sound egotistical. Ego springs from attitude, not language. A modest speaker can say "I know" and "I did" and "I was" with no problem. But I know a fellow who is so egotistical he can say "Good morning" and seem to take credit for it. Still, it's hard to imagine Caesar saying, "One comes, one sees, one conquers."

33   *GUIDELINE NUMBER SIX.* Be smooth. Speech demands uncluttered rhythm. Avoid clauses which interrupt your idea. It's a bit awkward for a speaker to say, "William Safire, former Nixon speech writer," but "former Nixon speech writer William Safire" flows a bit better. If you must add a clause, make a big deal out of it. For example, you might say, "Jogging—which can have a fantastically positive effect on your sex life—may clear up minor sinus problems."

34   Feel free to use contractions if they help the flow of the speech. In conversation the absence of contractions often becomes a device for emphasis. If you don't use contractions in speaking, you risk overemphasis.

35   In writing jokes into a speech, be sure to put the "they saids" *before* the quoted material, especially in punch lines. Observe the effect of reading: "Why does a chicken cross the road?" she asked. "To get to the other side," he answered.

36   *GUIDELINE NUMBER SEVEN.* Be aggressive. Don't use the loaded language of your enemies. Let me get my prejudice clearly before you. As a consumer, I deeply resent the careless use of the term "consumer advocate." As a breather of air and drinker of water and observer of sunsets, I resent the haphazard application of the term, "environmentalist" to anyone who can gather six friends in a living room to organize a Snailshell Defiance. My sympathy goes out to the engineer who finds it all but impossible to explain how fish like warm water without describing the fish as victims of thermal pollution.

37   I do not assume that American business and industry always have in mind the best interests of consumers, the environment, and fish, but we need to avoid one-sided language if we are to have an honest discussion of the issues. I would prefer to keep away from loaded words or to qualify them with "so-called" or "self-styled."

38   *GUIDELINE NUMBER EIGHT.* Be purposeful. Meaning is assigned to words by listeners; your intent is less important than your listener's perception. The controversy over sexism and racism in language can be settled if we remember words are symbols which listeners interpret. I will not use the phrase "girls in the office" because a significant number of people who hear me will react negatively. For the same reason, avoid "a black day" on the market, in favor of a bleak day or a bad day. We need not resort to awkward constructions. You might not want to say "unmanned boat," but this does not mean you must blunder along with "unpeopled boat." What about "a boat with no one aboard?"

39   *GUIDELINE NUMBER NINE.* Be eloquent. Use an occasional rhetorical device to enhance your expression of an idea. Indulge at times in a little light alliteration. Balance a pair of phrases: "Ask not what the country can do for General Motors, ask what General Motors can do for the country."

40   *GUIDELINE NUMBER TEN.* Be adaptable. Write to suit your speaker. A speech writer for Phillips Petroleum once described his role as being that of a clone. A writer must know the speaker's feelings and the speaker's style. And remember your speaker may need a tersely worded speech one week and a flowery one the next.

41   My guidelines are far easier to express than to execute. Writing a good speech requires talent, brains, and effort. If you write for others, add to the requirements a self-effacing attitude and a thick skin.

42   Our language will not be saved by the exhortations of evangelists in the Church of the Fundamental Grammar. It can be saved by writers and speakers with a grasp of function and a sense of quality. We should be proud of your organization's contribution; it enrolls and nurtures communicators who use language well.

QUESTIONS FOR DISCUSSION

1. Professor Tarver expresses the unconventional opinion that ads and graffiti can serve as models of good language use. Do you find his examples convincing? Can you cite other examples to support your agreement or disagreement with this idea?

2. Professor Tarver stresses the importance of results in speech making. On the basis of Professor Braden's speech earlier in this appendix, how do you think Professor Braden would feel about this point?

This speech, dealing with the role of women in communication, was given by Grace J. Fippinger, Vice President of New York Telephone. She delivered it at a conference of the New York Association of Women Business Owners, "Women in Business," in New York City on October 15, 1979.

This Is a Very Good Time

Women in Communications

GRACE J. FIPPINGER

1   I am delighted to be with you, who are in the business of communications, which, in one way or another, encompasses all who are here today. I say that because I've been the owner of several businesses. At the age of seven, I sold jelly apples. At 12, I ran a roadside stand. At 15, I was a babysitter. Today, of all things, I am the owner of a golf course. I have yet to discover how to conduct any business without communicating.

2   When you're asked, as I have been, to say a few words on the subject of women in communications, the field is wide open, ranging from Emily Bronte to Tokyo Rose.

3   I shall speak of none of these practitioners, except to say that it obviously was their gender that made their communications so compelling to their audiences.

4   It would have been exceedingly foolish if Mr. Tojo, for instance, had tried to stand in for the vacationing Tokyo Rose—and who among the great English novelists could have dared encroach upon the turf of Emily.

Reprinted by permission of *Vital Speeches of the Day*, January 15, 1980, pp. 222–224.

5   No, in certain uncontested matters, to paraphrase an old saying, no substitutions can be made.

6   But is that the case with women in business communications?

7   I don't believe so.

8   In most instances, gender is irrelevant when it comes to communications.

9   Let me cite a few outrageous examples.

10   Some of us here today may prefer that our personal physician be a woman. And yet, how eager would we be to go to that same doctor if she advertised herself as performing medicine according to the woman's point of view? That is, according to research and discoveries made only by women.

11   I'm sure we'd all say—"No, thank you." Medicine has little regard for whether the student is female or male. You treat goiter the same, be you Marcus Welby or Julie Farr.

12   Another ridiculous example: It's evening and you're relaxed in front of the TV looking at, who else—Pia Lindstrom, and she opens with: "Good evening, I'm Pia Lindstrom, and here is the news about Hurricane David from, of course, the woman's point of view." You'd never hear that from Pia.

13   Whether it's the profession of medicine, law, accounting—or the field we're concerned with today, communications, there are fundamentals which have to be mastered, and which have very little, if anything, to do with gender.

14   So, my first message is not that we should be more like men. My message is quite the opposite. There is no special male or female way to communicate. We all must begin with mastery of the rudiments. Carol Bellamy,* who excels in her field, achieved what she has not because she knows the fine print in Title VII of the Civil Rights Act of 1964. She studied law, period and went on to master other complicated matters. Ask her to discourse on the city budget, and you'll see what I mean.

15   Self-mastery is what it comes down to. If we women are serious about reaching for the prize, then we have to prepare for it.

16   And that is really what the awakening is all about in our nation today. Women don't want favors, they want the same opportunities. Gender is beside the point. Women have proved they are capable. They are proving it each day.

17   They are proving it in the publishing field. I sit on the board of Harcourt-Brace-Jovanovich and find the best seller list most interesting.

18   Month after month, this list has its share of women who write. Notice I say women who write, and not women writers. Their appeal transcends sex lines, and if you doubt that, look closely at what the men

*President, New York City Council

are reading on the commuter lines, going home at night. *The Thorn-birds, The White Album, A Distant Mirror, The Last Enchantment*—those are books that men and women alike are reading, and they all are best sellers written by women. That, I feel, is a remarkable indicator of how much the consciousness of our nation has changed. Yes, I suppose we could go back 30, 40, 50 years and find women authors whose works had great mass appeal. Margaret Mitchell and Edna Ferber undoubtedly come to mind. So do Pearl Buck and Katherine Anne Porter. There were others, and I don't mean to slight any of your favorites. But pick up today's best seller list, for instance, and you will see not one or two women on it, but more likely four and five.

19   There was a time when women writers often felt they had to follow the example of George Sand, and assume a false identity to make a dent in the publishing business. I doubt there's much of that anymore.

20   In my business, telecommunications, it once was that the men climbed the poles and the women sat at the switchboards. Now it often is the reverse. How in the world are you going to tell a young woman entering the telephone business today that pole climbing is man's work, that women are not inherently as agile as men? This generation of women coming out of our high schools and colleges has seen Olga Korbut and Nadia Comaneci doing somersaults on a high bar. Quite a few can swim faster than Johnny Weissmuller ever did, and every woman on the U.S. track team, vying for the Olympics, could have outrun the legendary Jim Thorpe.

21   The sacred preserves are not so sacred anymore. I know I'm never going to forget that match between Bobby Riggs and Billy Jean King.

22   But, let me be the first to admit that I would be very silly indeed to stand up here and claim that opportunities for women today are the same as for men.

23   Clearly, they are not. And, we all have to be disappointed by that fact. Women are getting there, but they're getting there slowly and on the average they continue to earn less than men for the same work. Business, labor, government—all have a way to go before the scales will have been balanced fairly. That is the residue of a culture of the past, a culture which unquestionably was biased. But not always vindictively. My mother and father gave me all the encouragement in the world to go out there and make a mark in whatever I set my sights on. But still, my father, open-minded as he was, never gave me a catcher's mask for Christmas in the hopes that Charlie Dressen might one day sign up Gracie Fippinger behind the plate at Ebbet's Field.

24   Culture. We live, as James Cagney is fond of saying, between our ears.

25   Well, now we are beginning to know better.

26   The old mores are on the run.

27   Of course, it's nice to help the process along whenever we can. So how can we do that?

28   Be positive, is my advice.

29   Emerson said: "This time, like all times, is a very good one—if we but know what to do with it."

30   And so it is with our time. It is a very good time.

31   The conventional wisdom says think not of the problems, think of the opportunities. In my opinion, women would do well to reverse that advice. Think not of the opportunities, think instead of the problems. For whether you know it or not, it is the problems that make the opportunities so abundant in our age.

32   There is more than enough opportunity for those who are willing to deal with the problems.

33   Consider the list of problems confronting us today:

34   How can we reclaim our cities? How do we make them livable and governable?

35   How do we improve the quality of public education?

36   How do we increase the efficiency of government, whether at the federal, state or local level?

37   Those are problems we desperately need answers to.

38   Take the economy:

39   How do we break the back of inflation?

40   Are we fated to see continuing declines in our nation's rate of productivity improvement? How do we reverse that?

41   What can we do to lessen our dependence on foreign oil?

42   Consider the problems of the aged:

43   How do we keep the social security system solvent without burdening the already over-burdened taxpayer?

44   How do we assure quality medical care for the aged?

45   Business, too, is not immune to problems that badly need solving.

46   How do we provide American workers with jobs that are rewarding, not only financially, but psychologically as well?

47   How do we restore confidence in business—indeed, how do we restore confidence in all our institutions?

48   Problems, problems, problems. And not a one has anything at all to do with gender. Not a one of these seemingly insurmountable problems is the special preserve of men or women.

49   Once, in the depths of crisis, the word went out: Send me a man who reads.

50   Today, in the midst of a myriad of problems, the call is: Send me a person who thinks.

51   As long as there are problems, there will be an abundance of opportunities for women.

52   Seek out the problems, is my advice.

53   Remember the Maid of Orleans who went to the Dauphin, Charles II, with a plan to rescue France from the enemy.

54   Now, we can't all be Joan of Arc. But just imagine this scene: We're in the Mayor's office. And there standing before him is a young lady, fresh from the Wharton School, the ink on her MBA not yet dry. And she has for the Mayor's consideration, just as Joan had for Charles, a rescue plan. Not only that, it's down on paper, in less than five pages. And it takes account of the realities—political, economical. And, by gosh, it looks like it could work. Can any one of us doubt what the Mayor's response would be to that young lady's plan? Three words—*you are hired!*

55   I come back to my original point: the door to opportunity for women is opening.

56   If it is not opening fast enough, then let us push it by mastering the rudiments of whatever pursuit it is we have in mind.

57   Let us seek out the problems, because that is where the opportunities are the greatest. That is where gender always is beside the point.

58   Be positive.

59   As for business communications, the rudiments are the same for women and men alike. This is one case where vive la difference only leads to babble, incoherence.

60   Along the way, yes, we may suffer the slings and arrows of chauvinists—there are those who still live between their ears.

61   I can only offer this solace which Oliver Wendell Holmes once offered to artists who worry about criticism. Holmes urged that the artists consider who was doing the criticizing, and then remember that:

> *Whenever God sculpts an artist*
> *He gathers the chips that fall,*
> *And out of them sculpts the critic,*
> *And that should explain it all.*

62   In conclusion: I'm terribly proud that all of us here are in the business of helping people to communicate, to reach out, to touch with words and images, to understand, to learn, to share, to reason—with others and with ourselves.

63   The introduction to the program you have before you puts it this way: The purpose of the week is to encourage cooperation, impart information and enrich the city's economy. It is important to get to know one another, to share knowledge and find out what others are doing.

64   In a word, my friends, communication.

65   Thank you ever so much. May all of you achieve your dreams. Don't turn from the problems; embrace them eagerly. And remember: "This time, like all times, is a very good one—if we but know what to do with it."

QUESTIONS FOR DISCUSSION

1. Ms. Fippinger asserts in this speech that gender is irrelevant when it comes to communications, or to our major societal problems. Assuming that she was addressing an audience mostly composed of women, do you think she adequately supported this point?
2. Assuming also that some of the audience members were concerned with problems of women's equality, did Ms. Fippinger adequately relate her ideas to this concern?

This speech is an example of the "scholarly paper," a type of speech in which the written manuscript is distributed to the audience. This paper was presented before the Indiana Bar Association by George P. Rice, professor of speech at Butler University. Professor Rice applies many of the principles dealt with in this text to courtroom communication. In doing so, he provides solid advice that will prove useful to any public speaker. His speech was presented April 20, 1979.

The Rhetoric of Appellate Advocacy

Theories and Standards

GEORGE P. RICE

1   Mr. Chairman, Honorable Judges, my Learned Friends: It is my pleasant privilege to talk with you this afternoon on some important aspects of the useful art of rhetoric to improve appellate advocacy in both oral and written communication. The invitation to discuss the topic reveals a discerning regard for a very ancient discipline which has been vitally concerned with the attainment of one of the noblest of human aspirations—the attainment of justice among men. The concept of appellate jurisdiction is of very ancient lineage, for it goes back to the year 700 B. C. when men of Athens established the Court of Areopagos to review decisions of inferior tribunals on issues of homicide and sacrilege. The discipline we call "rhetoric" is almost as old, for by the year 450 B. C. we had the first treatise dealing with the art of persuasion in forensic public speaking. By 335 B. C. Aristotle had produced his classic book, *The Rhetoric,* which defined the term thus:

Reprinted by permission of the author and *Vital Speeches of the Day,* May 15, 1979, pp. 473–476.

"Rhetoric is the faculty of discovering in the particular case what are the available means of persuasion." It was held a useful as distinguished from a fine art because it dealt with the probabilities of human affairs. Its aim was to influence the beliefs and behavior of hearers. Today and more simply we call rhetoric a body of rules governing good oral and written composition. But in addition to ideas and their appropriate expression rhetoric is also concerned with symbolic communication achieved by gesture, facial expression, stance, voice, dress, and decorum. The weapon forged by the Greeks was passed along to the Romans and from them to the medieval university as one of the Seven Liberal Arts and in the fullness of time came to us. I am on very firm ground when I say that there has been no distinguished forensic pleader from the Golden Age of Athens to the present who has not devoted much time and study to the mastery of rhetoric. Pleaders among Athenians include Pericles, Isocrates, and Demosthenes. The Romans had Caesar, Cicero, Tacitus, and Quintilian. The annals of British forensic eloquence are lighted by the brilliance of the Earl of Chatham, William Pitt the Younger, Edmund Burke, and Lords Mansfield, Erskine, and Brougham. We Americans point with pride to Hamilton, Adams, Clay, Webster, Lincoln, and John Davis. And let it be remembered that after John Adams had served as President of the United States, he did not think it beneath his dignity to serve as Boyleston Professor of Rhetoric in Harvard University.

THEORIES AND STANDARDS

2   What theories, models, and techniques were available to these men in the development of their art? Are these extant? They are. We shall now proceed to examine some of them.

3   The most basic premise is that the conditions which permit free speech for free men be fostered and protected, and this has been the great contribution of our profession in Athens, England, and in the United States. There must be freedom of speech, of course. Then, there must be great issues to discuss and debate and able men of high integrity to present all sides of the controversy before an audience of intelligent and educated men and women. The language used must be highly developed in its grammar and vocabulary, the best being Attic Greek, Latin, French, and English.

4   The advocate must also be constantly aware that every situation involving communication integrates four factors: the speaker or writer, the reader or listener, the subject of the composition, and the occasion and purpose of the presentation. Of these four factors, the appellate tribunal or audience is the most important because it holds the power of decision. Close study of the court and the individuals who compose it is important both for legal and psychological reasons.

PERSONAL ATTRIBUTES OF GREAT PLEADERS

5   There are five personal attributes, according to the greatest critic of style of antiquity, Longinus, which must be possessed by those who reach the peak of appellate excellence, the first two matters of natural endowment, the other three skills capable of acquisition by study and practice.

6   1. The advocate must be endowed with creative imagination, nourished by wide reading in the literature of his own and other professions, and able to see relations and draw inferences which escape the intelligence of lesser men.

7   2. He must be able to exert a high degree of emotional drive in the composition of his brief and in the oral argument before the court, and this must continue from beginning to end.

8   3. He must have an able command of metaphor, simile, and other figures of speech so as to employ memorable words, phrases, and figures, exemplified by Judge Learned Hand's remark in the New Masses case in 1919: "Words are not only the keys to persuasion, but the triggers of action."

9   4. He must be driven incessantly to increase his command of the language by which he communicates. The average person uses only 2000 words in daily talk. Yet the *Oxford English Dictionary* lists a word-hoard of over 416,000 words and definitions. His use of these words must be discerning. The basic criteria for choice of words are clarity for understanding and propriety for the speaker, for the listener, and for the subject. A good standard is set by the English novelist, Mr. Somerset Maugham in his book, *The Summing Up,* published in 1936: "Good diction lies in this—the choice, not of a good word, but of the inevitable word placed properly in the sentence."

10   5. Aristotle tells us in *The Poetics* that all things have a beginning, a middle, and an end. This emphasizes the importance of the architectonics or structure of the brief. Each part has a function to perform in and of itself and also in relation to the whole. These parts in turn must be connected by appropriate transitional devices to provide continuity. Proper punctuation, among other things, has its part.

RHETORICAL DEVICES FOR PROOF

11   Since the Age of Pericles we have been aware of what is called proof, that which makes us believe. Every pleader should be aware constantly that there are three forms of proof at his disposal—the ethical, the logical, and the pathetic.

12   Now ethical proof is represented by one's moral bent revealed as good or bad by choices he makes. Its influence is pervasive, but often unrealized by the pleader. Professor William Forney once phrased it thus: "Character is the tree and reputation the shadow which it casts." We reveal our ethical standards to the Bench in three

distinct ways. The first is by the reputation one bears as a result of previous action. The second is by the respect and goodwill displayed toward the listeners. The third is revealed by the sagacity or acumen revealed in the decisions we advocate. A good pleader is characterized not only by good moral bent, the desire to do what is proper and correct, but also the intellectual responsibility he shows by the close reasoning and careful research he puts into his preparation.

13   Logical proof is that which appeals to intelligence, reason, and intellect. It forms the core and center of the pleader's case. Rhetoric has furnished our profession with five useful tools for effective proof.

14   1. The first is *argument from sign.* This is predicated upon the supposition that one set of phenomena forms the basis for what logically must follow. We see snow fall and conclude that it is getting colder and winter has come.

15   2. The second of these devices is *argument from fact.* A fact may be defined as something accepted as true on the basis of the common experience of mankind, as with our belief that America was discovered in 1492. We apply certain tests for acceptance or rejection or argument from fact: (a) Are there sufficient units in the sampling to sustain the conclusion? (b) Do the findings agree with other known and established facts? (c) Is the material offered stated accurately? (d) Are the conclusions drawn from them within the pale of reason?

16   3. *Argument from causal relation* is our third weapon. It is based upon the establishment of a valid causal relation between two or more sets of facts or events. It assumes that every action has a discernible cause. The tests to determine the effectiveness of argument from causal relation include: (a) Has the causal relation been satisfactorily established? (b) Is the supporting cause adequate to produce the results asserted? (c) Are there any intervening factors which should have modified or changed the observed results?

17   4. The fourth, *argument from authority,* is a favorite of the legal profession for it emphasizes the importance of precedent and expert testimony. The importance of this type of logical appeal depends, of course, upon the weight of prestige of the authority or precedent and the accuracy and application with which it is used. We test its contribution to the strength of our case by questions such as these: (a) Does the source cited have access to data which justify his testimony? (b) Is there any evidence of prejudice which results in distortion? (c) Does the person quoted or the precedent cited have strict application to the issue involved? (d) What outside support is available to buttress this evidence?

18   5. The fifth and final logical device is *argument by analogy.* Here we stress factors of similarity between two or more sets of data or testimony.

FORMS OF SPEECH SUPPORT

19   In addition to these major weapons for the pleader's arsenal there are several other rhetorical devices called "forms of speech support" which add materially to the logical and literary qualities of a brief or an oral argument. Let us now review some of these.

20   1. The first is the *enthymeme* or generalization, commonly described as a categorial statement held to be true of a given class. For example, "All men are created equal in their civil and political rights in the U.S."

21   2. *Example* is defined as a specific instance said to be true of a class. Thus, "Alexander was one of the generals."

22   3. *Definition* of all important terms in the brief or argument is of the utmost concern to the pleader. We may say that definition is the description of a term which includes all that is relevant and excludes what is not. The subjective nature of language and the personalized meaning people give to the words they use (and which may be given yet others by listeners) are barriers to clear understanding. Words used should be concrete, vivid, and objective as possible. Abstract terms should be avoided whenever one can. The *Oxford English Dictionary* is the ultimate authority here. To illustrate definition: "Benjamin Franklin wrote that man was a tool-using animal."

23   4. *Anecdote* is a short, pointed, and relevant story. It has a place, but should be used sparingly and then only if the pleader is sure it will advance his oral argument or is responsive to question from one of the judges.

24   5. *Illustration* is an extended example.

25   6. *Statistics* involve the use of two or more sets of numbers for the purpose of comparison or contrast.

26   7. *Repetition* is a forceful device to present identical material more than once, retaining both idea and language, this for the purpose of emphasis. Patrick Henry's famous speech to the Virginia House of Burgesses in March of 1770 furnishes good usage.

27   8. *Restatement* expresses the same idea in variant language, and again, the purpose is to secure force and emphasis and rivet the attention of the judges on a particular argument or piece of evidence.

28   9. *Quotation,* (or citation) whether of a previous decision relied upon, testimony, or data from yet another source, is the verbatim repetition of material both because of its relevance to the point at issue and for its literary value.

29   10. *Rhetorical questions* are extremely important in every type of oral or written communication, primarily because they emphasize a point, because they stimulate the listener's interest and curiosity, and because they give the pleader time to arrange his own thoughts. In my experience, they are very seldom used during oral argument or in

public speaking generally. Their neglect should be remedied by discriminating use.

30   Examination of great forensic speeches of Greece, Rome, England, and The United States stresses the importance of laying an early foundation for matters on which there can be general agreement. These common grounds and received opinions include: expediency, the common welfare, wisdom of precedents and customs of ancestors, justice, the Bible, and the like.

STANDARDS FOR STYLE

31   All composition, but especially that intended for oral presentation, is judged in terms of material or content, structure or organization, and writing or oral delivery. The contributions of rhetoric to selection and use of rhetorical and literary devices have already been dealt with, while the technical aspects of organization or structure have been or will be discussed by highly qualified experts during our program. There remains the subject of style and delivery during argument.

32   Style may be defined as the expression of the speaker's personality and argument by his choice of *ideas and words.* There are two basic criteria for judgment of good style. The first is, is it clear? The second, is it appropriate to the subject, speaker, listener, and occasion? In general, the forensic pleader's level of excellence will fall into one or the other of three categories which derive from classical antiquity. Style is judged grand when the subject matter, level of forensic eloquence, and speaker's abilities are exhibited in the highest degree of perfection; we call it *plain* where the cause, speaker, and occasion stress simplicity, logic, and gravity, while the middle is a combination of the two.

33   Speaking style is determined by the speaker's personality, his training and experience, and by the treasury of ideas and words at his disposal. That speaker excels who commands integrity, knowledge, skill in rhetorical theory and its application, and self-confidence acquired from previous successful experience.

34   I suppose the first thing an appellate tribunal observes of counsel is his appearance in terms of dress and decorum. One's manner should be formal and respectful without self-deprecation. Dress and grooming are obviously significant. John Molloy's book, *Dress for Success,* is worthy of study. For example, he stresses the importance of color. Suits should be dark blue or gray. The tie should be blue or maroon. A white or blue shirt with buttoned down collar creates a good impression. Shoes should be black oxfords. Red, he says, should be avoided since it is an irritant. Mr. Molloy has even been audacious enough to recommend sartorial suggestions to the ladies of our profession.

35   Delivery is judged by rate, volume, pitch, and quality. A recom-

mended rate, unless interrupted by questions from the bench, is about 145 words per minute. Volume should be loud enough to be heard, probably 60 decibels as measured by an audiometer. Good eye contact with the Bench is a must. Too much dependence upon written notes or quotations from a brief already before the judges creates a bad impression. If counsel cannot come up with an answer to an intricate and perhaps undecided point, he should readily acknowledge it. Pitch refers to the evenness of tone of voice. Quality is total impression made in terms of individual performance. Facial expression, stance, and gestures should be in evidence with the ease and naturalness that careful preparation alone makes possible. If a question comes from the Bench, one should be sure that he understands it before attempting to answer. Several good studies on how to listen effectively have been published and should be consulted by those who have difficulties.

36   Tangential argument and irrelevant or obvious aspects of the case should be avoided. The Roman lawyer, Quintilian, stresses the importance of what he called *status*, the ultimate question or issue upon which decision depends. This should be determined with scrupulous precision and effectively adhered to. Every effort should be made to know the adversary's case and supporting arguments at least as well as one's own.

37   Now, one cannot talk well without the requisite command of English grammar and a fully adequate vocabulary. How to obtain these assets? I recommend the daily reading of a good dictionary, beginning with page one of the letter A while noting carefully the spelling, pronunciation, and meaning or meanings of each unfamiliar term. These should be noted on a card and used that day in conversation and dictation. At the end of a month one has read one page of each letter of the alphabet and for the next month is ready to begin with page two.

38   The model pleader will understand the distinctions made among pronunciation, diction, and articulation. Pronunciation stresses the ability to place an accent on the correct syllable of a given word. Diction is synonymous with vocabulary. Articulation refers to the full use of one's vocal apparatus to sound correctly each vowel, consonant, diphthong, and double consonant found in our language. My experience has been that most judges are lovers of language and they dislike liberties taken with its correct use. He who defiles the well of linguistic purity before an appellate tribunal will be noticed to his cost.

39   The correct use of English grammar is another must for the admired practitioner. Almost every mass media program, whether for entertainment or advertising, will demonstrate the baleful effects of illiterates upon the listening public. It follows that a general review of English grammar with the aid of a good text is in order. Suggestions

will be found in the bibliography included in this paper. The common errors, in addition to mispronunciation of words or misunderstanding of their meanings, are found with verbs like "sit" and "set" and "lie" and "lay," for example. "Imply" and "infer" are often confused. And most people do not know that when a sentence contains a singular pronoun followed by a prepositional phrase, the object of which is in the plural, the verb must be singular. To illustrate, we often hear "Everyone of them *are* ready." instead of "Everyone of them *is* ready." The successful advocate cannot afford these infelicities and outright errors, either in oral or written composition. It is written, "As a man speaketh, so is he."

SUGGESTED BIBLIOGRAPHY

40   Every time the advocate faces an appellate tribunal to sustain or attack a decision made below his reputation is on the line. Are there useful references dealing with rhetorical and psychological aspects of the art? Fortunately, the taste and industry of numerous judges and experienced pleaders have provided an extensive bibliography from which the following books and articles have been culled as exceptionally helpful. They should be reviewed at frequent intervals.

41   1. Mr. Justice Benjamin Cardozo's "The Nature of the Judicial Process," from the 1921 Storrs Lectures at Yale University School of Law.

42   2. Counsellor John Davis' "The Argument of an Appeal," published in 26 *American Bar Association Journal* at 895 in December of 1940.

43   3. Mr. Justice Robert Jackson's "Advocacy before the Supreme Court," published in 37 *American Bar Association Journal* at 801 in November of 1951.

44   4. Louis Nizer's *The Implosion Conspiracy,* published by Doubleday and Co., New York, 1973.

45   5. Lloyd Paul Stryker's *The Art of Advocacy,* Simon and Schuster, New York, 1954.

46   6. Finally for this category there is *The Lawyer's Treasury* edited by Eugene C. Gerhart, published by Bobbs-Merrill, Co., Indianapolis, Indiana, in 1956. It contains numerous informative and suggestive pieces helpful even to the experienced practitioner.

47   In addition to these titles there are many other books dealing more specifically with the art of rhetoric and with language which ought to be on a lawyer's shelf for immediate referral. Some of these are listed below.

48   1. H. W. Fowler, *A Dictionary of Modern English Usage,* 2nd ed., revised by E. Gowers, published by Oxford University Press, in 1965.

49   2. O. Jespersen, *Essentials of English Grammar,* published by Henry Holt Co., reprinted in 1964.

50   3. J. Sledd, *A Short Introduction to English Grammar,* published by Scott, Foresman and Co., in 1959.

51   4. H. Sweet, *A New English Grammar, Logical and Historical,* published by Oxford University Press in 1892.

52   5. Then, there is the absolute necessity of a good English dictionary, preferably *The Oxford English Dictionary* published by the Oxford University Press in 1933 in twelve volumes.

53   There is a final point to be discussed. Talk with several lawyers during the preparation of this paper has raised the question of the role of humor as a factor in persuasion during appellate argument. The best sources indicate that it has no place, except possibly and very rarely on behalf of criminal appellants. The reasons assigned are these:

54   1. Wit and humor serve best when used to crystallize or make more vivid a truth already partially perceived by the listener.

55   2. At best they serve to reinforce and strengthen existing attitudes or values already established rather than having the power to change them.

56   3. Wit and humor cannot produce conviction during the persuasive process by themselves alone.

57   The role of clear and appropriate language for human communication cannot be exaggerated. Our speech has been developing for possibly 500,000 years and came into use about the same time as tools and fire. Its exalted position cannot be expressed more beautifully than by the Greek poet, Sophocles, in *Antigone* when he wrote: "Wonders are many, and none is more wonderful than man . . . and speech and wind-swift thought hath he taught himself."

QUESTIONS FOR DISCUSSION

1. Professor Rice's speech is an example of a "scholarly paper." In this type of presentation the written manuscript is distributed to the audience. In your opinion, is the actual oral message necessary under those circumstances? Why or why not?

2. What are some of the changes that would be necessary if Professor Rice's manuscript was *not* handed out to his audience?

3. Because this speech was presented to a group used to specialized vocabulary, Professor Rice used some of that vocabulary in his speech. For example, he uses the term "appellate tribunal" instead of "appeals court." What other examples of specialized jargon did you notice in this speech?

4. Ross Smyth, in the fourth speech in this appendix, stated that "any person who has to give a speech . . . should insert a little humor or levity into it." Professor Rice, however, advises appeals lawyers that humor generally has no place "in persuasion during appellate argument." How do you account for the difference in these statements?

Index